The most heterogenous
ideas are yoked by violence
together — Samuel Johnson
re: John Donne

a brief forgiveness
between opposites ⟲
The death of Cuchulain

a difficult truce
of oil + water

On Baile's Strand

The Disappearances
The barricade

Modernists at Odds

THE FLORIDA JAMES JOYCE SERIES

UNIVERSITY PRESS OF FLORIDA

Florida A&M University, Tallahassee
Florida Atlantic University, Boca Raton
Florida Gulf Coast University, Ft. Myers
Florida International University, Miami
Florida State University, Tallahassee
New College of Florida, Sarasota
University of Central Florida, Orlando
University of Florida, Gainesville
University of North Florida, Jacksonville
University of South Florida, Tampa
University of West Florida, Pensacola

MODERNISTS AT ODDS

Reconsidering Joyce and Lawrence

Edited by Matthew J. Kochis and Heather L. Lusty

Foreword by Sebastian D. G. Knowles

UNIVERSITY PRESS OF FLORIDA

Gainesville / Tallahassee / Tampa / Boca Raton

Pensacola / Orlando / Miami / Jacksonville / Ft. Myers / Sarasota

This book may be available in an electronic edition.

20 19 18 17 16 15   6 5 4 3 2 1

Library of Congress Cataloging-in-Publication Data
Modernists at odds : reconsidering Joyce and Lawrence / edited by Matthew J. Kochis
and Heather L. Lusty ; foreword by Sebastian D. G. Knowles.
pages cm — (The Florida James Joyce series)
Includes index.
ISBN 978-0-8130-6047-7
1. English fiction—20th century—History and criticism. 2. Joyce, James, 1882–1941—
Criticism and interpretation. 3. Lawrence, D. H. (David Herbert), 1885–1930—Criticism
and interpretation. 4. Modernism (Literature)—Great Britain. I. Kochis, Matthew J.,
editor. II. Lusty, Heather L., editor. III. Knowles, Sebastian D. G. (Sebastian David Guy),
Author of introduction, etc. IV. Series: Florida James Joyce series.
PR6019.O9Z7284 2015
823'.912—dc23   2014033322

The University Press of Florida is the scholarly publishing agency for the State University
System of Florida, comprising Florida A&M University, Florida Atlantic University,
Florida Gulf Coast University, Florida International University, Florida State University,
New College of Florida, University of Central Florida, University of Florida, University
of North Florida, University of South Florida, and University of West Florida.

University Press of Florida
15 Northwest 15th Street
Gainesville, FL 32611-2079
http://www.upf.com

Contents

Figures

Foreword

According to Stephen Dedalus, the fundamental flaw in the hockey game that takes place after his history lesson is that "Cochrane and Halliday are on the same side." So it is with Joyce and Lawrence: in order for the great game of modernism to be played at its highest level, the two players must line up on opposite sides. According to T. S. Eliot, in his heretical book *After Strange Gods*, Lawrence is the heretic, and Joyce the orthodox writer, an unorthodox argument that Stephen Spender later overturned. But which is which? Would it not be fairer to say that Joyce is the more heretical writer, fledged on Ibsen's celebration of individual choice, while Lawrence remained true to the circumscribed world of the subject of his early literary study, Thomas Hardy? The answer provided in this excellent reappraisal is that they can be both, but not at the same time. They are contraries, in the Blakean sense: two elements in continual opposition. As Blake says in *The Marriage of Heaven and Hell*, "Opposition is true Friendship"; Joyce and Lawrence are eternally at odds, each a Scylla to the other's Charybdis. Modernism's original odd couple, as Earl Ingersoll calls them in this volume, they shared the same literary agent (James Pinker, whose death in 1922 was possibly the most significant literary event of that year, given a clientele that included Henry James, Ford Madox Ford, G. B. Shaw, and Thomas Mann), fought similar legal battles against the censor, and had the common distinction of being pirated by Samuel Roth. Louise Kane shows us how their work rubs together in the pages of the *Egoist*, tracking their movements through the literary magazines of the time. Brancusi's *Symbol of Joyce*, the rock and the whirlpool, is as much a symbol of Lawrence as it is a symbol of both.

In *The Good Soldier*, John Dowell famously likens Leonora and Florence to a greyhound and a retriever: that's as good an analogy as any for Joyce and Lawrence, both in life and art. They belong to the same great group: both are at once syncretists and fragmenters, bourgeois cosmopolitans, prudish libertines, displaced nostalgists. It is an interesting thought experiment to imagine Joyce as English and Lawrence as American, as by rights they both should have been. Neither would now be celebrated as the paradoxical figures that they are: it is their rebellion against their native lands, their un-Irishness and their un-Englishness, that makes them so compelling. "They usually lump us together," says Lawrence in 1922, and he is right as usual: Joyce and Lawrence are part of the same alloy, two complementary halves of a modernist whole. One cannot imagine Paul Morel being told that his mother is "beastly dead," or Bloom stripping naked to dance in the rhododendrons on the Hill of Howth. For Joyce, "Iron nails ran in" is a cosmic joke; for Lawrence it is no more than the physical truth. But Word requires Flesh and vice versa; as Martin Brick puts it in these pages: "[The two writers] look inside our experience with the physical world, and look inside our experience with the verbal world, and there find mystery."

Joyce and Lawrence, then, are oscillating poles; they serve as a magnetic north and south for modernism's rotating world. For Enda Duffy, this is an osculating world, in a superb analysis of the art of kissing in both writers. For Brick, it is the world of Isis and Osiris, against whom, and against Howard Carter's 1922 discovery of Tutankhamen's tomb and its confirmation of mythologies in Frazer's *Golden Bough*, both writers are usefully triangulated. For Eleni Loukopoulou, it is a world of ossified class struggle: where Lawrence styles himself as the voice of the proletariat, Joyce never saw a slum he didn't want to fly the nets of. For Ingersoll and others, the role that T. S. Eliot, Virginia Woolf, and F. R. Leavis played in officiating between the two during the style wars of the 1930s is kept carefully in mind. Kochis and Lusty, like Cochrane and Halliday before them, have shown themselves in full command of the playing field ("Hurray! Ay! Whrrwhee!"). But it is only fair to give Joyce the last word, with his laconic response to *Lady Chatterley's Lover*: "Lush."

Sebastian D. G. Knowles
Series editor

Acknowledgments

There are a number of people and organizations to whom we owe thanks: the International James Joyce Foundation, at whose 2009 annual convention in Prague we presented the first stage of this project as a panel on Joyce and Lawrence; the *D. H. Lawrence Review*'s editor, Eleanor H. Green, for furnishing a list of prominent Lawrentians and for promoting the initial call for papers; the University of Delaware Press for licensing the use of Zack Bowen's article in this collection; and the University Press of Florida for their early advice and support, as well as their patience and helpful guidance during the revision process. We would like to thank Margot Norris at the University of California, Irvine, who kindly allowed us use of her name as a contributor to this collection on the call for papers, and Dana Larson for her steadfast encouragement. We would also like to thank each of the contributors for their patience and flexibility during the editing process. Gerald Doherty, the first scholar to submit a manuscript as we began this collection project, sadly, passed away in January 2014, before he could see the book in print. His encouragement and enthusiasm for the project was infectious, and he is missed. Finally, to all of our colleagues who offered numerous bits of advice, support, and encouragement over the last three years—we thank you.

Abbreviations

Joyce Abbreviations

CW	*The Critical Writings of James Joyce*. Ed. Ellsworth Mason and Richard Ellmann. New York: Viking, 1959.
D	*Dubliners*. Ed. Robert Scholes in consultation with Richard Ellmann. New York: Viking, 1967.
FW	*Finnegans Wake*. New York: Viking, 1939; London: Faber and Faber, 1939. These two editions have identical pagination.
JJI	Richard Ellmann. *James Joyce*. New York: Oxford UP, 1959.
JJII	Richard Ellmann. *James Joyce*. New York: Oxford UP, 1982.
Letters I, II, III	*Letters of James Joyce*. Vol. 1. Ed. Stuart Gilbert. New York: Viking, 1957; reissued with corrections 1966. Vols. 2 and 3. Ed. Richard Ellmann. New York: Viking, 1966.
P1	*A Portrait of the Artist as a Young Man*. Definitive text corrected from Dublin Holograph by Chester G. Anderson. Ed. Richard Ellmann. New York: Viking, 1964.
P2	*A Portrait of the Artist as a Young Man*. Ed. Jeri Johnson. Oxford: Oxford UP, 2001.
SH	*Stephen Hero*. Ed. John J. Slocum and Herbert Cahoon. 1944. New York: New Directions, 1963.
SL	*Selected Letters of James Joyce*. Ed. Richard Ellmann. New York: Viking, 1975.
U + episode and line number	*Ulysses*. Ed. Hans Walter Gabler et al. New York and London: Garland, 1984, 1986. Published in paperback by Garland, Random House, Bodley Head, and Penguin between 1986 and 1992.

Lawrence Abbreviations

EC   *The Escaped Cock (The Man Who Died)*. Ed. Gerald M. Lacy. Los Angeles: Black Sparrow, 1973.

EY   John Worthen. *D. H. Lawrence: The Early Years 1885–1912*. The Cambridge Biography. Vol. 1. Cambridge: Cambridge UP, 1991.

1L   *The Letters of D. H. Lawrence*. Vol. 1. *September 1901–May 1913*. Ed. James T. Boulton. Cambridge: Cambridge UP, 1979.

2L   *The Letters of D. H. Lawrence*. Vol. 2. *June 1913–October 1916*. Ed. George J. Zytaruk and James T. Boulton. Cambridge: Cambridge UP, 1981.

3L   *The Letters of D. H. Lawrence*. Vol. 3. *October 1916–June 1921*. Ed. James T. Boulton and Andrew Robertson. Cambridge: Cambridge UP, 1984.

4L   *The Letters of D. H. Lawrence*. Vol. 4. *June 1921–March 1924*. Ed. Warren Roberts, James T. Boulton, and Elizabeth Mansfield. Cambridge: Cambridge UP, 1987.

5L   *The Letters of D. H. Lawrence*. Vol. 5. *March 1924–March 1927*. Ed. James T. Boulton and Lindeth Vasey. Cambridge: Cambridge UP, 1989.

6L   *The Letters of D. H. Lawrence*. Vol. 6. *March 1927–November 1928*. Ed. James T. Boulton and Margaret H. Boulton with Gerald Lacy. Cambridge: Cambridge UP, 1991.

7L   *The Letters of D. H. Lawrence*. Vol. 7. *November 1928–February 1930*. Ed. Keith Sagar and James T. Boulton. Cambridge: Cambridge UP, 1993.

8L   *The Letters of D. H. Lawrence*. Vol. 8. *Previously Uncollected Letters and General Index*. Ed. James T. Boulton. Cambridge: Cambridge UP, 2000.

LAH   *Love among the Haystacks and Other Stories*. Ed. John Worthen. Cambridge: Cambridge UP, 1987.

LCL   *Lady Chatterley's Lover and A Propos of "Lady Chatterley's Lover."* Ed. Michael Squires. Cambridge: Cambridge UP, 1993.

1P   *Phoenix: The Posthumous Papers of D. H. Lawrence*. Ed. Edward D. McDonald. London: Heinemann, 1936.

2P   *Phoenix II: Uncollected, Unpublished, and Other Prose Works by D. H. Lawrence*. Ed. Warren Roberts and Harry T. Moore. New York: Viking, 1968.

PO *The Prussian Officer and Other Stories*. Ed. John Worthen. Cambridge: Cambridge UP, 1983.

Poems *The Complete Poems of D. H. Lawrence*. Ed. Vivian de Sola Pinto and F. Warren Roberts. New York: Penguin, 1977.

R *The Rainbow*. Ed. Mark Kinkead-Weekes. Cambridge: Cambridge UP, 1989.

RDP *Reflections of the Death of a Porcupine and Other Essays*. Cambridge: Cambridge UP, 1988.

RHW "The Rocking-Horse Winner." *The Complete Short Stories of D. H. Lawrence*. Vol. 3. New York: Viking, 1961. 790–804.

S&L *Sons and Lovers*. Ed. Helen Baron and Carl Baron. Cambridge: Cambridge UP, 1992.

SCAL *Studies in Classic American Literature*. New York: Viking, 1964.

STH *Study of Thomas Hardy and Other Essays*. Ed. Bruce Steele. Cambridge: Cambridge UP, 1985.

TI *Twilight in Italy and Other Essays*. Ed. Paul Eggert. Cambridge: Cambridge UP, 1994.

WP *The White Peacock*. Ed. Andrew Robertson. Cambridge: Cambridge UP, 1983.

Chronologies

JAMES JOYCE		D. H. LAWRENCE	
1882	Born in the Dublin suburb of Rathgar on 2 February.	Born in Eastwood, Nottinghamshire, on 11 September.	**1885**
1888–1898	Attends Clongowes Wood College and Belvedere College.	Educated at Beauvale Board School, Eastwood, and Nottingham High School.	**1891–1901**
1898	Enrolls at University College, Dublin.		
1902	Graduates from university and goes to Paris.	Attends and graduates from University College, Nottingham.	**1902–1906**
1903	Returns from Paris. Receives telegram about his mother's death.		
1904	Meets Nora Barnacle. Stays briefly at the Martello Tower. Publishes three stories under the name Stephen Daedalus and begins writing *Stephen Hero*. Leaves with Nora for Trieste and Pola.		
1905	Continues writing stories for *Dubliners*. His son, Giorgio, is born in Trieste.		
1906	Moves to Rome.		

JAMES JOYCE	D. H. LAWRENCE
1907 Returns to Trieste, where his daughter, Lucia, is born. *Chamber Music* is published, and Joyce starts writing *A Portrait of the Artist as a Young Man.*	*A Prelude* is published under Jessie Chambers' name. **1907**
1909 Opens the Volta, the first cinema in Dublin.	Receives a teaching post at Davidson Road School, Croydon. Becomes engaged to Louie Burrows, which he later breaks off. Resigns his position after a lengthy illness. His mother, Lydia Lawrence, dies. **1908–1912**
1912 Makes his final visit to Ireland.	Returns to Nottingham-shire and meets Frieda Weekley. They elope and travel to Germany and Italy. Also during this time, pub-lishes *The Trespasser, Love Poems and Others,* and *Sons and Lovers.* **1912–1914**
1914 *Dubliners* is published; *A Portrait of the Artist* is serialized; and Joyce begins work on *Ulysses.*	Returns to England and marries Frieda (July). Publishes *The Widowing of Mrs Holroyd* and *The Prussian Officer and Other Stories.* **1914**
1915 Finishes *Exiles* and moves to Zurich because of the war.	During the war, he and Frieda are confined to England. In October 1915, *The Rainbow* is suppressed and banned in England. **1915–1917**
1918 Parts of *Ulysses* are serialized in America and England in *The Little Review.*	*New Poems* is published. **1918**

	JAMES JOYCE	D. H. LAWRENCE	
1919–1920	Returns to Trieste, then moves to Paris.	Travels to Italy and visits Sardinia and Switzerland. Publishes *Women in Love* (1920), *Aaron's Rod* (1922), and *England, My England and Other Stories* (1922).	**1919–1922**
1921	*Ulysses* is banned in America.		
1922	*Ulysses* is published by Shakespeare and Company, Paris.	Travels to Ceylon and Australia. Writes and publishes *Kangaroo*. Arrives in America in September.	**1922**
1923	Starts writing "Work in Progress" (known later as *Finnegans Wake*).	Visits Mexico and settles in Chapala. Also travels to New York, Los Angeles, and England. In 1924, travels to England, France, Germany, Switzerland, and Austria before returning to New Mexico. Death of his father, Arthur Lawrence. In Mexico City but returns to Taos after serious illness.	**1923–1924**
		Travels mainly in Italy, spending 3 months at Villa Bernarda, Spotorno. Finally settles at Villa Mirenda, Scandicci, near Florence. Last trip to Britain includes brief visit to Eastwood area.	**1925–1926**
1927	*Pomes Penyeach* published.	*Lady Chatterley's Lover* attacked in press (pirated copies begin to appear). Copies of *Lady Chatterley's Lover* and *Pansies* are seized by police. Paintings seized from exhibition at Warren Gallery, London. Lawrence moves to South of France at the end of 1929.	**1927–1929**

JAMES JOYCE	D. H. LAWRENCE
1931 Marries Nora. Death of his father.	Dies at Vence in South of France on 2 March. **1930**
1933 American ban on *Ulysses* is lifted.	
1939 *Finnegans Wake* is published.	
1940 Returns to Zurich because of the war.	
1941 Dies on 13 January and is buried at Fluntern Cemetery.	

Regardless of its title -- Modernists at Odds -- this collection is committed to reconciling two of the notoriously uncompatable Modernists

Truly odd couple
Contentious Couple
Dynamic Duo
Yoked together
Unmatched set

Introduction

Injoynted Perspectives

HEATHER L. LUSTY

This collection pairs two canonical figures generally treated as polar opposites—James Joyce and D. H. Lawrence. Literary modernism boasts a score of internationally renowned authors, often the focus of their own literary societies and considered fields unto themselves. Such insularism obscures the importance of sociohistorical contexts, however. For scholars, the porous framework of modernism encourages interdisciplinary approaches that have invigorated twentieth-century studies across fields. Modernism's inextricable engagement with external forces like the Great War, print culture, psychology, empire, architecture and design, commodity culture, and nationalism make modernist studies a rare pan-cultural, truly interdisciplinary movement. Yet as scholars of modernism work in myriad fields, the foundations are often neglected.[1] James Joyce and D. H. Lawrence, traditionally considered stylistic opposites, are reconsidered in this collection of essays by thematic categories, including religious/myth structures, social constructs, and cultural pastimes; the contributors find fresh and invigorating ways to reassess the writers, their contexts, and their art.

Joyce and Lawrence famously dismissed each other as creative rivals, as several of the essays in this collection note. Lawrence wrote to Aldous Huxley, "My God, what a clumsy *olla putrida* [sic] James Joyce is! Nothing but [. . .] deliberate, journalistic dirty-mindedness" (*6L 508*). Joyce's microfocus on detail annoyed Lawrence, and Lawrence's colloquial language and moralizing annoyed Joyce. Joyce considered Lawrence's *Lady Chatterley* "the usual sloppy English [. . .]" (*Letters I* 309). Stylistically, their work is diverse. Yet their brief criticism of each other's works shows that they viewed each other as popular, if not aesthetic, rivals. Lawrence understood that "Joyce would look as much askance on me as I on him," yet he noted that despite their mutual dislike, "We make a choice of Paola and Francesca floating down the winds of hell" (4L 340). Lawrence knew instinctively that despite their chasmal differences, history would view them in constant propinquity.

Joyceans and Lawrentians have historically had very little to say to each other. Despite the writers' differences in style, personally and professionally, their lives and careers bear striking similarities. Both Joyce and Lawrence wrote across genres, including essays, plays, poems, short stories, and novels, and incorporated music and singing into their writing. Their self-reflexive fascination with the struggling artist figure is evident in their early work. Thematically, however, Joyce and Lawrence engage in many of the same social concerns—sterility, political apathy, spirituality. As writers, each man also avowed preoccupations with his respective country's paralysis.[2] In their personal lives, both men were plagued by debilitating illnesses (eye disease and consumption), had tumultuous relationships with their partners, and struggled financially for the bulk of their respective careers. Both authors are towering figures in twentieth-century legal history, having been ensnared in infamous obscenity trials for their major works (*Ulysses* and *Lady Chatterley's Lover*). Finally, both Joyce and Lawrence chose a life of exile for personal and political reasons, which greatly impressed their work.[3] While these areas have been well explored in the scholarship of each respective writer individually, approaches that jointly consider these issues in concert have not.

Each man's place in the literary canon and importance to future readers and writers is indisputable. In *Modern English Literature* (1970), W. W. Robson outlines James Joyce and D. H. Lawrence as literary giants from a perspective unchanged over the last forty years. Citing both men as the most widely read of modern writers, he notes:

> Novel after novel, in England and America, reveals their influence. Their word divides opinions. Some readers dislike both. Some admire one and reject the other. Very few seem to care for both equally. This is because of the nature of their work. Each seems to make a claim for his kind of art as the *right* kind. (75)

This perhaps most succinctly identifies the polemic nature of Joyce and Lawrence studies in relation to each other. Their respective bodies of work are viewed as so different, so radically opposed in style, that areas of congruence seem an impossibility. Yet accepting this outlook requires deliberate oversights.

This volume illuminates some of these areas by making new connections or taking fresh approaches to familiar but restive ground.

JAMES JOYCE IS ONE of the twentieth century's most prominent and popular figures, associated with the radical breaks in form and focus that epitomize literary modernism. Students of all ages read his short stories, yet his novels are the epitome of high modern style. He enjoys wide attention in Irish studies as well, and his overshadowing presence in emergent scholarship on literary magazine production, myth structures, and linguistics has ensured his prominence across disciplines. While Joyce's popularity with scholars and readers has been consistent over the last half century, Lawrence scholarship has struggled against a variety of obstacles. Lawrence is often considered a unique, unclassifiable writer who does not gel well with others. Yet he is considered a master of the short story, an important poet, a respected critic, and a modernist to the core in his rejection of modernity and machinery. With so many avenues of exploration, perhaps the problem is one of too many radically diverse personae.[4]

Much of the damage to Lawrence's popular appeal stems from alternative readings by feminist scholars. Kate Millet's *Sexual Politics* (1970) severely crippled Lawrence's popularity in the public domain; her characterization of patriarchal sexism in his works (and that of Henry Miller and Norman Mailer) skewed future exploration of Lawrence's large body of work—for decades, Lawrence was reviled for his perceived misogyny. A. S. Byatt notes the importance of contextualizing these feminist attacks as coinciding with a more general social shift, in which

> literary criticism, and the teaching of literature, became a belief system, and indeed a societal structure almost independent of books and what was or is in them. A kind of moral fervour, accompanied by a glorying in their own power, led critics to cleanse the canon, to hunt out the little snakes of sexism, racism, cultural assumptions about superiority, aestheticism, and destroy them. People got on to [college] syllabus because they were virtuous and promoted sane and socially desirable values. (2)

Lawrence's work, while popular with Freudians, proved less hospitable to the many theory lenses popular in the 1980s. His shifting positions and the ever-fluctuating stance of his characters and their situations made single works approachable, but notoriously inconsistent within the larger body of his writing.

John Worthen, the author's most recent biographer, describes Lawrence as adored, despised, censored, and ignored: long a profoundly troubling figure in the literary canon. At the start of the twenty-first century, he notes, Lawrence is arguably once again the outsider he was during his lifetime: "More than seventy years after his death, although his books continue to sell, his reputation has fallen in the literary and academic world [. . .]" (xxiv).[5] Despite the decline in popular appeal and perception, Lawrence scholars have worked diligently over the decades on his corpus of work. Several important recent contributions have breathed new life into Lawrence studies.[6]

To date the only full book devoted to a comparative examination of the works of Joyce and Lawrence is Cynthia Lewiecki-Wilson's *Writing Against the Family: Gender in Lawrence and Joyce,* which examines the intersection of each author in relation to sexuality and class struggle, overdetermination, and Egyptian mythology and religion. Only a handful of shorter articles and chapters group the two authors.[7] Zack Bowen's classic essay, reprinted in this volume and originally appearing in a collection devoted to new interpretations of *Lady Chatterley's Lover,* is one of the notable instances of a successful pairing of Joyce and Lawrence. Despite the engaging approach, modernist studies in general seem to have continued the "separate but equal" stance with regard to studies of these authors' respective bodies of work.

Because of their keen attention to cultural and socioeconomic nuances, Joyce and Lawrence are stalwarts of the modern period, representative and paradigmatic figures of radical shifts in modernist style, language, social foci, and sexuality. The authors certainly have "[crept] into immortality together" (4L 340). Despite the robust body of scholarship on each author, very little considers them as contemporaneous artists with common ground. Yet their importance extends far beyond a genre or style; each writer is vital to the story of literary modernism itself.

THE ESSAYS HERE TOUCH ON just a few areas of intersection between James Joyce and D. H. Lawrence, reframing and refocusing attention to cultural contexts that inform congruous concerns and approaches. Many of these approaches reexamine social constructs of sexuality and marriage. Bowen's essay, which opens the collection, points out the many ways *Ulysses* and *Lady Chatterley's Lover* are interested in the same concerns. These two writers' styles were polemically opposed, their ideologies dissimilar, their backgrounds divergent, and the nature of their aesthetics made mutual admiration unlikely.

Yet, Bowen points out, in many ways *Ulysses* and *Lady Chatterley's Lover* are not so different.

Margot Norris explores similarities in the authors' respective portrayals of adultery in the same two novels, which reversed the *ethos* of nineteenth-century adultery. Norris suggests that these two works also share a deeper but less transparent preoccupation; besides focusing on the social and psychological causes and consequences of adultery, they also treat sexual desire and sexual activity as physical, biological, and natural phenomena. An ecocritical consideration of the novels draws attention to this reintegration of the body into nature and to the challenges this poses to the writers' stylistic strategies and techniques.

Earl G. Ingersoll reexamines gender issues in *Ulysses* and *Lady Chatterley's Lover*. Updating the territory Bowen explored in his gender assessment of Bloom and Mellors by examining some of the writing on gender in the intervening decades, Ingersoll suggests that Joyce and Lawrence anticipated future constructions of gender. Femininity and masculinity represent less the traditional binary of mutually exclusive poles than a continuum within which gender unmoors itself from its ties to sexual or biological identifications. This exploration of gender in Mellors and Bloom proposes a "New Man," no longer bound by nineteenth-century notions of masculinity or manhood.

The next two essays, which focus on religious aspects of each author's works, address another mammoth focus of these two men—blending intense personal examination of faith in the twentieth century with the historical genealogy of human faith across millennia. The forms of the English novel are deeply entwined with Christianity and the Bible, with its human stories and prophetic poetry (Byatt 1).[8] Gerald Doherty's essay looks beyond religion and sexuality to a third motif—sacrifice—a direct offspring of both. Because "The Dead" and "The Man Who Died" share common denominators in economies of sacrifice as a basis for both personal and institutional exchanges, highly intriguing convergences (and divergences) exist between them. Doherty traces the ways in which these stories are, in fact, very much engaged in similar explorations of sacrifice.

Martin Brick examines how Joyce and Lawrence rejuvenate Christianity in the modernist period through their use of "foreignization," or the intentional estrangement of the familiar, juxtaposing it with other religions—in this examination, the Egyptian myth of Isis and Osiris. Both *The Man Who Died* and *Finnegans Wake* address the resurrection of Christ—an event at the heart of Christian belief—asking readers to reimagine Christianity's core concepts: sin, death, judgment, and how individuals define or understand their relationship with God. Doherty's and Brick's essays show the depths of religious philosophy extant in the works of Joyce and Lawrence and suggest further exploration of ancient Egypt in both men's mythos.

The space of literary production is another shared arena. By the early 1920s, D. H. Lawrence and James Joyce were, F. R. Leavis claimed, "pre-eminently the testing, the crucial authors" of prose fiction (10). Louise Kane notes that against this backdrop, it is perhaps inevitable that critical comparisons of the two writers contributed to a Joyce/Lawrence dichotomy. Kane recognizes the men's shared artistic techniques with an examination of their contributions to the nascent periodical forum and connects their similar treatments of themes (love, the Great War, and religion) to dispute the myth of two separate, polarized types of Georgian and "high" modernism.

Eleni Loukopoulou also explores the publication background and cultural context of the writings of Lawrence and Joyce within a specific venue—the Criterion Miscellany Series—and highlights how Lawrence and Joyce coexisted largely due to Eliot's role as their publisher. This engagement with periodicals and little magazines demonstrates a shared engagement in everyday culture that critics traditionally view as the antithesis of modernism: the culture of commerce. Joyce's and Lawrence's career trajectories share a path of creative publications in small magazines and local newspapers. The last decade has enjoyed a flourishing of "little magazine" studies, to which these examinations of literary production contribute.

New psychoanalytical approaches are also presented. Hidenaga Arai's essay identifies common ground between the two writers in terms of concepts introduced by Jacques Lacan and Slavoj Žižek, particularly the idea of the Real. Arai notes that in *After Strange Gods*, T. S. Eliot compares "The Shadow in the Rose Garden" (1914) and "The Dead" (1914), considering Lawrence, who wrote the former, to be "an almost perfect example of the heretic" while appreciating Joyce, who wrote the latter, as "the most ethically orthodox" of the eminent writers of his time (Eliot 38). In spite of Eliot's polarizing view of the two modernist writers, differences between "The Dead" and "The Shadow in the Rose Garden" suggest a fundamental affinity between the works.

Johannes Burgers and Jennifer Mitchell explore ideological masochism, an oft-overlooked but critical element within the modernist literary movement, and argue that both Lawrence and Joyce actively react against the socially accepted sexological definitions of masochism. The two writers, famous for their frank or irreverent attitudes toward sex, had complex relationships that included indulging in bondage fantasies (Joyce and Nora) and theatrical public fights (the Lawrences). This essay delves into the genealogy of scholarship about sexuality in Lawrence and Joyce and teases out the proclivity for pleasure through pain in modernist writing, which has generally been explored through the lens of "sadomasochism."

Finally, aspects of modernist popular culture occupy the focus of our last two essays. Enda Duffy puts the professional lives of the two literary giants into context with the emerging technological culture with an examination of public affection and the kiss in *Portrait* and *The Rainbow*. Suggesting that the kiss as a public declaration of sexual desire is a modernist invention, Duffy considers the multiple mediums in which the passionate kiss as public spectacle revolted against propriety and connects judgments of Joyce and Lawrence's focus on discourses of sexuality.

Joyce's and Lawrence's attention to the minutiae of culture is explored in Carl F. Miller's consideration of the significant role of horse racing in Joyce's *Ulysses* (1922) and Lawrence's "The Rocking-Horse Winner" (1926). Horse racing, perhaps the most culturally ubiquitous sport in the early twentieth century, is utilized by both Joyce and Lawrence as a cultural touchstone. Miller explores the perverse economic and social system such a culture produced and the dramatic significance of racing and gambling in each of these memorable works.

While we hope that the essays included here show what productive conversations and valuable perspectives can arise upon closer examination of these two epic figures in concert, we also hope to encourage readers and future scholars to continue this pursuit, as numerous other areas of congruence remain virtually unexplored. Examining these figures together, rather than choosing one over the other, may freshen restive areas of modernist studies and propel new critical approaches.

Notes

1. See Chris Baldick's introduction to *The Modern Movement: 1910–1940,* vol. 10 of *The Oxford English Literary History.*

2. In a letter to Constantine Curran, written in July 1904, Joyce states of the work that will become *Dubliners*: "I am writing a series of epicleti—[. . .]. I call the series Dubliners to betray the soul of that hemiplegia or paralysis which many consider a city" (*SL* 22). In a later letter to his publisher Grant Richards, he reiterates this idea, explaining that his intention was to write a chapter of the moral history of his country, and he chose Dublin for the scene because that city seemed to him the center of paralysis.

For Lawrence, the industrial age created a spiritually stagnant environment in which the land and people were stifled; social class is the marker that restrains individuals and against which they strain in their efforts to "find themselves." Clifford Chatterley embodies the most literal evocation of cultural paralysis and sterility, but stories like "The Horse Dealer's Daughter" and "The Rocking-Horse Winner" among others emphasize the general malaise of England's Midlands.

3. Lawrence eloped with Frieda von Richthofen in 1914, and the couple spent a few years wandering around Austria, Germany, and Italy. Trapped in England during World War I, unable to secure passports due to Frieda's nationality, the Lawrences emigrated in 1919 and spent the next decade between Italy and shorter stints in Ceylon, Australia, Mexico, and New Mexico. He, too, was prolific during his nomadic years. Lawrence's residences in Italy span from 1912 to his death in 1929; during the years Joyce was writing in Trieste, Lawrence published his first two travel-writing works, *Twilight in Italy* (1916) and *Sea in Sardinia* (1921); the play *Touch and Go* (1920); the collection of poems entitled *Bay* (1919); the story "The Sisters," which developed into *The Rainbow* (1915) and *Women in Love* (1921); and the group of so-called "Italian novels": *The Lost Girl* (1920), *Aaron's Rod* (1922), and *Mr. Noon* (1920–21).

4. Howard J. Booth notes that while effective theoretical approaches to Lawrence's work have slowly emerged, a historical contextualization has been slower in coming; he cites a need to understand from whence Lawrence comes as a writer, his relationship to his own era, and how his reception shaped the way we approach his texts (3).

5. This fall is the subject of two newer works that examine Lawrence's treatment over the decades. Gary Adelman's *Reclaiming D. H. Lawrence: Contemporary Writers Speak Out* (2002) examines the precarious legacy of and frequent aversion to Lawrence in academia and offers insightful, personal reflections on how Lawrence has been presented, rejected, and refigured by the last generation of writers. Barry Scherr's *D. H. Lawrence Today: Literature, Culture, Politics* addresses the author's marginalization as a result of what he terms "ideological shifts" in the types of literature society preferred.

6. Monographs focusing on Lawrence before the recent surge include Michael Bell's *D. H. Lawrence: Language and Being* (1992), Fiona Beckett's *D. H. Lawrence: The Thinker as Poet* (1997), and *The Cambridge Companion to D. H. Lawrence* (2001), among others. Contemporary works include *The Cambridge Edition of the Letters and Works of D. H. Lawrence*—the culmination of decades of work begun in 1979 to produce definitive editions of Lawrence's writings—which will produce more than forty separate volumes, each an authoritative base for academics, critics, reference, and research. Howard J. Booth's *New D. H. Lawrence* (2009) addresses the author's output using current and emergent themes in English studies and offers a wide range of essays exploring topics including (but not limited to) early marketing strategies, death and modernist ethics, psychoanalysis and war, ecocritical approaches, and comedy/gender. See also *Ecocritical Theory: New European Approaches,* ed. Axel Goodbody and Kate Rigby (Charlottesville: U of Virginia P, 2011).

7. See, for example, Michael Bell, "Varieties of Modernist Mythopoeia," *Literature, Modernism and Myth: Belief and Responsibility in the Twentieth Century* (Cambridge: Cambridge UP, 1997); Mary Burgan, "Androgynous Fatherhood in *Ulysses* and *Women in Love*," *Modern Language Quarterly* 44.2 (1983): 178–97; Alan M. Cohn and Richard F. Peterson, "Frank O'Connor on Joyce and Lawrence: An Uncollected Text," *Journal of Modern Literature* 12.2 (1985): 211–20; James C. Cowan, "Lawrence, Joyce, and the Epiphanies of *Lady Chatterley's Lover*," *D. H. Lawrence's 'Lady': A New Look at Lady Chatterley's Lover* (Athens: U of Georgia P, 1985) 91–115; H. M. Daleski, "Life as a Four-Letter Word: A Contemporary View of Lawrence and Joyce," *D. H. Lawrence in the Modern World* (Cambridge: Cambridge UP, 1989) 90–103; Paul Delany, "'A Would-Be-Dirty Mind': D. H. Lawrence as an Enemy of Joyce," *Joyce in the Hibernian Metropolis: Essays* (Columbus: Ohio State UP, 1996) 76–82; Monroe Engel, "Contrived Lives: Joyce and Lawrence," *Modernism Reconsidered* (Cambridge: Harvard UP, 1983) 65–80; Ian Gregor and Mark Kinkead-Weekes, "Lawrence and Joyce: A Critical Comparison," *The English Novel* (London: Sussex, 1976, 1977) 133–52; Dennis Jackson, "*Lady Chatterley's Lover*: Lawrence's Response to *Ulysses*," *Philological Quarterly* 66.3 (1987): 410–16; Charles Rossman, "A Metacommentary on the Rhetoric of Reviewing the Reviewers: Paul Eggert on the New Edition of *Ulysses* and *Women in Love*," *D. H. Lawrence Review* 21.2 (1990): 219–22; Charles Rossman, "Henry Miller on Joyce vs. Lawrence," *Joyce Studies Annual* 3 (1992): 248–54; John E. Stoll, "Common Womb Imagery in Joyce And Lawrence," *Ball State University Forum* 11.2 (1970): 10–24; and Raymond J. Wilson III, "Paul Morel and Stephen Dedalus: Rebellion and Reconciliation," *Platte Valley Review* 11.1 (1983): 27–33.

8. Byatt notes that Joyce's *Ulysses* is a theological novel, out of a Catholic culture, that plays with hierarchies of interpretation. Lawrence, coming from a culture of Protestant exhortation and preachments, sees his novels as necessarily written from the depth of his religious experience (1).

Works Cited

Adelman, G. *Reclaiming D. H. Lawrence: Contemporary Writers Speak Out.* Lewisburg, PA: Bucknell UP, 2002.

Baldick, Chris. *The Modern Movement: 1910–1940.* Vol. 10 of *The Oxford English Literary History.* Oxford: Oxford UP, 2004.

Booth, Howard J., ed. *New D. H. Lawrence.* Manchester: Manchester UP, 2009.

Bowen, Zachary. "*Lady Chatterley's Lover* and *Ulysses*." *D. H. Lawrence's "Lady": A New Look at Lady Chatterley's Lover.* Ed. Michael Squires and Dennis Jackson. Athens: U of Georgia P, 1985. Reprinted in this volume.

Byatt, A. S. "The One Bright Book of Life." *New Statesman.* 16 December 2002. Accessed 1 July 2013. www.newstatesman.com/node/144489.

Eliot, Thomas S. *After Strange Gods: A Primer of Modern Heresy.* London: Faber and Faber, 1934.

Joyce, James. *Occasional, Critical, and Political Writing.* Oxford: Oxford UP, 2000.

Leavis, F. R. *D. H. Lawrence: Novelist.* London: Chatto and Windus, 1955.

Lewiecki-Wilson, Cynthia. *Writing Against the Family: Gender in Lawrence and Joyce.* Carbondale: Southern Illinois UP, 1994.

Robson, W. W. *Modern English Literature.* London: Oxford UP, 1970.

Scherr, Barry J. *D. H. Lawrence Today: Literature, Culture, Politics.* New York: Peter Lang, 2004.

Worthen, John. *D. H. Lawrence: The Life of an Outsider.* New York: Perseus, 2005.

1

Lady Chatterley's Lover and Ulysses

ZACK BOWEN

D. H. Lawrence and James Joyce, the two giants of modern British fiction, did not, as has been often cited, think much of each other's writing.[1] Lawrence, referring to Joyce's work, wrote to Aldous Huxley, "My God, what a clumsy *olla putrida* [*sic*] James Joyce is! Nothing but old fags and cabbage-stumps of quotations from the Bible and the rest, stewed in the juice of deliberate, journalistic dirty-mindedness" (*6L* 508). Of *Ulysses*, Lawrence said, "The last part of it is the dirtiest, most indecent, obscene thing ever written. Yes it is, Frieda [. . .]. It is filthy" (Brett 81). While Joyce's plethora of detail annoyed Lawrence, Lawrence's language and didacticism annoyed Joyce. Referring to *Lady Chatterley*, Joyce wrote to Harriet Shaw Weaver, "I read the first 2 pages of the usual sloppy English [. . .] which is a piece of propaganda in favour of something which, outside of D.H.L.'s country at any rate, makes all the propaganda for itself" (*Letters I* 309). The two writers' styles were polemically opposed, their ideologies dissimilar, and so each refused to recognize the genius of the other, partly because of their divergent backgrounds and their rationalizations for their perceived shortcomings, and partly because of the nature of their aesthetic. But Joyce did buy *The Rainbow* when he had little money, and Lawrence did admit to reading bits of *Ulysses*.

On the surface their work seems as divergent as any could be by two novelists who were such close contemporaries. Yet, in many ways *Ulysses* and *Lady Chatterley's Lover* are not so different. Each represents the mature work of its author and culminates his career. Joyce's great novel was to be followed by his magnificent experiment, *Finnegans Wake*. But *Ulysses* is a statement of middle age, and experimental as it is, it was his last work still recognizable as a novel. It is often said by Lawrence's critics that his last novel is a summation of themes developed through his entire canon. Both of the books had long and difficult trials in the courts and elsewhere before their publication, and both became the centerpiece for momentous legal decisions. Indeed, the 1933 decision on *Ulysses* figures prominently as a precedent in the 1959 *Lady Chatterley* case. Both books were accused of being pornographic; both were widely popular before publication in England or the United States; and both were published in pirated editions. Lawrence's sympathy with Joyce, expressed by his joining other writers in signing a petition against Samuel Roth's unauthorized publication of *Ulysses*, was prophetic because Roth was later to pirate *Lady Chatterley's Lover* in America.

Moreover, Lawrence and Joyce were each exiles from countries with which they had love-hate relations. Both felt themselves outsiders, yet curiously they were spokesmen for their heritage. Lawrence, born into a lower social class than Joyce, saw life in part as a contrast between the beauties of nature and the horrors of mechanization and the coal pits. Emancipated from a life of economic determinism, he married a woman of higher social standing. Joyce, of a moderately well-off middle-class parentage, saw his family's fortunes reduced to poverty. In Joyce's curiously egalitarian Irish-Catholic society, in which everyone was poor, class distinctions did not loom as large as they did in England, divided by both aristocratic lineage and money into a more rigid structure. Joyce, if anything, married beneath his class, a B.A. taking up with a barmaid. Marriage evidently meant more to Lawrence than it did to Joyce, who refused—even after two children had resulted from his relationship with Nora—to succumb to the formal marital state until, worried that after his death inheritance rights might be denied his family, he officially married at age forty-nine. While Lawrence dwelt outside England and in later works portrayed foreign scenes and countries, Joyce, for all his exile, never left Ireland and more specifically Dublin in his fiction. Pastoral or rural scenes appear only in Joyce's poetry, whereas Lawrence often set his fictional scenes in nature, scarred by man and machine.

Yet both men did live in the same age, and it would stand to reason that, for all their differences, some areas of commonality can be addressed. Certainly the alienation theme is a basis for the action both of *Lady Chatterley* and *Ulysses*, as I suppose it is for every twentieth-century work from *The Wizard of Oz* to *The Texas Chainsaw Massacre*. But in a number of ways the two novels in question bear a much closer resemblance than might be suspected on first reading, and some insights into each novel may be gained by comparing their treatment of sex, language, geography, social structure, characterization, and art.

The most apparent similarity and obviously the most prominent historically is their candid treatment of sex, which permeates all the areas to be considered in this essay. It is the topic invariably discussed by critics comparing Joyce and Lawrence and certainly a major preoccupation of Lawrence. I had not thought the same was true of Joyce until I began thinking about this essay. Molly Bloom's language and her general preoccupation with matters sexual, coupled with Bloom's memory of their lovemaking on Howth and his masturbation on Sandymount Strand seem to have caught the imaginations of the censors and prurient readers of *Ulysses* to the exclusion of almost everything else, but the preoccupation throughout Bloomsday with matters at least partially sexual had not seemed so far removed to me from everyday behavior that it called attention to itself. However, Strother Purdy sees *Ulysses* as a sexual epic, its heroism portrayed entirely in sexual terms of infidelities, comic masturbation, a heroine in bed throughout, a masochistic orgy in which the hero changes sex, etc. Its message, Purdy asserts, is "How inescapably sexual is life!" (28–29). Of course, Bella Cohen's brothel and Molly Bloom's bed are by no means the entire essence of *Ulysses*. There are thoughts, conversations, and themes that deviate from the purely sexual. But these are fewer than I had thought: Stephen's day begins with Mulligan's blasphemous ribaldry; with Stephen's oedipal preoc-cupations, linked to Hamlet's own; with the rivalry for the favor of the old milkwoman, and, by extension, Ireland; with Deasy's cattle and their fertility symbolism. Bloom's day begins with the sensuous Calypso, Molly, and his trip to the pork butcher's to walk home behind the moving hams of a female shop-per. His odyssey includes trips to the cemetery, where he conjures up visions of the caretaker copulating; to All Hallows, where he hopes to stand "next to some girl" and leaves worrying about his trousers being unbuttoned; to the library, where Anne Hathaway seduces Shakespeare in a Dedalus analogue; to the Ormond bar, where siren songs are sung while the phallic white baton beer-pull is being fondled; to a maternity hospital, where all aspects of procre-ation are examined; to a brothel; and finally to Ithaca, where the quoits of the bedstead, which have occupied Bloom's thoughts during the day, jingle. Only, it seems, in Barney Kiernan's, with the Citizen and assorted asexual barflies, is sex to be escaped, though not entirely even in this male bastion. Bloom, for all his Christian charity, is never far from awareness of his adulterous wife and the assignation about which his mind revolves during the entire day. Molly is at the center of his universe, a Gea-Tellus figure, the personification of the sexual experience. What makes *Ulysses* seem so normal is that it accurately depicts everyday life, which in itself is inextricably bound to sex.

G. Wilson Knight sees both Joyce and Lawrence as rump-oriented. For them the ultimate answers lie in the posterior. The affirmation of Knight's thesis is Bloom's kissing Molly's behind before he goes to sleep and the preoccupation of Mellors with the beauty of Connie's "arse." Both Joyce and Lawrence, Knight claims, "labour to interpret and redeem man in natural and human terms," but "Lawrence tries hard to keep his mysticism close-locked to physical creation" (Knight 413). Therein lies one of the profound differences between the two. For Joyce, sex is an integrated part of life, which his characters accept as part of their beings, below as well as above the conscious level. Lawrence's characters constantly raise sex to the conscious level through rational discussion or the experience of spiritual sexual ecstasy. During the scene with the girl on the beach, at the end of chapter 4 of *A Portrait of the Artist as a Young Man*, Joyce attempts a Lawrencean combination of spiritual ecstasy and the eroticism of orgasm, but the conjunction is in Stephen's mind. The scene is parodied in "Nausicaa" by the all-too-fallible Gerty MacDowell and the literal-minded, masturbating Bloom. No topic is so sacred as to escape parody in Joyce's comic vision, in which importance and solemnity have nothing in common. This view is fundamentally different from the exultations of Lawrence's didacticism. Lawrence could describe the sublimity of the sex act without self-consciousness, through direct description, poetic language, and exalted emotion. Joyce, steeped in literary tradition and a parodist by temperament, could never unblushingly relate a coital experience, even when its source is the mind of Stephen Dedalus. For Joyce, writing about sex was to deal didactically with subjects for which there were no ultimate truths and about which everything had been said centuries before. But for Lawrence, sex achieves an elegant mysticism, the fullest appreciation of it linked with a transcendental participation in the core of being. It is not like Joyce's view of everyday life as casually permeated by sex; it becomes rather the source of divine understanding in Lawrence's work, particularly *Lady Chatterley's Lover*.

The individual love scenes between Connie and Mellors mark new levels of increased spiritual awareness by Connie and dictate the pattern of her subsequent behavior. As such they are each important structural elements in the novel, as nature and a full life in communication with that nature are linked increasingly with the love scenes. The plot progression of *Lady Chatterley's Lover* is largely a history of Connie's developing sensibility. The sense of continuity in the book in large measure derives from explicit sexual conduct, resulting in Connie's progress toward a oneness with nature. The language of these scenes is elevated and lyrical, and the experience of sex, the orgasm in particular, is the pathway to life in harmony with transcendental being. The gamekeeper, after his and Connie's first sexual encounter, declares:

"Now I've begun again."

"Begun what?"

"Life."

"Life!" She re-echoed, with a queer thrill.

"It's life," he said. "There's no keeping clear. And if you do keep clear you might almost as well die." (*LCL* 165)

It was not in Joyce, however, to deal so straightforwardly and explicitly with sex as the entry to God and the essence of being. It is there in *Ulysses*, but in Joyce's usual comic parody. If Bloom emerges triumphant over the suitors at the end of his Odyssean day, it is because he accepts with equanimity the outrages perpetrated upon him. In this he is not unlike Clifford, when he assumes initially that he will triumph over the men who merely plant seeds in Connie's womb and that the mental bond of friendship will overpower the passionate bond of sex. Clifford is wrong; sex wins. But the case of Bloom is more ambiguous. His home is threatened, his peace of mind jarred, his existence impaired by the adultery of his wife and her sexual passion. His reflection on this subject is outlined in "Ithaca."

> Why more abnegation than jealousy, less envy than equanimity?
>
> From outrage (matrimony) to outrage (adultery) there arose nought but outrage (copulation) yet the matrimonial violator of the matrimonially violated had not been outraged by the adulterous violator of the adulterously violated. (*U* 17.2195–99)

Like Mellors and Connie, Bloom finds equanimity in his recognition that sex is a manifestation of the natural order of things.

> Equanimity?
>
> As as natural as any and every natural act of a nature expressed or understood executed in natured nature by natural creatures in accordance with his, her and their natured natures, of dissimilar similarity. As not so calamitous as a cataclysmic annihilation of the planet in consequence of a collision with a dark sun. As less reprehensible than theft, highway robbery, cruelty to children and animals, obtaining money under false pretences, forgery, embezzlement, misappropriation of public money, betrayal of public trust, malingering, mayhem, corruption of minors, criminal libel, blackmail, contempt of court, arson, treason, felony, mutiny on the high seas, trespass, burglary, jailbreaking, practice of unnatural vice, desertion from armed forces in the field, perjury,

poaching, usury, intelligence with the king's enemies, impersonation, criminal assault, manslaughter, wilful and premeditated murder. As not more abnormal than all other parallel processes of adaptation to altered conditions of existence, resulting in a reciprocal equilibrium between the body organism and its attendant circumstances, foods, beverages, acquired habits, indulged inclinations, significant disease. As more than inevitable, irreparable. (*U* 17.2177–94)

The question arises from these two parodies of catechism or scientific observation, whether this is a true picture of Bloom's views and identification with nature, or, like some other distorted views in "Ithaca," a false representation. Whatever falseness there is in "Ithaca" stems from the misimpressions of Bloom and not from their fidelity to his conscious or unconscious mind. The question of whether Joyce could handle the topic seriously, as Lawrence did, or whether he had to deal with it on the sophomoric level of a dirty joke is not the issue here. What is, is that in a curiously comic way, the universe as Joyce depicted it is similar to Lawrence's universe. Their methods were entirely different, their self-consciousness of presentation and roots in the past widely divergent, but their views of the natural order coincide.

Lawrence's repeated explicit descriptions of foreplay, coition, and postorgasmic satisfaction are erotic in their realism and essential to the author's intent. We participate with the characters in the immediacy of the action. Joyce, on the other hand, filters the actual sexual experience through the minds of his characters. The five sex scenes in *Ulysses* include both Bloom's and Molly's versions of the episode on Howth, Bloom's unconscious projection of Molly's copulation in the afternoon, Bloom's vicarious sex act with Gerty MacDowell and concomitant masturbation, and Molly's recapitulation of her afternoon with Boylan. While all of these are explicit and realistic in their narration, in none of them except the masturbation (vicarious in itself) does the act occur as an actual event in the book. Rather they occur in the minds of the characters either as speculation or retrospection. The secondhand quality of the sex in *Ulysses*, particularly in Molly's soliloquy, has prompted some harsh criticism of Joyce from critics such as Strother Purdy, who claims that Jung was mistaken in praising Joyce's knowledge of women's minds because Molly's is really only a compendium of male jokes and popular erotic literature (29). Lawrence's realism, on the other hand, has just as often been seen as either courageous, honest art or adolescent indulgence.

Stemming from the sexual metaphor is the basic linguistic similarity between Joyce and Lawrence, the use of four-letter vernacular words by the two most basic characters, Molly Bloom and Oliver Mellors. When four-letter words occur elsewhere in *Ulysses*, as in the dialogue of Private Carr, they are such a natural part of the linguistic landscape that they go nearly unnoticed. Only Molly commands our special attention in her use of four-letter words in "Penelope" to describe the vitality of her feelings. This is not unlike Mellors' employment of "obscene" words to give an exalted quality to the paradox of the sublime arising from the ostensibly filthy. F. R. Leavis and the many others who find Lawrence's four-letter words objectionable criticize them as being out of place and hence an artistic flaw (Leavis 74). Even W. W. Robson, who sees Lawrence's language as deliberate, is unwilling to excuse him for it:

> What the orthodox stigmatize as lust, as shamelessness, as unnatural sexual practices, become cardinal virtues. Essential to this undertaking is the notorious use of the four-letter words. The shocking effect is deliberate. This deliberateness is unattractive: and it suggests a certain falsity. *The class in which Lawrence was brought up was unprudish but decent* [italics mine]. Lawrence seems to have forgotten that when he drew Mellors. His motives were in part noble. He hoped to cleanse the sexual relationship of guilt and fear. But we suspect other motives. *Lady Chatterley's Lover* is one of those books [. . .] which seem to be written out of resentment. They are powerful, but the atmosphere is constricting. The reader feels he is being got at. (91)

Yet the use of such language by Mellors, who modulates his accent to project himself as either a gentleman or a peasant, seems perfectly natural as one of his affectations. Here the linguistic similarity between the two authors generally ends. Lawrence's use of dialect as a device by some of his male characters reflects his preoccupation with class distinction. Joyce uses dialect for different purposes. In *Ulysses* a low Dublin accent is occasionally afforded characters for comic effect, as in the extensive use of dialect in "Cyclops," where the barfly-narrator has a comic patter all his own, and in "Eumaeus," where W. B. Murphy affects a low Dublin accent sprinkled with salty nautical metaphors. For Lawrence, the extensive use of linguistic variation and experimentation is neither an artistic nor a thematic concern. However, for Joyce, who attempted a microcosm of Western man in his universal novel, the experimentation in language is all-pervasive, from the history of rhetorical styles in "Oxen of the Sun" to the range of narrative devices in the last twelve chapters of *Ulysses*. It would be surprising if four-letter words did not appear somewhere in *Ulysses*, so closely linked is linguistic and rhetorical variety with the variety of human experience depicted in the microcosmic action of the book.

Growing out of the sexual metaphor and its relation to nature are the geography of the two novels and its relation to meaning. In Lawrence, place is associated with fixed ideas, fixed classes, fixed metaphors, but with Joyce, geography represents flux and the basis of ambiguity. Just as the ultimate meaning is intertwined with setting in *Lady Chatterley*, the ambiguous meaning of Joyce's egalitarian novel is in large measure due to the book's being set in the city. Joyce, one of the first urban novelists, depicts characters who are all city dwellers, not separated by caste or economic status but diversified by occupation and idiosyncrasy of habit. Bloom's urban livelihood as an advertising salesman depends on society, on people, as a service industry. His thoughts are largely preoccupied with social service, schemes for the betterment of mankind, or schemes for better ads. He is without a key to his own house and wanders all day a "competent keyless citizen." If there is a bower of bliss at No. 7, and if nature is identified with Molly, they are of a different variety from Lawrence's. Bloom's day is spent mostly in public. References to natural life, flowers and the like, are confined mostly to Bloom's memory of the rhododendrons on Howth. His younger counterpart in the novel, Stephen Dedalus, is also denied a key and even at the novel's end has no place to go. Their day is spent wandering, either in solitary thought or in the company of others. But as Joyce scholars have pointed out, the geography of the city, like the geography of the Mediterranean and Aegean in the *Odyssey*, provides the basis for the plot itself, a journey motif where people and places are part of the adventure. The Gardiner Street Church, the Ormond Bar, Barney Kiernan's, Davey Byrne's, the Mosque of the Baths, the cemetery, the hospital, the brothel, the cabman's shelter, and the detailed map of Ulysses-Bloom's wanderings are part of a novel of public behavior. Bloom's character is drawn in no small part through his interactions with others, and much of his stream of consciousness is associated with the geography in which he finds himself. The geography of the city is so all-pervasive that maps are available in every bookstore in Dublin for Joyce lovers to trace one or another of the Bloomsday paths. The odysseys of other characters such as Father Conmee are also recorded, rendering *Ulysses*, in effect, a topographical map of Dublin on 16 June 1904. When Bloom finally returns home and has to lower himself ignominiously over the area railings and climb through a basement window in order to get in, he is hardly in harmony with natural surroundings. Plumtree's ad comically emphasizes the difference between Mellors' Edenic bower and Bloom's city row house:

> *What is home without*
> *Plumtree's Potted Meat?*
> *Incomplete.*
> *With it an abode of bliss.* (U 5.144–47)

At day's end, Bloom finds flakes of Plumtree's meat in his bed—a tinned prod-uct of a packing plant, of society, a confinement metaphor, a death image, and a pun on Boylan's afternoon activities. The urban diversity leads to ambiguity of meaning and unresolved answers to unclear questions.

Lady Chatterley's Lover draws fixed meaning rather than ambiguity from place. As Mark Schorer poetically puts it, "In the background of this picture black machinery looms cruelly against a darkening sky; in the foreground, hemmed in and yet separate, stands a green wood; in the wood, two naked human beings dance" (298–99). The estate is divided spiritually and physi-cally into two parts. Wragby Hall is the intellectual pole of rational discourse, achieving a relationship of economic determinism with the dingy village out-side. The Edenic wood is the seat of passion and nature, scarred by the rav-ages of war when Clifford's father cut trench timbers. The wood contains the hut and the gamekeeper's cottage, twin bowers of bliss, the first where the initial knowledge is gained and the second—where knowledge is broad-ened—providing a transition from Edenic intimacy to the outside world. Julian Moynahan best summarizes the geography of this novel in terms of the sacred wood with its life mysteries, standing between the manor house and the village with their social and economic hostility and yet their joint wor-ship of money, power, property, and the mechanistic organization of human affairs (146–47).

In the wood all of nature complements the sex act, which is performed both outdoors and in: the raising of the game in the safety of Mellors' cages until it can be freed, the budding flowers, the changes of season, and the plethora of natural imagery that enhances the awareness of Connie and Mellors as they begin to commune with their surroundings. Yet Lawrence seems to realize that the lovers' participation in a transcendental life in the seclusion of their bower is but a moment in the life of Mellors and Connie, and that a permanent free existence has got to be gained in the world outside. If that world threatens the lovers in *Lady Chatterley*, it also provides a hope of salvation. Mellors, it seems, has found in farming the one vocation besides game keeping that provides gainful employment and interaction with nature. What hope there is for the couple's future is predicated on living outside the sacred wood. That hope is the difference between the book's being a tragedy of high, doomed emotion or a comedy that offers a chance for a satisfactory free life in an outside world still in harmony with nature. Mellors will certainly never be a public, Bloomian figure, but there is the hope that he may be able to exist in an uneasy truce with the rest of society. The question of whether the couple will live happily . . . is left in the air, but the issues are not ambiguous, thanks to their associations with the setting.

The war between nature and mechanized society is intertwined in Lawrence's didacticism with another force that militates against nature, the division of society into classes and into the owners and the oppressed. If Clifford Chatterley can afford to maintain his sanctuary in Wragby Hall, it is because he is separated by the woods from the encroachment of the grimy town and the collieries on which much of his income depends. In the days of "Merry olde England" the division between feudal lord and serf was not so destructive because all classes lived in harmony with natural surroundings. But during the Industrial Revolution the classes all began to cooperate in destroying their natural surroundings by building collieries and the horrible towns surrounding them, or canals such as the one dividing the Brangwen property in *The Rainbow*. Both classes, while perpetuating the distinction between themselves in the new order, begin a ceaseless war with nature in which nature inevitably suffers. It is like the degradation of God. Clifford's failure as an artist is early revealed in his inability to write literature of a lasting value, presumably because it does not recognize the truths of nature, and his subsequent failure as a man is sealed by his embracing the new mechanization, which suits his paralyzed state and his twisted temperament.

The pattern begins with the inability of his mechanized wheelchair to operate in the woods and extends to his subsequent immersion in the mindless sounds of his radio. If to the town he achieves a kind of superior manhood through his inventions and his mechanical pervasion of nature, his inner soul and manhood crumble simultaneously into an infantile state in private life. Mrs. Bolton provides his last contact with the humanity of the town through her stories and pampering. The nurse, too, has known the joy of sexual fulfillment and detests Clifford at the same time she is compassionate toward him. At first she is overawed by his class position, but she ultimately becomes scornful when she realizes that his inadequacies transcend class origins. Manhood cannot be defined through such arbitrary divisions. In a way her disgust and loyal service reflect the situation of an entire class of servants. Money makes slaves of all classes in the new society. Both Connie and Mellors reiterate repeatedly their condemnation of monetary greed as the principal preoccupation of all people rich and poor.

But Lawrence's novel is based primarily on the relation of sex to class distinction. It is, after all, about a love affair between a woman of the upper classes and her gamekeeper. The fact that their social positions are so divergent is a statement of the polemic and one possible resolution to the class struggle and social determinism that permeate all of Lawrence's novels about England. Had Connie indeed taken, as Clifford suggests, a lover of her own class for the father of her child, or had Mellors stuck with a wife of his own class or accepted another lover of his own class, there would, in effect, have been no point to the novel. Their sexual intercourse, which obliterates class distinction, is the novel's paradise, while mechanization and the industrial society, which impose a much harsher class determinism than the feudal system ever did, are the novel's hell. Clifford's literal descent into his own pit, his rejuvenation of the mines and industry, and ultimately his talent for enhancing the artificial class struggle, parallel his personal perversions in a satanic portrait.

Undoubtedly social class was linked with sexual tension in Lawrence's own life. The apparent disparity of his marriage to the daughter of a German baron and their search for sexual and intellectual values bridging the class distinction provided him with the basic dilemma of *Lady Chatterley's Lover* as well as a rationalization for his own marriage. The battle of sexes over economics, which is a primary source of lower-class marital discontent, was a part of Lawrence's youth, vividly portrayed in *Sons and Lovers* and closely intertwined in many of Lawrence's novels and short stories. But mere lovemaking is not the only resolution to the problem of class disparity. In *Lady Chatterley's Lover*, Connie's father and the gamekeeper reach a reciprocal respect transcending class origin by their mutual veneration of the physical. But Lawrence also seems to be retreating from the unrelenting sexual polemic of earlier works when he makes Mellors more gentlemanly in his natural demeanor than even the higher born or economically endowed: "Yet, she saw at once, he could go anywhere. He had a natural breeding which was really much nicer than the cut-to-pattern class thing" (*LCL* 342). Lawrence also emphasizes Mellors' gentility of speech gained in part at the tutelage of his army commander, so that Mellors' gentlemanliness has a learned aspect complementing its natural sources.

Joyce, on the other hand, was less concerned with social strata or the economic and social system than with intellect in determining the actions of the characters in *Ulysses*. His life with a former barmaid constituted less of a gap in social class than in intellectual ability for Joyce. Nora Barnacle was a primitive life force, a prototype for Molly Bloom, who is closer to nature than any other character and who unites the novel with her sensuality and vital energy. If Joyce felt inferior to Nora, it was like the situation in *Exiles* where Richard Rowan feels inferior because of his wife Bertha's natural understanding of sexual security. The biggest difference between Stephen on the one hand and Bloom and Molly on the other is not that of age, class, or marital status, but of intellect. Half of the dilemmas of the novel are the products of Stephen's allusive intellectual nature. Where the intellect in *Ulysses* is important enough to be both hallowed and ridiculed, in Lawrence—at least in *Lady Chatterley's Lover*—it runs a poor second behind sensual experience. Leopold Bloom, the "allroundman," is a partaker of both the intellectual processes and the experience of life. Class distinctions, such as they are, play little part in Molly's affair with Boylan, or Bloom's with Mrs. Breen, Gerty MacDowell, or Lizzie Twigg. Instead, sympathy, image, and intellect, all mental states, pervade these liaisons: Bloom's pity for Mrs. Breen, his romantic image of Gerty MacDowell, and his intellectual-artistic connections with Lizzie Twigg ("smart lady typist to aid gentleman in literary work" [*U* 13.326–27]). Art of another kind, vocal, is the basis of (or excuse for) the relationship between Molly and Blazes. The largely classless society of Irish literary and theatrical audiences obliterates social distinctions in art, and the general poverty in Roman Catholic Ireland obviates the need for economic distinctions as a basis for fiction.

It is perhaps in an examination of the characters that the most informative comparisons between the sensibilities of Joyce and Lawrence may be explored. Despite the title of Lawrence's novel, the central consciousness of the book is not Mellors but Connie Chatterley. As in *The Rainbow* and most of Lawrence's work, the development of the female character's awareness and perceptions constitutes the main interest of the story. The males exist as satellites of Connie Chatterley, as they shape her mind and decisions. This is not to say that Mellors does not learn anything or that his character remains static throughout the book; rather that our main interest remains with the mind of Connie Chatterley with whose history we are familiar long before we meet Mellors. *Ulysses*, on the other hand, is shaped largely by a male perspective. Of the three major characters in *Ulysses*, Bloom is clearly the predominant figure, both in the length of his narrative portion and in the detailed exploration of his mental outlook. The plain fact is that we do not know whether Bloom learns a great deal about himself or life, or in that sense whether there is a progression of action in the book. Most of us speculate that he has and that the action does progress. At any rate our interest is clearly with Bloom's dilemma, his problems, his answers, his sensibility throughout the day, much more than with Stephen's or Molly's. Molly, though the strongest advocate of a philosophical or life position in *Ulysses*, is really, like Stephen Dedalus, a satellite of Bloom, and the females in the book, Mrs. Breen, Bella Cohen, and Gerty MacDowell, mere influences on his sensibility.

Bloom and Mellors are similar in a number of ways. Both are outside the establishment and the society in which they have to live. Both are identified as having female as well as male sensibilities. Bloom is called the "new womanly man" (*U* 15.1798–99), while Mellors is similarly characterized: "They used to say I had too much of the woman in me," he says (*LCL* 344). Bloom possesses the same sort of gentility as Mellors; both have pretenses of knowledge as well as catholicity of reading. The terms in which Bloom is described by Lenehan as "a cultured allroundman" (*U* 10.581) could easily have been attributed to Mellors. Finally, both men are sensualists, and both have a strong sexual instinct.

In the story line, however, Bloom's situation is much closer to Clifford's. The difference is that Lawrence is very careful not to allow Clifford's plight and paralysis to enlist the reader's sympathy, while Joyce opens the floodgates of pity and terror for Bloom's universal plight. Clifford is cuckolded, defeated, and reduced to childishness in his inner life, while he achieves supermanhood in his external business dealings. Bloom's home and marital prerogatives are usurped, but he remains unbeaten. Clifford's literary and industrial victories likewise enable him to carry on. The difference is that Clifford's handicap is symbolic of his spirit, which forces him into a life of the outside world because of his shriveled personal life. Bloom, however, chooses of his own free will to face a hostile outside world, and the same spirit, love, and equanimity that he manifests in that world are brought to bear on his home life. On the other hand, Bloom is like Clifford in many ways, occasionally infantile, masochistic, and weak. But ironically from this he emerges stronger, his torments by the end of the day fended off mainly by the strength of his own personality. No one can say that Bloom is insensitive after being privy to his thoughts about his companions in "Hades" and his wife in "Lestrygonians" and "Sirens." But he never completely surrenders to suffering because he is better able to cope, self-sufficient from masturbation, and sympathetic to the plight of others.

On the literal level, Mellors and Boylan, his counterpart in *Ulysses*, represent male energy. While it is to Lawrence's credit not to succumb to the longitudinal fallacy of equating manhood entirely with penis size, Boylan's prodigious ability to produce sexual satisfaction is in direct proportion to his equipment. The jaunty jingling of Boylan's cart harnesses, his jaunty atmosphere of self-assurance, as described in "Sirens," is similar to Mellors' self-assured peacock pride in dealing with women. Here Mellors resembles both Molly and Boylan. Molly's sensuality and vitality are obvious to men, who generally see her in sexual terms. Her uninhibited espousal of sex almost as a political and religious cause closely allies her with Mellors, as do her innate self-assurance based on sexual principles and her ability to move in different classes (due to her artistry and sensual attractions). Mellors represents a way of life that is individualistic and, like Molly's, close to nature. Like her, he is a judgmental character who is set in his ways and, in touch with a natural sexual reality, measures all people and things against that standard.

While Mellors and Clifford both, even in the most charitable eyes, exhibit a neuroticism born of past and present injustices, Connie, despite her past, is essentially as whole a person as Bloom and Molly. But Connie and Mellors both have pasts that so color their perspectives that their love assumes an attitude of desperation. It is in a sense Mellors' last stand and Connie's discovery of life after the deadness of marriage and meaningless copulation. While Bloom and Molly have had a less-than-blissful marital history, neither one has been permanently disfigured, nor have their perspectives been substantially warped, though many shocked readers of "Circe" and "Penelope" may claim otherwise. An attitude of comedy, of universality, and of congenial and steadfast strength permeates their characters throughout the book. Mellors' alternating ecstasy and gloom lead him to focus on salvation. Only at the end of *Lady Chatterley* has his faith in life been restored enough for him to hope again for a happy existence with someone loving and caring. Mellors is a rebel hero. Like Molly, he has only his faith in sensuality to sustain him. That sexual base in nature provides what tentative resolutions there are in both books as the thoughts and judgments of Molly and Mellors close the novels.

Bloom of the womanly sensibility is like Connie Chatterley the discoverer. His poignant lovemaking with Molly on Howth among the rhododendrons is the turning point of his life, and it influences his thoughts and actions during the day, providing him with a major buffer against self-derision and the slights of others. To both Bloom and Connie, offspring have great meaning. It is the coming of the child that shapes Connie's future more than any inner stasis or awareness of her own spiritual being. The pregnancy is a certainty. The possibility of having a child had been discussed by Connie and Clifford long before her pregnancy, but the impossibility of her continuing to live at Wragby Hall with the child after her consciousness is altered by Mellors leads to her leaving. The child is the hope for the future, the symbol of her union with Mellors and life, not to be stifled in the perversions of Wragby Hall. Mellors' earlier child with Bertha Coutts is for him dead. His future also lies in the birth of a new child. Likewise, Bloom's hope for a son in his future has, since the death of Rudy, never completely died. On this sixteenth day of June, Bloom's search for vicarious fatherhood goes on unabated. Will Stephen and Bloom become spiritual father and son? Stephen is only a parody of Telemachus, and there is certainly no indication that any permanent relationship will come to pass. Happiness in any tangible form such as the child represents is more likely to be the reward of Connie and Mellors than Molly and Bloom. In Joyce's world there are other compensations.

For Joyce's characters, art has always provided a means of salvation, personal as well as political. Bloom and Molly feel that Stephen could create great art in their company: Bloom's idea is that Molly would contribute to Stephen's musical education and that Bloom could manage their joint concert tours, while Molly thinks that she will inspire Stephen to write great poetry and that she would be preserved and enshrined in his art. For Joyce, art is the primary reason for being, and as such it is of paramount importance in his work.

The subject is less pervasive in Lawrence, though his great novels all have artists in them. Very often, like Will Brangwen, they are craftsmen rather than individuals gifted with the ability to create deathless art. Similarly, Clifford's artistic endeavors in *Lady Chatterley's Lover* bring the rewards of popularity to someone merely able to craft pleasingly. In both *Ulysses* and *Lady Chatterley's Lover* artists are often degraded as human beings. Stephen, who by the beginning of *Ulysses* has produced little other than the villanelle, is certainly not a particularly admirable figure, any more than Shem of *Finnegans Wake* or Richard Rowan of *Exiles*. They are as neurotic as Lawrence's Clifford and Duncan. Bloom, the would-be artist, seeing himself, like Philip Beaufoy, earning a guinea per column, defaces the artist's "maturer work," "Matchem's Masterstroke," by wiping his behind with it, as he thinks of the whole artistic enterprise principally in terms of its profit. He is not unlike Clifford and Michaelis in this regard. The theme running through both works is that artists use art as a rationalization for their own failings and psychological inadequacies.

Both Joyce and Lawrence as literary artists established credentials in another art form, though certainly Lawrence's painting has gained a greater notoriety and respect than Joyce's music. But both Joyce and Lawrence used the second art to enhance the first. Lawrence's visual imagery and Joyce's musical imagery are the sources of such memorable passages as Connie's first spring walk in the woods or the opening of the "Sirens" episode of *Ulysses*. While art provided stylistic devices and subject matter in the perfection of art and the imperfections of artistic people and would-be artists, both writers were careful to give art a realistic place in the actions, if not the minds, of their characters. None of Lawrence's artistic characters are deluded enough to see themselves as saviors of their race or nation, but Joyce's primary artist, Stephen Dedalus, will "go to encounter for the millionth time the reality of experience and to forge in the smithy of [his . . .] soul the uncreated conscience of [his . . .] race" (*P* 252–53). Stephen's preoccupation must not have been so different from Joyce's when he wrote *Dubliners* and acknowledged his own messianic urges: "My intention was to write a chapter of the moral history of my country" (*Letters II* 134). Whereas Joyce's treatment of Stephen in *Portrait* is ironic, by the time he wrote *Ulysses*, Joyce had matured enough to be able to see genuine comedy in the artistic impulse, when he made artistic, civic-minded Bloom a parodied savior of Ireland. On the other hand, Lawrence never deviated from his own preoccupation with saving England from contemporary tawdriness. Lawrence finally kicked the traces of social didacticism and concentrated on the freedom of self in a human relationship, though tempered by the surrounding evil of a mechanized and money-grubbing society. The didacticism had merely shifted to a salvation stemming from an inner strength to ward off the encroachments of an increasingly meretricious world. Although Lawrence's characters do not find salvation revealed in art, and although Lawrence is not the reflexive novelist that Joyce is, still *Lady Chatterley* itself is a didactic work. At the end of his career Lawrence still maintained a serious messianic spirit, something the later Joyce heavily disguised, if indeed Joyce did not finally decide merely to reveal truth and let societal betterment go its own way.

The validity of this thesis may be tested by comparing the endings of the two novels. In *Lady Chatterley's Lover*, Mellors is able to blend his love of nature and natural processes with the necessity of living in the world. While we do not know whether Clifford will divorce Connie or whether Connie and Mellors eventually will be married and happy, the lovers' determination to be together seems to presage a bright future. That optimism is reinforced by our wanting them to succeed without regard to the artistic merits of such a conclusion to the novel. They have enlisted our sympathy, and we share the author's idea of what an ideal world should be.

Ulysses presents us with a different proposition. We make much of Molly's "yes" in the end, not only as an affirmation of life but as her response to Bloom's request for breakfast the next morning. Has Bloom like his Greek precursor won the day and vanquished the suitors? Is Boylan to return no more? Is the

Citizen to throw no more biscuit tins? Is Bloom finally to publish to critical acclaim his experiences in a cabman's shelter, or does any of that really make any difference? It is difficult to find readers from whom Bloom has not elicited sympathy. It is equally difficult to find many who favor some sort of assertion of Bloom's will over Molly, or who seriously feel that Stephen would become a great artist if he would come to live with Bloom. The ending of *Ulysses* is ambiguous only if we wish to read a moral lesson in it; it is another slice of reality, as gripping and as poignant as any moment in Bloom's day. But its meaning goes beyond any lesson we may apply in practical terms to our own lives, any conception of good or evil. It is essentially a comic vision of life that plays a Sancho Panza to Lawrence's Quixote, the elemental contrast between the sensibilities of the two great figures in twentieth-century British fiction.

Notes

1. Delaware University Press allowed the inclusion of this essay by Zack Bowen, which first appeared in *D. H. Lawrence's "Lady": A New Look at Lady Chatterley's Lover*, ed. Michael Squires and Dennis Jackson (Athens: U of Georgia P, 1985).

Works Cited

Brett, Dorothy. *Lawrence and Brett: A Friendship*. Philadelphia: Lippincott, 1933.

Knight, O. Wilson. "Lawrence, Joyce, and Powys." *Essays in Criticism* 11.4 (1961): 413.

Leavis, F. R. *D. H. Lawrence: Novelist*. Chicago: U of Chicago P, 1955.

Moynahan, Julian. *The Deed of Life: The Novels and Tales of D. H. Lawrence*. Princeton, NJ: Princeton UP, 1963.

Purdy, Strother B. "On the Psychology of Erotic Literature." *Literature and Psychology* 20.1 (1970): 23–29.

Robson, W. W. "Joyce and Lawrence." *Modern English Literature*. London: Oxford UP, 1970.

Schorer, Mark. "On Lady Chatterley's Lover." *Modern British Fiction*. Ed. Mark Schorer. London: Oxford UP, 1961.

Vivas, Eliseo. *D. H. Lawrence: The Failure and the Triumph of Art*. Bloomington: Indiana UP, 1960.

2

Love, Bodies, and Nature
in *Lady Chatterley's Lover* and *Ulysses*

an ecocritical analysis

MARGOT NORRIS

James Joyce's *Ulysses* and D. H. Lawrence's *Lady Chatterley's Lover* brought the nineteenth-century adultery novel to modernity. Although their female protagonists are indeed adulterous, they are no longer consigned to the social punishments that led the heroines of Flaubert's *Madame Bovary* and Tolstoy's *Anna Karenina* to suicide. But the modernist novels of Joyce and Lawrence go beyond merely averting the catastrophic fate of the adulteress by reconfiguring sexuality as a much broader phenomenon with significance and satisfaction beyond the social and the interpersonal. Nature is a very powerful force in the works of Joyce and Lawrence, although its function as a topic of serious literary analysis was obliged to await the emergence of ecocriticism in the twenty-first century. That moment has arrived, and D. H. Lawrence's 1923 *Studies in Classic American Literature* is now cited as a proto-ecological literary analysis by such critics as Scott Russell Sanders (*The Ecocriticism Reader* 182–84) and Lawrence Buell (*The Environmental Imagination* 33–34).[1] Joyce is entering this field more slowly, although a June 2010 conference in Limerick on "Ireland and Ecocriticism" featured a panel titled "Eco-Joyce."

The field of ecocriticism is itself currently undergoing challenging discussions, and in this context my own formulations of an exploration of Joyce's and Lawrence's use of nature images in relation to love and sexuality in their novels hew to the rather loose description offered by Cheryll Glotfelty in her introduction to *The Ecocriticism Reader*. "What then *is* ecocriticism?" she asks. "Simply put, ecocriticism is the study of the relationship between literature and the physical environment" (xviii). She goes on to add, "Despite the broad scope of inquiry and disparate levels of sophistication, all ecological criticism shares the fundamental premise that human culture is connected to the physical world" (xix). At the same time, Timothy Morton in *Ecology without Nature* argues that ecological writing fashions compelling images of "nature" that nonetheless get in the way of "properly ecological forms of culture, philosophy, politics, and art" (1).

Bonnie Kime Scott points out that despite the lack of attention from many modernist authors and later critics, "modernism takes an abiding interest in nature, human interdependencies with it, and even in its preservation" (219). This interest is linked to the modernist fascination with "non-human life, particularly animals and trees, that overlaps an interest in the primitive world, locus of vital sexual and spiritual energies [. . .]" (221). I would therefore like to conjoin Lawrence and Joyce as writers with a shared vision of nature, and of landscape as no mere setting for love and sex, but as "the energized *medium* from which human lives emerge and by which those lives are bounded and measured" (Sanders 183). Both *Lady Chatterley's Lover* and Molly Bloom's musings and memories in the "Penelope" episode support this premise. I will organize my ecocritical discussion of these two novels loosely around four thematic topics—flowers, animals, the body, and the land—set against the backdrop of marriage, adultery, sexuality, and vitality. These topics will interrelate in untidy and complicated ways but with the same result: the demonstration of a common ecological sensibility in Joyce and Lawrence.

On the surface, the adultery themes in Lawrence and Joyce appear to have much in common. In both texts, married women are driven to adultery by sexual frustration stemming from a husband's sexual dysfunction, the result of significant trauma. Clifford Chatterley is a paralyzed war veteran, and Leopold Bloom is haunted by the problematic conception of an only son who died soon after childbirth. Interestingly, mere sex is an inadequate solution for the frustrations of both women. Connie Chatterley first has an unsatisfactory affair with a young Irish dramatist named Michaelis before she begins her intense relationship with the gamekeeper Oliver Mellors. And it is by no means clear that Molly Bloom's affair with Hugh Boylan will offer her the emotional intimacy and vital connection with a man that she craves and needs. The evocation of nature in relation to the women's intimacies with men therefore plays an important role in sorting out the ways in which sexuality alone is or is not capable of providing satisfaction and healing the symptoms of loneliness and disaffection that their marital problems have produced. The symptoms are dramatized much more clearly in *Lady Chatterley's Lover* and precede the affair with Mellors by some time: "Vaguely she knew herself that she was going to pieces in some way. Vaguely she knew she was out of connection: she had lost touch with the substantial and vital world" (*LCL* 20). Molly Bloom, who is kept virtually out of sight for much of the novel until "Penelope," expresses her needs and desires more directly and generically, as lovemaking with *someone*— "I wish some man or other would take me sometime when hes there and kiss me in his arms theres nothing like a kiss long and hot down to your soul" (*U* 18.104). This is less than Connie's lost touch with the vital world, but it still implies Molly's need to feel fully alive again.

In both novels the most satisfying experiences of love and making love occur in a vital connection with the outdoors. Flowers play a highly significant role for both, although less as aesthetic objects than as vivid, living creations. Lawrence sets the romance between Connie and Mellors in the spring—a season already configured as a time of rebirth and sacred renewal by T. S. Eliot and the mythic inspirations of Jessie Weston and James Frazer.[2] Her depression is lifted both by the sight of the blooming daffodils as well as by her memory of having earlier seen Mellors bathing, "the keeper, his thin, white body, like a lonely pistil of an invisible flower" (*LCL* 85). Bloom—his name transliterated from Virag, the Hungarian word for flower—also names himself Henry Flower in his sexualized incarnation with Martha Clifford, who responds by attaching a flower to her letter. And, like Mellors, Bloom in his bath is also characterized with a phallic floral image: "the limp father of thousands, a languid floating flower" (*U* 5.571).

But *Lady Chatterley's Lover* surpasses any flower evocation in Joyce's work with the climactic "flower wedding" in chapter 15 of the novel. The lovers have shared a number of satisfactory and unsatisfactory experiences by this time, when they come to a troublesome pass, with Connie scheduled to go to Venice with her family at a time she believes she may be pregnant with Mellors' child. Connie cavorts in the rain on this day, and Mellors gathers flowers that they then entwine in hair, moustache, navel, and pubic hair, throughout their bodies: "He had brought columbines and campions, and new-mown hay, and oak-tufts and honey-suckle in small bud. He fastened fluffy young oak-sprays round her breasts, sticking in tufts of bluebells and campion: and in her navel he poised a pink campion flower, and in her maidenhair were forget-me-nots and wood-ruff" (*LCL* 227–28). He then pronounces their marriage in their private sexual incarnations as "John Thomas marryin' Lady Jane" (*LCL* 228).

In *Ulysses* it is not their wedding, which is largely elided, but the day of the proposal that is studded with memories of flowers for Molly. Molly and Bloom, too, have romantic moments in the rain—"he did look a big fool dreeping in the rain splendid set of teeth he had made me hungry to look at them" (*U*

18.306). But their day is the sunny day of Bloom's proposal on Howth Head in May when the rhododendrons are in bloom. Their experience closely follows Molly's first romantic encounter with Mulvey, also in May, when she was a girl in Gibraltar. And she deliberately maneuvers the timing of the proposal to take place not in her kitchen, but in the lovely outdoor setting of Howth overlooking the sea. Mulvey seems to have given her flowers on their first youthful encounter: "I got him excited he crushed all the flowers on my bosom he brought me" (*U* 18.777). We learn that Bloom, too, has given her flowers on her birthday, something that pleased her enormously: "I liked the way he made love then he knew the way to take a woman when he sent me the 8 big poppies because mine was the 8th" (*U* 18.329–30). But Bloom's gift to Molly on Howth is to transform *her* into a flower: "yes he said I was a flower of the mountain yes so we are flowers all a womans body yes" (*U* 18.1576). Molly's equation of a woman's body with a flower points more to vitality and living than merely aesthetic beauty, and Bloom, sensing that it pleases her, repeats the appellation in his proposal—"then he asked me would I yes to say yes my mountain flower" (*U* 18.1605). When Bloom remembers the same scene earlier in the novel, he recalls not that he called her his mountain flower but that "Flowers her eyes were, take me, willing eyes" (*U* 8.910).

The ecstatic role that flowers play in the romance and lovemaking of Connie and Mellors and Molly and Bloom is contrasted with the far less satisfying function of flowers in relationship with other partners. For Clifford Chatterley, flowers inspire poetic effusion: "'Thou still unravished bride of quietness,' he quoted.—'It seems to fit flowers so much better than Greek vases'" (*LCL* 93). This drives Connie into a silent outburst: "She was angry with him, turning everything into words. Violets were Juno's eyelids, and windflowers were unravished brides. How she hated words, always coming between her and life: they did the ravishing, if anything did: ready-made words and phrases, sucking all the life-sap out of living things" (*LCL* 93). Bloom's strategy of turning a bride into a flower rather than a flower into a bride clearly works much better for Molly. Interestingly, both Bloom's and Molly's other love interests on this day present them with flowers, but to far less pleasing effect. Martha Clifford attaches a flower to Bloom's letter, and Boylan takes the red carnation plucked from a vase in Thornton's shop to his assignation with Molly. But neither Bloom nor Molly is particularly impressed or charmed by these gestures—"who gave him that flower he said he bought," Molly wonders (*U* 18.125). Flowers have their most potent romantic effect on Bloom when they remain grounded. Bloom has particularly fond memories of the young Molly at a party at Mat Dillon's in Roundtown, in another month of May when the lilacs were in bloom: "Full voice of perfume of what perfume does your lilactrees" (*U* 11.730). Martha Clifford is interested in the perfume of Henry Flower's wife presumably to gauge her attraction, but the metaphorical perfume of Molly's voice singing the song "Waiting" that evening is infused in Bloom's memory with the actual heady fragrance of the lilac trees.

[Animals play a less significant and less tidy role than flowers in the romantic relationships of the Lawrence and Joyce couples.[Mellors, his job as gamekeeper notwithstanding, can be quite brutal, as when he makes his little girl cry by killing a cat he calls a "poacher." His treatment of his sobbing little girl is no less cruel—"Ah, shut it up, tha false little bitch" (*LCL* 58). It is impossible to think of Bloom treating either a cat or his daughter Milly like that. Bloom actually remembers a sad moment in Milly's childhood involving an animal: "Dead animal even sadder. Silly-Milly burying the little dead bird in the kitchen matchbox, a daisychain and bits of broken chainies on the grave" (*U* 6.951).[And although the Blooms' cat may be less a pet than a practical mouse catcher, Bloom treats her with considerable empathy:]"They call them stupid. They understand what we say better than we understand them," he thinks and wonders how he appears to her, "Wonder what I look like to her? Height of a tower? No, she can jump me" (*U* 4.26).[3] Molly interestingly displays a similar curiosity about the cat: "I wonder do they see anything that we cant staring like that when she sits at the top of the stairs" (*U* 18.936). In *Lady Chatterley's Lover* it is Connie who is alive to the animal, a tiny chick she discovers in one of Mellors' coops on "a lovely sunny day with great tufts of primroses under the hazels, and many violets dotting the paths" (*LCL* 114). The little chick seems to her "the most alive little spark of a creature in seven kingdoms" as Connie watches it "in a sort of ecstasy. Life, life! Pure, sparky, fearless new life" (*LCL* 114). The chick moves Connie so greatly that when Mellors sees a tear fall on her wrist, he suddenly feels "the old flame shooting and leaping up in his loins" (*LCL* 115).[The tiny chick becomes the catalyst for both Connie and Mellors to become alive again[No animal plays a similar role in *Ulysses*, although Bloom's empathy for animals does find a counterpart in Molly. Bloom feeds the cat and the seagulls and has brought home a stray dog, much to Molly's consternation—"like the night he walked home with a dog if you please that might have been mad" (*U* 18.1086). But she, in her turn, is horrified at the Gibraltar bullfights that hold no romance for her at all, "ripping all the whole insides out of those poor horses" (*U* 18.633) while the "brutes of men" and women in white mantillas cheer.

However, the animal plays another role in both novels when it is perceived in the human body as a living organism. In *Lady Chatterley's Lover* the healthy perception of the body as creatural is set in contrast to an opinion voiced during one of Clifford's evenings with his friends: "'So long as you can forget your body you are happy,' said Lady Bennerley. 'And the moment you begin to be aware of your body, you are wretched'" (*LCL* 74). Connie first becomes acutely aware of the body when she stumbles on the gamekeeper, naked to the hips, washing himself in the forest and is surprised by a "visionary experience" (*LCL* 66). She sees Mellors as "a creature that lives alone" and is struck by "a certain beauty of a pure creature" (*LCL* 66). It is not aesthetic beauty that touches her "but a lambency, the warm, white flame of a single life, revealing itself in contours that one might touch: a body!" (*LCL* 66). Bloom has a similar response to seeing Molly's body in bed in the morning, without any visionary fanfare: "He looked calmly down on her bulk and between her large soft bubs, sloping within her nightdress like a shegoat's udder. The warmth of her couched body rose on the air, mingling with the fragrance of the tea she poured" (*U* 4.304). After seeing Mellors, Connie goes home and there removes her clothes to study her naked body in the mirror. What she sees distresses her, her body looking flattened and "a little harsh" (*LCL* 70). She sees her body as a living thing deprived of the conditions to flourish: "It was as if it had not had enough sun and warmth; it was a little greyish and sapless" (*LCL* 70). After Mellors has awakened her, Connie is likened to "a forest, like the dark interlacing of the oakwood, humming inaudibly with myriad unfolding buds. Meanwhile the birds of desire were asleep in the interlaced intricacy of her body" (*LCL* 138).

Although Bloom does not invoke animal tropes to remember Molly's body on Howth, or his own, his remembrance is studded with natural images and a sense of vitalism. Both plants and animals are a vivid part of the scene as they lay hidden "under wild ferns." There are "earwigs in the heather scrub," and they hear a "nannygoat walking surefooted, dropping currants" (*U* 8.904, 911). Although Bloom's erotic imagination is generally strongly shaped by pornographic theatrics, his actual sexual experience with Molly is focused on the immediacy of bodily sensation, on touch ("[c]oolsoft with ointments her hand touched me"), taste ("she gave me in my mouth the seedcake warmed and chewed"), and temperature ("[h]ot I tongued her") (*U* 8.904). Molly's body itself is described as pulsing and dilating, "her stretched neck beating" and her "fat nipples upright" (*U* 8.913). His memory echoes refrains from Lawrence's lovers, when he thinks "Young life, her lips that gave me pouting" (*U* 8.909). He describes his own response to the experience as "Ravished over her I lay, full lips full open, kissed her mouth" (*U* 8.906). Bloom clearly uses the word "ravished" in a very different sense from Clifford's poetic echo of Keats. Connie objects to "ravish" because she associates it with violation, "sucking all the life-sap out of living things" (*LCL* 93), while the ravished Bloom feels overcome with the joy and pleasure of experiencing the life-sap of the living body and the living scene on Howth. Sadly, after the memory of that glorious lovemaking on Howth fades, Bloom's thoughts turn to nonliving statues and sculptures, "[s]hapely goddesses, Venus" and "women sculped Junonian" (*U* 8.920, 8.928)—as though he had become a Pygmalion in reverse. Connie Chatterley would not approve: "She was angry with him. Violets were Juno's eyelids, and windflowers were unravished brides" (*LCL* 93).

Molly's own appreciation of the body on the day *Ulysses* is set is focused not on her husband, however, but on her experience with her lover of that afternoon, Boylan, who seems indeed to have ravished her in a narrow version of Bloom's sense of the word. Like Connie, Molly is prompted to reflect on her own body, but instead of finding it flat or harsh, she finds her breasts juicy and stiff—"yes I think he made them a bit firmer sucking them like that so long he made me thirsty" (*U* 18.535). She is less enchanted with "what a man looks like with his two bags full and his other thing hanging down out of him or sticking up at you like a hatrack no wonder they hide it with a cabbageleaf" (*U* 18.542). Boylan's own apparatus is admired for its dilated vigor, although Molly's language has none of Connie's lyricism—"he must have come 3 or 4 times with that tremendous big red brute of a thing he has I thought the vein or whatever the dickens they call it was going to burst" (*U* 18.143). She does associate Boylan's potency with animals, "like a Stallion driving it up into you," and thinks "he must have eaten oysters I think a few dozen" (*U* 18.148). But in some respects her sense of ravishment is more violent than poetic, thinking of her encounter with Boylan: "thats all they want out of you with that determined vicious look in his eye" (*U* 18.152). Connie's early encounters with Mellors too have their rough edges: "[S]he had to lie down there under the boughs of the tree, like an animal, while he waited, standing there in his shirt and breeches, watching her with haunted eyes" (*LCL* 133). But the effect, once the lovemaking is under way, becomes quite wonderful with "new strange trills rippling inside her" that are "exquisite, exquisite and melting her all molten inside. It was like bells rippling up and up to a culmination" (*LCL* 133). Molly, too, has a similar sensation after "coming for about 5 minutes with my legs round him [. . .] I feel all fire inside me," she says, as she remembers the scene (*U* 18.585).

Finally, the setting of lovemaking in the context of the outdoors and in connection to the land is significant for intensifying the vitality of the experience
for lovers. In *Lady Chatterley's Lover* the woods around Wragby are inscribed
with English myth and history. "The wood was a remnant of the great forest
where Robin Hood hunted" (*LCL* 41), we are told, although when Clifford returns maimed after World War I, the forest, too, has been crippled and ruined
in order to supply trench timber to the front: "[T]here was nothing but a ravel
of dead bracken, a thin and spindly sapling leaning here and there, big sawn
stumps, showing their tops and their grasping roots, lifeless" (*LCL* 42). The
wildlife that had once populated the wood is also virtually gone by this time:
"A jay called harshly, many little birds fluttered. But there was no game: no
pheasants. They had been killed off during the war, and the wood had been
left unprotected, till now Clifford had got his game-keeper again" (*LCL* 41–42).
This is Mellors' job, then, to revitalize the woods with pheasants, and in the
spring when they are brooding, Connie visits them every day—"they were the
only things in the world that warmed her heart" (*LCL* 113). And it is in this setting that Connie and Mellors both come back to life again, like the forest itself,
after their times of isolation and hibernation. But as if offering an ecological
prophecy, Mellors speculates that the days of the forest are numbered and that
technology and civilization would soon intrude again and finish the destruction begun with the war: "Soon it would destroy the wood, and the bluebells
would spring no more. All vulnerable things must perish under the rolling and
running of iron" (*LCL* 119).[4]

Ulysses is, of course, set a decade before World War I, and so although its
setting is urban Dublin, the surrounding countryside remains unspoiled. The
dichotomy between indoor lovemaking and outdoor lovemaking that under-
lies the ambience of *Lady Chatterley's Lover* is also operative in *Ulysses*. Connie's arid affair with Michaelis takes place in her boudoir at the manor house,
while her vital encounters with Mellors occur either in a cottage or outdoors
in the woods. Molly's affair with Boylan takes place indoors in her home.
But her memorable encounters with Mulvey, Gardner, and Bloom take place
outdoors. Molly and Gardner kiss good-bye on the canal bank, and Mulvey
first kissed her under the Moorish wall. Molly's romantic and other youthful memories of Gibraltar are largely set in outdoor spaces. She told Mulvey
she was tired, presumably so they would lie down together—"we lay over
the firtree cove a wild place" (*U* 18.789). Much of her play with Mulvey takes
place outdoors: "I was jumping up at the pepper trees and the white poplars
pulling the leaves off and throwing them at him" (*U* 18.851). But even beyond

romance, Molly's memories of Gibraltar seem to have conditioned in her a passionate love of nature:

> O and the sea the sea crimson sometimes like fire and the glorious sunsets and the figtrees in the Alameda gardens yes and all the queer little streets and the pink and blue and yellow houses and the rosegardens and the jessamine and geraniums and cactuses and Gibraltar as a girl where I was a Flower of the mountain. (*U* 18.1598)

The feelings inspired by those early delights in Gibraltar have clearly intruded into Molly's present life: "I love flowers Id love to have the whole place swimming in roses God of heaven theres nothing like nature the wild mountains then the sea and the waves rushing" (*U* 18.1557). Bloom catches her passion that day on Howth, it seems: "[T]he sun shines for you he said the day we were lying among the rhododendrons on Howth head in the grey tweed suit and his straw hat the day I got him to propose to me" (*U* 18.1571).

I concur with Glotfelty and Morton that *Lady Chatterley's Lover* and *Ulysses* do indeed rely on arguably benign and even sentimental fantasies of "nature" to make their point, that certain intense emotional and erotic intimacies between men and women are intensified by connections to elements of the environment such as flowers and animals, and to the human body and its sensations. But while these representations may have Romanticist overtones and otherwise appropriate the concept of "nature" rather than interrogating it in ecocritically profitable ways, they nonetheless usefully complicate the more common socially oriented analyses of the nineteenth- and twentieth-century adultery novel. Marriage and its discontents are grounded in sexual dysfunction in both works. Yet both novels demonstrate that the intensity of connection between partners is not resolved by sexual activity alone, but by something deeper and more fundamental, namely by a connection of human bodies and their perceptions and sensations to nonhuman forces in the environment, to flowers, animals, woods and forests, and to their own vitality as sensate organisms. In the end, nature is, of course, reduced to language in these works, like all thematic elements of fiction. But its poetic effect in these similarly themed works by D. H. Lawrence and James Joyce is extraordinarily powerful.

Notes

1. In Howard J. Booth's 2009 collection *New D. H. Lawrence*, Fiona Becket notes that one turn Lawrence studies might take is toward the author's "nuanced handling

of human and non-human nature in his writing, in particular in the context of green thinking and the development of a workable green cultural critique" (148). Trevor Norris reaffirms the importance of an ecocritical examination of D. H. Lawrence, whose attention to Western societies' industrialization he termed a crisis of civilization; Norris connects Lawrence's concerns to Heidegger's development of a phenomenology that encouraged a return to self-understanding, or authenticity, that allowed proper ethical relations between man and his environment (115).

2. Buell writes, "The foregrounding of the seasons as the central subject of a major work of English literature came only on the eve of the scientific and industrial revolutions, and partly in reaction to the experience of social displacement wrought by urbanization" (222). While the seasons are not a central theme in either *Lady Chatterley's Lover* or *Ulysses*, their emphasis at moments in the works does work in contrast to displacements produced by industrialization in Lawrence's Midlands and by urbanization in Dublin. See Tim Wenzell's *Emerald Green* for a discussion of Irish urbanization (1).

3. Bonnie Kime Scott discussed Bloom and his cat in "Greening Joyce: Does Joyce Have a Place in Ecocriticism?," a paper delivered at the conference "California Joyce Redux" on 30 January 2010 at the University of California, Irvine.

4. Tim Wenzell sounds a similar warning about contemporary Ireland, although his culprit is urban sprawl rather than industrialization: "This new topography of pavement is threatening to undermine the rich natural history of Ireland and the rich legacy of nature literature from the beginning of Irish civilization" (1).

Works Cited

Becket, Fiona. "D. H. Lawrence, Language, and Green Cultural Critique." *New D. H. Lawrence*. Ed. Howard J. Booth. Manchester, UK: Manchester UP, 2009. 148–68.

Bowen, Zack. "*Lady Chatterley's Lover* and *Ulysses*." *D. H. Lawrence's "Lady": A New Look at Lady Chatterley's Lover*. Ed. Michael Squires and Dennis Jackson. Athens: U of Georgia P, 1985. 116–35. Bowen's essay has been republished in this volume.

Buell, Lawrence. *The Environmental Imagination: Thoreau, Nature Writing, and the Formation of American Culture*. Cambridge: Belknap Press of Harvard UP, 1995.

Delany, Paul. "'A Would-Be-Dirty Mind': D. H. Lawrence as an Enemy of Joyce." *Joyce in the Hibernian Metropolis: Essays*. Ed. Morris Beja and David Norris. Columbus: Ohio State UP, 1996. 76–82.

Ellis, David. *D. H. Lawrence: Dying Game 1922–1930*. Vol. 3. Cambridge: Cambridge UP, 1998.

Glotfelty, Cheryll. Introduction. *The Ecocriticism Reader: Landmarks in Literary Ecology*. Ed. Cheryll Glotfelty and Harold Fromm. Athens: U of Georgia P, 1996. xv–xxxvii.

Morton, Timothy. *Ecology without Nature: Rethinking Environmental Aesthetics*. Cambridge: Harvard UP, 2007.

Norris, Trevor. "Martin Heidegger, D. H. Lawrence, and Poetic Attention to Being." *Ecocritical Theory: New European Approaches*. Ed. Axel Goodbody and Kate Rigby. Charlottesville: U of Virginia P, 2011.

Sanders, Scott Russell. "Speaking a Word for Nature." *The Ecocriticism Reader: Landmarks in Literary Ecology*. Ed. Cheryll Glotfelty and Harold Fromm. Athens: U of Georgia P, 1996. 182–95.

Scott, Bonnie Kime. "Green." *Modernism and Theory: A Critical Debate*. Ed. Stephen Ross. New York: Routledge, 2009.

———. "Greening Joyce: Does Joyce Have a Place in Ecocriticism?" Paper delivered at the conference "California Joyce Redux," 30 January 2010, at the University of California, Irvine.

Wenzell, Tim. *Emerald Green: An Ecocritical Study of Irish Literature*. Newcastle upon Tyne, UK: Cambridge Scholars Publishing, 2009.

Woolf, Virginia. *The Letters of Virginia Woolf*. 6 vols. Ed. Nigel Nicholson and Joanne Trautman. New York: Harcourt Brace Jovanovich, 1975–80.

———. *A Writer's Notebook*. Ed. Leonard Woolf. San Diego: Harcourt, 1982.

3

The "Odd Couple" Constructing the "New Man"

Bloom and Mellors in *Ulysses* and *Lady Chatterley's Lover*

EARL G. INGERSOLL

Gender issues, a common element in Joyce's and Lawrence's writing, deserve further attention in these two writers' most (in)famous novels, *Ulysses* and *Lady Chatterley's Lover*. Having conceived of exploring Leopold Bloom and Oliver Mellors as the focus of gender issues, I returned to Zack Bowen's essay, which I had read when it appeared a generation ago. I discovered to my chagrin that Bowen had opened up the very territory I assumed I would be the first to explore. After beginning his essay dramatically with a sampling of the unpleasant comments Joyce and Lawrence made about each other's novels, Bowen moves on to his real concern: an extensive survey of how much their writing shares in common, especially *Lady Chatterley's Lover* and *Ulysses.* Bowen briefly notes that Bloom at one point is identified as the "new womanly man" (*U* 15.1798–99), and that Mellors admits that he has been told he has "too much of the woman" in him (*LCL* 344), generalizing that Mellors and Bloom reveal "female as well as male sensibilities" (Bowen 23). By implication at least, these characteristics, traditionally considered "womanly" or "feminine," appear in a context where such identification calls into question the manhood of Bloom and Mellors.

My project is to revisit Bowen's brief gender assessment of these two literary figures and to bring to bear on gender identification some of the relevant theoretical writing that has appeared in the intervening decades. I propose to locate Bloom and Mellors along the spectrum of gender to which most of us have become accustomed in thinking about these issues. In this context, femininity and masculinity represent less the traditional binary of mutually exclusive poles than a continuum within which gender unmoors itself from its older ties to sexual or biological identifications. At its extreme, this exploration opens out into the possibility that at the beginning of the last century Lawrence and Joyce found in the much-touted "New Woman" the license to offer in Bloom and Mellors a "New Man," characters not bound by nineteenth-century notions of masculinity or manhood.]

It needs to be noted at the outset that this heuristic effort to explore similarities between two central figures in the banned novels of two major modernists is obviously appropriating the indeterminate term "New Woman" to coin yet another, "New Man," as a means of focusing attention on the transcoding of elements in traditional gender identifications. Although neither Lawrence nor Joyce would have been likely to subscribe to such "labels," in large part because both Mellors and Bloom are more complex literary constructions than the term "New Man" can connote, the value of provoking a re-viewing of Bloom and Mellors is sufficient to tolerate the term's looseness. Furthermore, the term "New Man" borrows some of its agency here from Joyce's own term "new womanly man," as Bloom is satirically denoted in the "Circe" chapter.

[The logical place to begin this examination of Joyce's and Lawrence's contributions to the notion of a New Man is *Ulysses* and Leopold Bloom, largely because Joyce began to construct Bloom by 1915, more than a decade before Lawrence began to think about Lady Chatterley's lover, Oliver Mellors.] Although the *Little Review*'s March 1918 issue began the serialized version of *Ulysses*, it is unlikely that Lawrence would have read any of Joyce's novel before it appeared as a book, six years before *Lady Chatterley's Lover* (1928). Much as Lawrence was aware of the notoriety of *Ulysses,* how much he was aware of the novel itself is a matter of speculation.

What Lawrence read, he did not like. He wrote: "Joyce wearied me: so like a schoolmaster with dirt and stuff in his head: sometimes good, though: but too mental" (4L 275). Lawrence *was* willing to acknowledge there was something "good, though" in his rival's scandalous novel. The Lawrence biographer David Ellis indicates that when Lawrence's publisher Thomas Seltzer suggested he might want to publish "brief, off-the-cuff remarks" about *Ulysses,* Lawrence demurred at first: "Do you really want to publish my James Joyce remarks? No, I don't think it's quite fair to him" (4L 345). Those remarks did finally appear, however, in Lawrence's essay "Surgery for the Novel—Or a Bomb," in which he lumps Joyce together with Proust and Dorothy Richardson as writers whose novels he finds excessively "mental.] Lawrence spoofed that annoying "mental" self-absorption of Joyce and Co: "'Did I feel a twinge in my little toe, or didn't I?' asks every character of Mr Joyce or of Miss Richardson or Monsieur Proust" (STH 151). Lawrence read enough of *Ulysses* to call it a "filthy book," but we can

[margin, handwritten, rotated: Lawrence thought Joyce's too mental" — here]

only guess how extensive his reading was. Like Virginia Woolf, Lawrence saw Joyce as a "competitor [. . .] on another track," not in any similarities in their approaches to narrative, as was the case in Woolf's disparagement of Joyce, but in their investments in representing sexuality, particularly the hitherto under-represented sexuality of women.

However much Lawrence read of *Ulysses*, the scandal of its being censored must have encouraged him to recall his own novel *The Rainbow* (1915). It, too, was banned for its representation of female sexuality, even though Lawrence's novel did not use the full range of the English language Joyce did in his pro-vocative novel. In 1915, it might be noted, Lawrence was still working in the context of publishing firms supplying lending libraries such as Mudie's, which had no willingness to risk offending their patrons with graphic sexuality or colorful English. Even so, Lawrence dared to allow *The Rainbow*'s Anton Skre-bensky, in an early sexual encounter, to implore his lover Ursula Brangwen, to let him "come." Perhaps Lawrence's editor was unfamiliar with the word's non-standard English deployment as a synonym for reaching orgasm or expected few "ladies" a century ago to understand its predominantly male currency.

The background of Joyce's awareness of the New Woman is easier to docu-ment than Lawrence's because it was extensively explored by feminist critics decades ago. As Bonnie Kime Scott explains in *Joyce and Feminism* (1984), Joyce came to maturity in a Dublin where the larger movement for Irish indepen-dence had subsumed the women's movement, whose goals included not only suffrage but access to higher education and the professions. The resuscitation of the women's movement after the Second World War elevated Joyce to a posi-tion of high prominence among writers/theorists such as Hélène Cixous and Julia Kristeva as well as American academics such as Marilyn French in *The Book as World* (1976), Margot Norris in *The Decentered Universe of* Finnegans Wake (1976), Carolyn Heilbrun in *Women in Joyce* (1982), and Scott in *Joyce and Feminism.*

[Scott extensively explored Joyce's attraction to the New Woman, as well as the hostility to much of the women's movement among his young Irish contemporaries.]That "hostility" found its center in the "purist" impulse of the movement represented by Joyce's friends/colleagues such as Francis J. C. Sheehy-Skeffington and the Sheehy Sisters[Joyce was appalled by the purists who considered sexuality merely a necessary evil for procreation, one they would have gladly eliminated, even within marriage.] Scott reminds us that although Joyce was romantically attracted to Mary Skeffington, he found the country girl Nora Barnacle more appealing because she was very much *not* one of these upper-middle-class women whose obsession with "purity" had turned her against sexuality. Given the puritanical view of sexuality evident in the women's movement, Joyce undoubtedly knew he could anticipate cold comfort in the marriage bed, while in Nora he found a "good girl" who also made it clear that she understood the reality of sexual desire. The first time Joyce and Nora "walked out together"—to Ringsend, where "An Encounter" is set—Nora opened Jim's flies and masturbated him to orgasm (*SL* 182). Nora may not have been a New Woman in the conventional sense of an intellectual agitating for women's suffrage, but sexually she was light-years from the feminist Margaret Cousins, who was unsettled by the rigors of performing her "wifely duties."

Similarly, although he concurred with his fellow Irishman, or more precisely *Anglo*-Irishman, George Bernard Shaw, in his support of the New Woman, Joyce found the dramatist's rendition of the construct unacceptable. Like Joyce's friend Sheehy-Skeffington, Shaw was hardly a fan of sexuality in the New Woman, or in any woman—or, for that matter, any *man*. It was no coincidence that Shaw was a virgin until he was twenty-nine. His marriage to the suffragist Charlotte Payne-Townsend was, at her request, never consummated. To Shaw, sexuality was merely a vehicle of the Life Force, moving the species toward the "Superman." Indeed the portrayal of Ann Whitefield in *Man and Superman* is scarcely flattering, as Shaw depicts her as a predatory womb hungering for the semen of a visionary realist such as John Tanner to help her produce what could be the *Übermensch*.

Even more than Shaw's work, the writing of the dramatist Henrik Ibsen encouraged Joyce to find the New Woman an attractive figure. Scott prefaces her comments on Joyce's high regard for Ibsen by noting the efforts of Joyce scholars, such as Richard Ellmann, to diminish the role of Ibsen's female characters in the construction of Joyce's response to the New Woman. Scott respectfully disagrees with Ellmann, offering evidence of Joyce's interest in not merely Ibsen's technique as a dramatist and his commitment to representing the "truth" but also Ibsen's feminism. She cites Joyce's rebuke of Arthur Power, often quoted by feminists: "The purpose of *The Doll's House*, for example, was the emancipation of women, which has caused the greatest revolution of our time in the most important relationship there is—that between men and women, the revolt of women against the idea that they are the mere instruments of men" (qtd. in Scott 47–48).

The first readers of *Ulysses* would have found Bloom an unconventional male for 1904. "Mr Leopold Bloom" steps on stage in the kitchen of 7 Eccles Street, performing domestic chores conventionally assigned to women: feeding the cat, shopping for and then cooking his own breakfast, and so forth. Even more unconventional to readers a century ago, Bloom has asked his wife, still in bed, "You don't want anything for breakfast?" and read her "Mn" as negative (*U* 4.55, 57). When he returns from getting his breakfast kidney, the morning mail has arrived, and he delivers it to Molly, after having read the envelope of a letter addressed to her as "Mrs Marion Bloom," *not* Mrs. Leopold Bloom, the addressee's name written in a "[b]old hand" (*U* 4.244).

This meticulously rendered scene continues with the description of Bloom's response to Molly's question, "Who are the letters for?" The narrative foregrounds the fastidiousness of his response as the product of Bloom's exquisite, one might even say "feminine," sensibility; we read: "A letter for me from Milly, he said *carefully*, and a card to you. And a letter for you" (*U* 4.251–52, italics added). Bloom's womanly "scrupulosity" in maneuvering through the minefield of the morning mail cannot be exaggerated. The letter from Milly is addressed to her *father*, not her parents: Has she been removed from the household to protect her innocence from her mother's incipient adultery? The unidentified card is addressed "to" *Molly*; the letter, however, is "for" her, as Milly's letter was "for" him, suggesting that the letter addressed in a "bold hand" is "personal," for her eyes only. To avail her of the opportunity to deal with the letter "for" her and allow himself to furtively observe her response, Bloom adjusts the "blind" while she reads the card from Milly: Molly receives a card; Bloom, a letter. He notes with a "backward eye" how she will merely "glance at the letter and tuck it under her pillow" (*U* 4.256–57). Molly orders him to get her tea and to scald the pot, giving her more time to read Boylan's letter concerning "private" matters—presumably involving the "privates"—in Poldy's absence. Bloom risks angering Molly by asking, "Who was the letter from?" and she says, "O, Boylan [. . .] He's bringing the programme" (*U* 4.310, 312)—and more, as she undoubtedly anticipates, despite her transparently covert casualness in "O, Boylan."

As her chapter will demonstrate profusely, Molly represents an overt sexuality that undoes the gender straitjackets of the nineteenth-century assumptions that sexual frankness is the monopoly of men, a "masculine" characteristic inappropriate for all but a few women who are not "ladies." Bloom rushes out to rescue his burning kidney and then to retire to the privy, the only place as an Irishman he can be "king," since 7 Eccles Street is the domain of Molly, the Queen Bee. Bloom is launched on the stage as the husband who will not contest his wife's right to commit adultery, and the plot is set in motion.

This episode deserves attention because in the narrative's present, Bloom's day, it offers the longest "scene from a marriage." The narrative offers only one other marriage scene in the present, the brief and quite vague "scene" in the wee hours of the next day when Bloom recaptures the marriage bed vacated by Blazes Boylan. The other scenes from this marriage exist mainly in memory only—just as the "Circe" scenes exist mainly as fantasies—for this is a marriage of the middle-aged. It is also a "modern marriage," since Molly certainly is not a conventional early-twentieth-century woman. She may not be an ideal New Woman—single, feminist, championing the vote for her sex—perhaps because she is wise enough to recognize that the vote has not done much for the other sex in her class. However, she does enjoy an independence that most women in turn-of-the-century Dublin would have envied. As an artist of a sort, Molly is not confined to the house and conventional domesticity. Whatever domestic chores need attention at 7 Eccles Street, beyond those taken care of by the charwoman, Mrs. Fleming, are done by Bloom, Molly seeming never to have learned to do housework. Ironically, the domestic arrangements in the Bloom household are uncannily similar to those in the many places the Lawrences lived, in which he did the cooking and scrubbed floors while Frieda read and smoked cigarettes.

Molly's independence extends to an incipient affair. This is not to say, of course, that she is the first female character in a novel to stray from her marriage vows; however, unlike the affairs of earlier "heroines" such as Emma Bovary, this is clearly not a "romance." Molly has no illusions of being "in love" with Boylan. Instead, her expectation is for the most part sexual gratification, "pure and simple," just as that has been the expectation of countless men who have begun affairs in and outside of literature. Boylan is little more to her than a flesh-and-blood avatar of a male character from her latest encounter with what might now be called "supermarket romances," or "bodice rippers." With his conventionally macho manner, Boylan promises her the distinct probability of achieving orgasm. His function has been reduced primarily to agency, to providing the instrument of gratification in her bed, where presumably she has had to be content with "solitary pleasures," produced through the agency of erotica such as the books of "Paul de Kock. Nice name he has" (*U* 4.358), as she purrs to her husband.

The episode also provides an important introduction to Bloom as the progenitor of the later-twentieth-century "sensitive male." Because he is dancing "carefully" around the associations of the marriage bed in which he senses Boylan may be supplanting him later that day, his "sensitivity" is apparent in his performing the role of complaisant husband, or willing cuckold. These centuries-old terms remind us that Bloom is hardly the first man, in literature or out of it, to turn a blind eye to his wife's turning to another man, or woman. What begins to make him "modern," however, and a candidate for the identification New Man lies not in the older acknowledgment of weakness in cuckoldry, or in his powerlessness to forestall "betrayal," but in Bloom's recognition that Molly is a New Woman in at least one seemingly limited sense. As Bloom himself may well surmise, she can no longer deny her need for sexual gratification, after recognizing that erotica has its limitations, and she must pursue that gratification with another man as "honestly" as she can.

It is without any large measure of irony that we can say Molly pursues gratification "honestly." Whether Emma Bovary is intent on sexual gratification is not clear because her two affairs are "romances" in which she is scripting herself as the romantic heroine of one of the cheap romance novels she gluts herself on as an antidote to a comfortable but boring marriage. Molly is honest enough to jettison such self-deluding sentimentalities. She all but announces to her husband that she intends to practice more than her voice with Boylan that afternoon, by being "careless," in an almost deliberate manner, not concealing the letter's author. She may even be working on the assumption that her husband *wants* her to have an affair to satisfy herself sexually, once again an extension of her possible masturbation with "Paul de Kock" in her bed. At the same time, Molly is "sensitive" to the potential calamity of her husband's happening in on her "rehearsal" with Boylan. That she is willing to risk hurting Bloom—going so far as to invite Boylan into the marriage bed in which she conceived her two children with Bloom—is a silent testimony to the depth of her need, making the Molly-Bloom-Boylan narrative thread at least in part, to borrow Spike Lee's film title, a matter of *She's Gotta Have It.*

And Molly is forced to resort to a vulgarian like Boylan because, as we all know, Bloom is the Modern Man with ED, even though he is not yet forty; indeed, he is thirty-eight, the exact age of Mellors. The severity of Bloom's sexual dysfunction, however, is unlikely to be ameliorated by Viagra or Cialis, for he suffers from the kind of neurosis more likely to have been associated a century ago with the upper-middle-class women who reclined on Sigmund Freud's famous couch in his office at Berggasse 19. After Rudy died at the tender age of eleven days, Bloom reflects: "Could never like it again" (*U* 8.610). The "it" here is presumably sexual intercourse, because "it" could produce another child who might follow Rudy to an early grave. Because the phrase is within his interior monologue, the "it" can remain appropriately unspecified since even eleven years later sexual intercourse with Molly is still an intensely tender topic. Also the absence of a subject for the verbal phrase "never like it again" might even refer to Molly. Indeed, it is not until the last chapter of Molly's "soliloquy" that readers gain access to her frustrations with Bloom's obviously minimal performance: he clearly still loves her and wants to express it sexually, but typically their efforts lead to failure to reach orgasm and to mutual frustration.

The genesis of Bloom's neurosis, however, is more complicated, especially for a man who passes himself off as a rationalist, even a "man of science." The problem is much more than his simple loss of interest. Bloom has constructed an "old wives' tale"[2] to facilitate the acknowledgment of his own responsibility for Rudy's death. Bloom is sexually inhibited by a bizarre genetic fiction of his own making, concerning a baby's health or lack thereof: "If it's healthy it's from the mother. If not from the man" (U 6.329).[3] Without a shred of empirical evidence for this belief, Bloom allows himself to be clasped by the icy grip of impotence, frustrating *him* to be sure but, as even he surmises, frustrating Molly as well, given that lovemaking inevitably ends in coitus interruptus.

Clearly Bloom is not always impotent. Stimulated by the exhibitionism of Gerty MacDowell, for example, he masturbates to orgasm. His fantasy of masturbating during his bath adds another dimension to this neurotic complex, for he foresees his penis in the bath water as "the limp father of thousands, a languid floating flower" (U 5.571), savoring the irony of the frustrated procreation of what is probably closer to millions than to "thousands," and yet he cannot father even *one* more child. Given that Bloom is grateful at the climax of the Gerty episode that he did not reach orgasm in the morning bath scene, if he masturbated at all, suggests that Bloom may never have been a sexual athlete. Alternately, Bloom's fixation on "absence," that is, his failure to produce another child, credits the "presence," or potential, to produce a plenitude of issue. In the need to guarantee the survival of the species, spendthrift Mother Nature wastes untold resources held in reserve. This is a Joycean fixation: the "Oxen of the Sun" chapter offers a pastiche of a sermon on the nightly slaughter of the innocents through contraception: "those Godpossibled souls that we nightly impossibilise" (U 14.225–26).

Although women have had no monopoly on neurosis, it has been—like hysteria—associated more often with women than with men. Similarly, the power of empathy evident quite literally in Bloom's daily life, of which *Ulysses* offers a huge slice, has been traditionally gendered feminine. That said, as Bloom himself is aware, he is not alone in his capacity to empathize with others. In the "Hades" episode, we see Bloom startled to recognize that Martin Cunningham is also a man of compassion. Married to a woman with serious psychological problems, Cunningham feels Bloom's pain when the "masculine" men among the mourners carelessly agree that suicide is the worst sin, because it thwarts Providence, while Cunningham is aware Bloom still mourns for a father who took his own life eighteen years earlier.

Bloom seems never to have experienced "compassion fatigue." His empathy for others ranges from Dilly Dedalus, who is forced to sell her brother Stephen's books to put food on the table, through Josie Breen, who lives with a deranged husband intent on suing for slander the unidentified sender of a possibly derogatory postcard, to yet another woman, Mina Purefoy, who has been in labor three days with her eighth child. In addition to these Dubliners he knows by name, there is also the "blind stripling," who complicates Bloom's empathy: much as he would like to offer his arm to help the young man cross the street, he is inclined to hold back, lest his offer be misconstrued as patronizing.

Like much else about Bloom, his concern for others is misunderstood as "womanly" by the "masculine" Dubliners. They suspect him of having bet on Throwaway and then furtively leaving the pub to "gather in the shekels," to quote Lenehan, and upon his return refusing to buy a round "like a man," to share his good fortune (*U* 12.1551, 1663), when in fact he has stepped out to contribute to a fund for the Widow Dignam's well-being. These are the same men who mock Bloom's doing household chores such as shopping for "a tin of Neave's food six weeks before the wife was delivered" (*U* 12.1651–52). The narrator adds that Bloom is "one of those mixed middlings," and according to Pisser Burke, Bloom is in bed "once a month with headache like a totty with her courses" (*U* 12.1658–60). It is also suggested that Bloom's children had to have been fathered by another man because he is too sexually challenged to impregnate Molly. And when Bloom talks about his race as a victim of injustice, John Wyse replies: "Stand up to it then with force like men" (*U* 12.1475). The empathy Bloom demonstrates is clearly a form of "tenderness." And Bloom has the "courage" to expose it at the risk of other men's mockery and disdain, even to face hazards to life and limb in Barney Kiernan's pub, particularly if the Citizen were not too inebriated to be able to hit him with a boulder or a biscuit tin.

Further characteristics of Bloom's personality that might be identified as traditionally "feminine" become more apparent in the closing hours of his day. His "fathering" of Stephen Dedalus might be seen as more like the "mothering" of a young man who is patently unable, for example, to take care of his own money, much less himself. After taking Stephen's money for safekeeping—who among the other male Dubliners, except Martin Cunningham, would have done the same?—Bloom takes this surrogate son in and feeds him, even offers to put him up for the night. Bloom's charitable impulses are not pure, of course, since he fantasizes a "proposition" in which Stephen might help Molly with her pronunciation of Italian in exchange for room and board. This proposition has shadier dimensions as Bloom envisions Stephen servicing Molly in order to eliminate the potentially more disruptive presence of Boylan in his bed (*U* 17.937–39).

Yet another more traditionally "feminine" characteristic, associated with this "proposition" of Stephen's helping out Molly, is Bloom's sense of accommodation. The long Q-and-A section of the "Ithaca" chapter has as its burden Bloom's effort to "rationalize" but also to accept Molly's "infidelity" with Boylan. Central to Bloom's thinking about the day's main event is his effort, and the narrative's, to restore a sense of perspective disrupted by the morally righteous, intent on making the commandment against adultery bear as a great a sense of sin as any of the other nine. Similarly, as we see from the initial episode, Bloom sees Molly as different but equal in the partnership. As a woman she needs and deserves sexual fulfillment as much as he does as a man. She may need to ask him what "metempsychosis" means, not because she is stupid but because she is even more undereducated than he is. Tellingly, he resists the impulse to "correct" her grammar when she tells him that the book she was reading "must have fell down" (*U* 4.326) under the bed.

Like the notion of the New Woman, the construction of the New Man is difficult to theorize because many of us have not yet succeeded in shedding the influence of the gender/sex identifications consolidated by patriarchy in the nineteenth century—the very identifications against which the New Woman and, I would propose, the New Man have struggled for their independence. Just as the New Woman a century ago fought to liberate herself from the stultifying role of the "Angel in the House," frail, passive, dependent, yet saintly, the New Man has struggled to find a place *in* the House and to free himself from the equally life-denying role of the Beast in the Jungle. Because facets of our humanness have been arbitrarily designated "feminine" or "masculine" and then parceled out to either women or men as a means of keeping all women and most men in their places so that a few men at the top could enjoy absolute power, both men and women were forced to live a half life publicly and a fuller life secretly. Those who refused to lead a half life have been identified as "androgynous," a term that has faded because it is grounded in the arbitrary schema of deciding what is feminine or masculine and insisting that such features "belong" only to women or to men, respectively Joyce in *Ulysses* and Lawrence in *Lady Chatterley's Lover* were among the first male authors to develop male characters who refuse to wear the straitjackets of "masculinity," even in the face of others' disdain. Just as Bloom is not a "man" to the crowd in Barney Kiernan's pub because he has a place in the House and has no need to turn the pub into his home away from Home, where he wastes his resources in drink, so, as we shall see, Mellors is not a "man" to some because he raises game but has no need to shoot it because he refuses to "get ahead" through labor for money in work that denies his humanness.

Molly may not be a New Woman in the broadest sense, but she demonstrates independence as an equal partner in the marriage Bloom mutely acknowledges. His respect for his wife's independence is matched in her monologue, in which she pays homage to him as a New Man, despite or perhaps because of his sexual disabilities. In the monologue Molly may continue to titillate herself, and probably masturbate, as she recalls the size of Boylan's "member" and the number of orgasms he achieves—a count that curiously increases in her memory from "3 or 4 times" (*U* 18.143) to "4 or 5 times" (*U* 18.895). And yet she remains "true" to Bloom. Despite his sexual athleticism, Boylan is clearly not satisfactory as a lover because he treats Molly as though she were a side of beef and has no concern for her either as a person or as a woman with sexual needs of her own. In yet another uncanny connection between this novel and Lawrence's, Connie Chatterley will eventually expel her lover Michaelis from her bed because while he cannot help her reach orgasm, he criticizes her savagely for making him the instrument of her sexual gratification, even though that is exactly what he has done to her. Molly ends up as Bloom's true Penelope— faithful in her fashion because, of course, she is "Molly," not merely "Mrs. Leopold Bloom."

SURPRISINGLY ENOUGH, D. H. Lawrence's attitudes as a young man toward feminism and the New Woman were strikingly similar to Joyce's, despite the perception a generation ago that Lawrence was a misogynist. In her 1993 book on Lawrence, *Sex in the Head*, Linda Ruth Williams, for example, notes his notoriety two decades ago when she writes: "Lawrence, perhaps more than any other writer, is feminism's *bête noire*, the monster it loves to hate" (16). Lawrence was very aware of the women's movement through several women of his acquaintance who were suffragists. Among the women a generation older than Lawrence, Sarah "Sallie" Hopkin was a strong feminist; she and her socialist husband, William "Willie" Hopkin, were good friends of Lawrence. Another feminist, Blanche Jennings, was important to Lawrence as a beginning writer because she was a "lady," that is, a woman well-off enough not to have to work for a living or marry for financial support. Lawrence asked Jennings to critique the manuscript of his first novel, *The White Peacock*, in part because she was a member of the middle class he foresaw as his future audience. One other feminist was Alice Dax, through whom he became more intimately aware of the women's movement.

Alice Dax was the wife of an Eastwood pharmacist and optician, and the mother of two small children. Before she moved to Eastwood and married Dax, she was a leader in the socialist movement and active as a suffragist in Liverpool, where she was born. "Dax," as she was known to her friends, became a name in Eastwood, beginning a nursing association and taking an active role in the Workers Educational Association. Like Lawrence, she was a reader of progressive thinkers such as Ibsen.[4] As the Lawrence biographer John Worthen notes, Lawrence shared his copies of the *English Review*, in which Dax read the serialization of *Tono-Bungay* by H. G. Wells, and she lent him books by Edward Carpenter, the late-nineteenth-century socialist poet, philosopher, and gay activist. Dax wrote poems and plays, attended the "Eastwood Debating Society," and most of all was, according to Worthen, "deeply interested in the Women's Movement" (360).

Dax was a New Woman in her radical individualism, which her small-town community came to disdain. The people of Eastwood, especially the women, considered her "individualism"—laughing too loudly in public, wearing gray when other wives wore black, being too outspoken about social issues—unwomanly eccentricity. As Worthen notes, the community avenged itself on Dax by threatening to stone her windows because she violated the custom of dressing them with lace curtains. Then, too, she outraged the community's mores by receiving her milk delivery with no stockings on. Eventually, when the community boycotted the business, the Daxes were forced to sell the apothecary shop and move to another town. The young Lawrence braved the sharpness of her tongue by asking her to be the first reader of *The White Peacock*'s manuscript. Relatively little evidence has been found of the impact Dax's critique of that manuscript had on the novel as it appeared in 1911. Alice Dax, the New Woman in young Lawrence's life, had a far greater impact on his later work.

Early in 1910, Dax made it clear to Lawrence that she had fallen in love with him. Although she later vehemently denied that their affair served as the basis for Paul Morel's relationship with Clara Dawes in Lawrence's breakthrough novel, *Sons and Lovers* (1913), there is little doubt that it did. When her daughter was conceived, Dax fervently hoped the father was Lawrence rather than her husband. Even if Lawrence was not biologically responsible, Dax considered him her daughter's "father" because it was her passionate love for Lawrence that effected the conception in her intercourse with a husband whom she had married not for love but from desperation. She told her daughter Enid Hilton that she had "never found sex exciting, or thrilling, or even very pleasant until D. H. came along" (qtd. in Worthen 367). When Lawrence's wife, Frieda, for whom he left Dax to elope to Germany in the spring of 1912, published *Not I, but the Wind* (1934), Dax wrote Frieda, generalizing about the affair: "we were never, except for one short memorable hour, whole; it was from that one hour that I began to see the light of life" (qtd. in Worthen 368). The "hour" Dax recalls is rendered as the "peewits" episode in *Sons and Lovers*. Even more importantly, the shared experience of Clara and Paul's baptism in the fire of passion is recuperated many times over in the transformation of Connie Chatterley and Mellors in Lawrence's last novel.

Through his relationship with Dax, and then in the early months of his "marriage" with Frieda in 1912, before it became official in 1914, Lawrence began to think of himself as a "feminist." From Italy late in 1912, he offered Sallie Hopkin a prospectus for his future writing: "I shall do my work for women, better than the suffrage" (*1L* 490). The Lawrence biographer Mark Kinkead-Weekes notes that the final phrase was added "somewhat cheekily, given Sallie's suffragism" (64). Brief though Lawrence's reference may seem, it offers a clear indication of his strong commitment to the empowerment of women, before the nightmare of the "Great War" engulfed his hopes for a brighter future. Through the writing of *The Rainbow* (1915) and *Women in Love* (1920), Lawrence believed he was offering in Ursula Brangwen a model of radical independence for women. Just before her transfiguration in *The Rainbow*, Ursula acknowledges that her long childhood, her family and friends are now dead to her, and she has given birth to herself as an independent and self-reliant woman. This is the novel he had conceived of as a major feminist narrative whose contribution to the emancipation of women would be more important than the pursuit of suffrage—which would only make women as self-deluded as men regarding the value of their votes in a patriarchal, or more precisely an oligarchic political structure, enshrining power primarily in the upper classes. Ursula Brangwen's self-liberation in the closing pages of *The Rainbow* and her clearly equal status with her husband, Rupert Birkin, in *Women in Love* more fully represent an epic model of an empowered woman than any female character in Joyce's oeuvre.

In turning back to Bonnie Kime Scott's extended examination of the investment of feminists in Joyce's work close to a half century ago, those with an investment in Lawrence as well as Joyce are likely to feel an acute sense of irony in the import of her single allusion to D. H. Lawrence. Among the many feminists she points to as having a sympathetic response to Joyce, Scott includes the polemicist Kate Millett, whose best seller *Sexual Politics* (1971) tars with a large brush a number of writers such as Henry Miller, Norman Mailer, and D. H. Lawrence as male chauvinists. According to Scott, Millett applauds among other things in Joyce his celebration of "the eternal feminine" and goes on to assert that to Lawrence the New Woman was the "enemy" (Scott 127).[5] As a "sexual" politician herself, Millett can comfortably avoid commenting on Lawrence's background in early-twentieth-century feminism, and Scott is either unaware of or ignores Lawrence's early inclination to support feminism.

If Leopold "Poldy" Bloom offers the best entry to *Ulysses*, Constance "Connie" Reid Chatterley offers Lawrence's counterpart.[6] Connie is center stage from the beginning, indicating that Lawrence saw *Lady Chatterley's Lover* as *her* story, not Mellors.' Connie's "Lover" is referenced only obliquely, and he is not allowed to enter until the narrative gives him his cue. The postponed appearance of Mellors enhances Connie's power as the object of focalization. Like her "sister" Molly, Constance Chatterley is an independent woman who pursues sexual fulfillment not found in a marriage to an impotent husband.

Readers are expeditiously apprised of Connie's credentials as a modern woman. As adolescents, she and her sister were students in Dresden, where they talked and sang and camped in the woods with male friends who were so "craving" the sisters could hardly do less than give themselves, even though the "love-making" was only an interruption of the "discussions," a "primitive reversion," "an anti-climax" (*LCL* 7). Connie and her sister were "free," but in a patently superficial manner that never allowed them to find the means to any meaningful sexual gratification that might have transformed them into genuinely "Free Women."[7] Following the conventional pattern of young men, they "sowed their wild oats" as an accepted prelude to marriage and motherhood.

When the action begins a decade later, Connie is attempting to live cheerfully with the aftermath of the war. Her husband, Clifford, has survived his two elder brothers and their father to inherit the Chatterley estate and title at the cost of paralysis from the waist down. Lawrence has encountered some severe criticism in constructing Clifford as sexually disabled, but the text makes it amply clear that he married Constance Reid because his father wanted a grandson to inherit Wragby, lest Clifford join his brothers in the next world before producing an heir. The narrative indicates that in his mid-twenties Clifford "had been virgin when he married: and the sex part did not mean much to him" (*LCL* 12). The "month's honeymoon" did not generate an heir, perhaps because Clifford was convinced the "sex part" was only "one of the curious obsolete organic processes which persisted in its clumsiness, but was not really necessary" (*LCL* 12).

In the novel's present, Connie has taken a lover—Michaelis, a rising, young Irish playwright whom Clifford has invited to Wragby Hall. Clifford is intent on "being known" as a British writer "over there" in America. Since Clifford will eventually encourage Connie to take a lover to produce an heir and keep Wragby in the family, perhaps Michaelis is the beginning of that campaign. In any case, Michaelis is Connie's lover until she breaks off the affair, which she sees as hopeless from the beginning. The narrative indicates that to her, "Mick *couldn't* keep anything up" (*LCL* 31), perhaps a "Freudian slip" indicating her ultimate dissatisfaction with him as a lover.

The orchestration of Michaelis' departure from Connie's life is carefully timed. Before Michaelis returns to Wragby Hall one last time in February 1923 with the first act of a play he is drafting, with "Clifford as a central figure" (*LCL* 50), Clifford has introduced Connie to Mellors, who has returned from the army to take up his former position as Wragby's gamekeeper. Clifford and Mick have developed a perverse rendition of blood brotherhood in their shared pursuit of "success: the bitch-goddess" (*LCL* 50). Indeed it appears that in his final episode of "love-making" with Connie, Michaelis has become impatient to get on with it so he might rejoin her husband for the real purpose of his visit.

The consequence of this impatience is among the most painful scenes Lawrence ever wrote. Connie finds Michaelis "a more excited lover that night with his strange, small-boy's excitement and his small-boy's frail nakedness" (*LCL* 53). The brevity of his "excitement" leaves Connie not only unsatisfied but also somewhat distressed because Michaelis has aroused a deeper and potentially perverse passion through "his little boy's nakedness and softness" (*LCL* 53). She is forced to pursue her own release, "while he heroically kept himself up and present in her" until her "wild crisis" (*LCL* 53). Perhaps envious of her deeper and more powerful sense of release, Michaelis attacks her in the most violent manner any lover can brutalize another in the moment of greatest openness and vulnerability.

With Mellors' entry into Connie's life, the dynamics of the coming Clifford-Connie-Mellors love triangle here recalls the Bloom-Molly-Boylan triangle of *Ulysses*. Clifford has just reminded his wife that their lives have become "interwoven" in an intimacy more meaningful than sex and that he could understand her having an affair with another man as long as it might produce a child—a male child, of course, and with the right genes—to inherit Wragby. Minutes later Mellors appears and declares his independence as a man by "star[ing] straight into Connie's eyes with a perfectly fearless, impersonal look, as if he wanted to see what she was like" (*LCL* 46). His gaze denotes what Lawrence's audience a century ago would have understood as a gross violation of his role as a servant by daring to look into her ladyship's eyes for more than a second, if at all. She, in kind, demonstrates her independence as woman by returning his gaze, denoting that she is a "lady" with a difference, empowered by *his* violation to compound it with her own in "look[ing] him in the eyes" (*LCL* 46). Although she may not have *consciously* focused upon Mellors as an alternative to Michaelis and his ilk, the gamekeeper's presence in the scene with Mick is the prime mover of her effort to slough off a lover who violates her tenderness. Connie senses what Gudrun learned in her unfortunate experience with Gerald Crich: a woman whose lover brings out the mother in her learns to her sorrow that lovemaking can turn into something like rape.

These issues of how lovers respond to the openness and vulnerability in any genuinely meaningful lovemaking foreground themselves in a conversation late in *Lady Chatterley's Lover*. In this crucial scene Mellors is still adjusting to Connie's news that she is pregnant. This pregnancy raises questions of how Connie will deal with the child they have produced and how he will cope with the unmanning possibility that she "used" him merely as an unwitting sperm donor. When Mellors asks Connie what she wants, she responds "simply," "I want to come and live with you always—soon" (*LCL* 211). Given her position as the wife of a wealthy aristocrat, Mellors can respond only that he has nothing to offer her. Were Mellors one of Clifford's circle, readers might suspect him of false modesty to encourage Connie to say he has "more than most men" and to add, "Come, you know it" (*LCL* 276). To his credit, Mellors admits, "I know it" and then pauses to think.

His thoughts comprise the important passage Bowen briefly notes: "They used to say I had too much of the woman in me—" (*LCL* 276). Mellors explains that by "the woman" he means more than the part of him that chooses not to kill birds (but to nurture their chicks), or the major part of him that is not focused on making money to get on. He could have easily gotten on in the army, were it not for the "twaddling, bossy impudence of the people who run this world" (*LCL* 276), in the army and out. At its base it is the "impudence of money [. . .] and class" he hates so much that he believes he has nothing to "offer a woman" (*LCL* 276).

In this brief scene the narrative covers much territory, with Connie serving as essentially the interlocutor, offering Mellors the opportunity to expose his gender construction through his responses. It is significant that his assertion that "They used to say I had too much of the woman in me" comes in response to Connie's telling him she wants to live with him, announcing the need to structure a relationship in which, as he reads it, *she* will have the "masculine" position because she has the power of her money and position, and *he* has been "feminized" by his vulnerability as the servant of a rich and powerful master, who could "turn him out," at best, and prosecute him for rape, at worst (*LCL* 276).

The narrative offers Mellors the opportunity to express in fairly simple terms a Lawrentian notion, evident as early as *The Rainbow*—that is, the man needs some sense of meaning in his life, outside the relationship with the woman; if this meaning is lacking, the relationship cannot succeed. And more specifically, as Lawrence writes in his essay "The Crown," the couple, troped as the lion and the unicorn, must have equal power to push against each other or they lose their balance and collapse. More than anything, Mellors is concerned with the sexual implications of her empowerment through money and social position. As he phrases it, "I can't be just your male concubine. [. . .] The money is yours, the position is yours. [. . .] I'm not just my lady's fucker, after all" (*LCL* 276).

As the scene moves to its culmination, it is Connie who delivers the narrative's pronouncement on what it is that Mellors has and other men do not: "It's the courage of your own tenderness, that's what it is: like when you put your hand on my tail and say I've got a pretty tail" (*LCL* 277). After the narrator cues the reader that Mellors is thinking again, presumably about the "courage" of his "tenderness," he returns to his experience in the army and his relationships with the men. Thus the gamekeeper is circling back to where he began, after Connie emphatically asserted that he knew what separated him from other men. Explaining that he disliked the army because of its inane sense of leadership, he adds: "I could manage the men all right: they liked me," then repeats himself, "I like men, and men like me" (*LCL* 276).

In accepting Connie's encomium to his courage to be "tender," it is instructive that he first grounds his agreement in the context of his relationships with men: "I knew it with the men [. . .]. I had to be bodily aware of them—and a bit tender to them [. . .] in a proper manly way. Makes 'em really manly [. . .]

[I]t's tenderness, really; it's really cunt-awareness" (*LCL* 277). Since this is but one occasion on which the narrative authorizes Mellors to use the signifier *cunt,* which led to Robbie Turner's "rise" to good fortune with Cecilia Tallis and tragic fall in Ian McEwan's *Atonement*, it requires further attention.

First and foremost, *Lady Chatterley's Lover* is intent on retrieving the ancient Old English signifier "cunt," along with "cock" and "fuck," from their later currency as demeaning and pejorative terms. To Mellors these old signifiers are all positive expressions of sexual/spiritual pleasure. Although he may occasionally refer to Connie's genitals as "cunt," Mellors more frequently employs the term to represent their lovemaking. Kate Millett is dead wrong when she asserts that "Connie is 'cunt,' the thing acted upon" (240), first because she perhaps deliberately ignores Mellors' more frequent use of the term for lovemaking, and second because she uses the term in its contemporary pejorative sense, as Mellors never does, even in describing his wife, Bertha Coutts.

In this context, the world of Mellors is less "modern" than Bloom's. Mellors and Bloom are coincidentally the same age and demonstrate a generally optimistic outlook. Such optimism is evident in the letter Mellors writes to Connie, pregnant with their child, which serves as the novel's conclusion, and in Bloom's loving acceptance of Molly's adultery in the later pages of the "Ithaca" chapter. These two literary figures part company, however, in relation to the word "cunt." By the time Mellors introduces the term "cunt-awareness," readers have already learned that "cunt" is never a pejorative term, as Mellors uses it. It is never a means of putting down a woman—or a man—but always a positive expression of not only the female genitals, but the joyful sexual love it generates. Bloom's world, on the other hand, has a "cunty Kate" in it, and even Bloom's consciousness reveals an attraction to its most pejorative associations.

Early in his day Bloom surprisingly experiences a rare moment of "desolation," perhaps generated by his suppressed depression in becoming aware of Molly's incipient adultery that afternoon. Bloom's "desolation" is couched within the context of his ethnic roots in Palestine, a world rendered as the "cities of the plain [. . .]. All dead names. A dead sea in a dead land, grey and old [. . .] the grey sunken cunt of the world" (*U* 4.222–23, 227–28). Bloom's world teems with "manly men" who exercise their masculine power by policing the gender lines. In that capacity these men view Bloom's "femininity" in a negative manner that stops just short of damning him with the word that even Bloom in his own dark moments allows into his consciousness as a pejorative reference.

When Connie tells Mellors he has the "courage of [his] own tenderness" (*LCL* 277), she means, of course, the courage to be tender with her. His desire may be too insistent for him to engage in foreplay, and on at least one occasion he "takes" her as though they were animals because of the urgency of his need. But he has no impulse to hurt her physically—or psychologically, as Michaelis does when he criticizes her for working toward her own orgasm, requiring his "heroic" effort to help produce satisfaction for her. Mellors is that rare person, especially a male, to whom vulnerability calls up tenderness, whether the creature is a pheasant chick or a Lady Chatterley. It is a tenderness traditionally identified as "womanly," or more specifically "motherly," and that may be the reason he responds to Connie's insistence on his *knowing* what he has "got more [of] than most men" (*LCL* 276). And we ought not to forget that the first time Connie rouses desire in Mellors is the episode in which he notices a teardrop on her wrist as she holds the pheasant chick, an emblem of her own sense of vulnerability.

Connie's "courage" in celebrating the courage of Mellors' tenderness and identifying it by adopting his—a *man's*—language deserves attention. It is her willingness to risk his overpowering her in the relationship, after she defers to his language, which is crucial. Her strength in clearly expressing herself positions her toward the "masculine" end of the gender spectrum and frees him to reveal his further movement toward the "feminine" end of the scale. Mellors is courageous enough to risk Connie's hostility by revealing his relationship with the men he led: "I had to be in touch with them [. . .] bodily aware of them— and a bit tender to them [. . .]" (*LCL* 277). The risk he takes, of course, is her potential misapprehension, post-"Freud," that Mellors is dancing around the repressed confession that he is "latently homosexual." This is a view projected by Millett in her footnote: "One remembers that Mellors' first love was his colonel. With the exception of *Sons and Lovers* and *The Rainbow*, every Lawrence novel includes some symbolically surrogate scene of pederasty" (241), an unconventional use of "pederasty," which usually denotes a man's love for boys.

Actually those conventional preoccupations with physical intimacy between men have been raised much earlier in the text, thanks to a thunderstorm that keeps Connie and Mellors confined in his hut. Connie asks him about his experience in the army when he was a lieutenant and an officer and a gentleman (*LCL* 216).[8] She goes on to ask if Mellors "loved" his colonel. Answering in the affirmative, Mellors describes the colonel as an officer twenty years his senior who "loved the army" through whose ranks he had risen, "very intelligent," a "passionate man," and a South Asian under whose "spell" he lived until his colonel died, and with his death Mellors recognized that "another part of me was finished" (*LCL* 216).

The conversation between Connie and Mellors continues after the narrative adds a trope that expands this dialogue beyond two lovers discussing the past in the midst of a thunderstorm: "The thunder crashed outside. It was like being in a little ark in the Flood" (*LCL* 216). When Connie notes that he has "such a lot *behind*" him, Mellors comments: "Do I? It seems to me I've died once or twice already" (*LCL* 216). The conjunction of the Flood trope and the concept of death and rebirth recalls *The Rainbow*'s ending as read by Kate Millett, who maliciously attacks *Lady Chatterley's Lover* in the opening of her chapter on Lawrence: "Having polished off the unfortunate man [her lover Anton Skrebensky], Ursula beholds the vision of the rainbow and the promise of a new world, for the old is drowned in the flood. She alone survives, the new woman awaiting the new man" (262). Three sentences later, Millett begins: "*Women in Love* presents us with the new man arrived in time to give Ursula her comeuppance and demote her back to wifely subjection" (262). The implication seems clear that Millett would have preferred Ursula to remain single for "another kind of love."

Perhaps more than Bloom and Molly in the early hours of 17 June 1904, Connie and Mellors in the closing scenes of *Lady Chatterley's Lover* more fully demonstrate the immense power of a woman's contribution to the construction of a New Man. Unlike the New Woman, who needed no man to achieve that status—indeed, some would deny that status to any woman who did need one—the New Man requires a woman, not necessarily a New Woman, but certainly a woman who has broken free of the ties that bind her to the nineteenth-century position of the Angel in the House. As strong, independent women, Molly and Connie have clearly demonstrated that by moving toward the traditionally "masculine" end of the spectrum they have liberated their male partners from the stress of living up to an older, restrictive construction of masculinity forcing them into the pursuit of a half life, an existence in which they could maintain respect only by eradicating from their performance of masculinity all that could be identified as "feminine." When both sexes can freely range across the gender spectrum, women *and* men have some hope of living together outside the oppressive gender identifications traditionally offering them no more than a partial life.

Notes

1. Scott points to Joyce's acquaintance Margaret Cousins, among the earliest Irish suffragists to be imprisoned, for breaking windows at 10 Downing Street. In her mem-

oirs, Cousins reveals her ignorance of sex and reliance on the newlyweds' "aspirations to build purity and beauty into [their] lives and into the world," an idealism that gave way to disenchantment: "Every child I looked at called to my mind the shocking circumstance that brought about its existence [. . .]. I found myself looking on men and women as degraded by this demand of nature" (qtd. in Scott 34).

2. One tale holds that if a mother is nursing a baby boy she must be careful not to allow any of her milk to touch the boy's penis, lest he one day become impotent.

3. Another index of Bloom's self-deprecation is apparent in his consciousness supplanting "father" with "man," as though no "man" could consider himself a "father" if his bad seed produced his child's ill health or death.

4. Lawrence read more widely in Ibsen's work than most and recommended his work to others, encouraging his fiancée Louisa ("Louie") Burrows, for example, to read *Lady Inger of Östrat* (see Earl G. Ingersoll, "*The Rainbow*'s Winifred Inger").

5. Millett's noting of Joyce's celebration of Goethe's "eternal feminine" may surprise many today, for later, "postfeminists" would be likely to respond to the term: How like a man to arrogate to himself the power to restrict women to an essentialist "feminine" categorization. But then Millett was undoubtedly influenced by *The Feminist Mystique* (1963), which even Betty Friedan saw the need to reconstruct in the 1980s.

6. The names of Bloom and Connie tell their own story. He is known only to Molly as "Poldy" and to everyone else as "Bloom." Lady Chatterley is known to friends and family as "Connie," except to Mellors, whose first name, "Oliver," is spoken only by Clifford's housekeeper/nurse Ivy Bolton and Connie's sister, Hilda. When Hilda notes that her sister never refers to the gamekeeper as "Oliver" or even "Mellors," his servant name, Connie is startled into recalling that she and the gamekeeper never reference each other with names other than their "phallic" names, coined by Mellors, "John Thomas" and "Lady Jane." I use "phallic," as Jacques Lacan does, to encompass female as well as male genitalia.

7. The term "Free Women" occurs as an ironic response to the difficulties of women in achieving freedom in *The Golden Notebook* by Doris Lessing, who told me at some length about the formative power of Lawrence's writing on her as a young woman.

8. It ought not to be ignored that Mellors' promotion to lieutenant would have been unusual for someone who had been a servant, given a rigid class system. Paul Fussell describes at length the separation between officers and soldiers during the "1914–18 War." On the march, officers fell out on one side of the road to relieve themselves and their men on the other, just as both groups faithfully patronized only brothels appropriate to their own ranks.

Works Cited

Bowen, Zack. "*Lady Chatterley's Lover* and *Ulysses*." *D. H. Lawrence's "Lady": A New Look at Lady Chatterley's Lover*. Ed. Michael Squires and Dennis Jackson. Athens: U of Georgia P, 1985. 116–35. Bowen's essay has been republished in this volume, and the parenthetical citation refers to the present work.

Ellis, David. *D. H. Lawrence: Dying Game 1922–1930.* Vol. 3 of The Cambridge Biography of D. H. Lawrence. Cambridge: Cambridge UP, 1998.

Ellmann, Richard. *James Joyce.* Oxford: Oxford UP, 1982.

French, Marilyn. *The Book as World: James Joyce's Ulysses.* Cambridge: Harvard UP, 1976.

Friedan, Betty. *The Feminine Mystique.* New York: Norton, 1963.

Fussell, Paul. *The Great War and Modern Memory.* New York: Oxford UP, 1975.

Henke, Suzette, Elaine Unkeless, and Carolyn G. Heilbrun. *Women in Joyce.* Urbana: U of Illinois P, 1982.

Ibsen, Henrik. *Lady Inger of Östrat. The Works of Henrik Ibsen.* Ed. William Archer. New York: Willey, 1911.

Ingersoll, Earl G. *D. H. Lawrence, Desire, and Narrative.* Gainesville: UP of Florida, 2001.

———. "*The Rainbow*'s Winifred Inger." *D. H. Lawrence Review* 17.1 (Spring 1984): 67–69.

Kinkead-Weekes, Mark. *Triumph to Exile 1912–1922.* Vol. 2 of The Cambridge Biography of D. H. Lawrence. Cambridge: Cambridge UP, 1995.

Lacan, Jacques. *Écrits: A Selection.* Trans. Alan Sheridan. New York: Norton, 1977.

———. *The Four Fundamental Concepts of Psycho-Analysis.* Trans. Alan Sheridan. Ed. Jacques-Alain Miller. New York: Norton, 1978.

Lawrence, Frieda von Richthofen Weekley. *Not I, but the Wind.* New York: Viking, 1934.

Lessing, Doris. *The Golden Notebook.* New York: Simon and Schuster, 1962.

McEwan, Ian. *Atonement.* New York: Doubleday, 2001.

Millett, Kate. *Sexual Politics.* New York: Equinox, 1971.

Norris, Margot. *The Decentered Universe of* Finnegans Wake: *A Structuralist Analysis.* Baltimore: Johns Hopkins UP, 1976.

Scott, Bonnie Kime. *Joyce and Feminism.* Bloomington: Indiana UP, 1984.

Shaw, George Bernard. *Man and Superman.* Cambridge: Cambridge UP, 1903.

Williams, Linda Ruth. *Sex in the Head: Visions of Femininity and Film in D. H. Lawrence.* Detroit, MI: Wayne State UP, 1993.

Woolf, Virginia. *The Letters of Virginia Woolf. 6 vols.* Edited by Nigel Nicholson and Joanne Trautman. New York: Harcourt Brace Jovanovich, 1975–80.

Worthen, John. *D. H. Lawrence: The Early Years 1885–1912.* Vol. 1 of The Cambridge Biography of D. H. Lawrence. Cambridge: Cambridge UP, 1991.

Lady or Priestess of Isis ? (handwritten)

4

The End of Sacrifice

Joyce's "The Dead" and Lawrence's "The Man Who Died"

GERALD DOHERTY

In an interesting essay entitled "A Would-Be-Dirty Mind," Paul Delany narrows the literary rivalry between James Joyce and D. H. Lawrence down to two nodes of contention that made them impossible readers of each other's work: their writing styles and their treatment of sexuality. While Joyce almost certainly never read Lawrence's two masterpieces—*The Rainbow* and *Women in Love*—and dismissed *Lady Chatterley's Lover* because of its impoverished style and because it makes "propaganda in favour of something which [. . .] makes all the propaganda for itself" (*SL* 359), Lawrence assumed that Joyce, as "the inheritor of nineteenth-century realism," was ill-equipped to do the work Lawrence thought modern writing should do (Delany 78). As for sexuality, their mutual blindness is even more radical. Dwelling obsessively on indirect or incomplete modes of consummation, Joyce is fascinated by everything that may "intervene between desire and performance" (Delany 80). Lawrence, by contrast, is obsessed with sexuality's potential for self-transformation, and the negative forces within that block total fulfillment. As to religion, Delany suggests that while both writers were heterodox, their heterodoxies took different forms, largely determined by their respective inheritances: Roman Catholicism and evangelical Protestantism (Delany 80). Joyce's defection from Catholicism took place in his mid-teens, and Lawrence broke with Congregationalism when he was twenty-two.[1]

The present essay takes neither religion nor sexuality as its primary focus but concentrates on a third motif—sacrifice—a direct offspring of both. In order to explore these motifs, I shall take two of Joyce and Lawrence's finest short stories—"The Dead" and "The Man Who Died"[2]—in which all three motifs interact in an intensive critique of each other. Because both stories have their common denominator in economies of sacrifice as a basis for both personal and institutional exchanges,[3] highly intriguing convergences (and divergences) exist between them. For both writers, these were their final short stories, though their modes of finality differ: Joyce, who wrote "The Dead" in 1907, went on to complete *A Portrait of the Artist*, *Ulysses*, and *Finnegans Wake*, while Lawrence died shortly after completing "The Man Who Died" in September 1929.

In a recent essay, Mark Singleton shows that from the opening "paragraph of *Dubliners* to the last page of the *Wake*, Joyce's work forms a prolonged exploration of the consequences of sacrifice" (321). Already in a 1905 letter to his brother Stanislaus, Joyce indicates his awareness of how deeply in Ireland an economy of sacrifice—a rationalized investment in expectation of a return—is embedded: the same people in Ireland who call his "moral nature oblique" are precisely those "who think that the whole duty of man consists in paying one's debts" (*SL* 70).[4] The same profound suspicion of sacrifice is evident in Lawrence's work from one of his earliest novels—*The Trespasser* (1912)—to *Lady Chatterley's Lover* (1928).[5] In a December 1912 letter to his sister-in-law, Else Jaffe, he asserts that the "worst of sacrifice is that we have to pay back. [. . .] It put[s] the recipient under the obligation of making restitution, often more than he could afford" (*1L* 486). Defining his own personal attitude to all future exchanges, Lawrence affirms, "it costs more courage to assert one's desire and need, than it does to renounce" (*1L* 486). In his earliest antisacrificial pronouncement, he declares that the "real way of living is to answer to one's wants" (*1L* 504).

It is important to distinguish between interior personal sacrifice, which involves an economy of small (often financial) losses and gains, from exterior ritual sacrifice, which involves suffering and death and for which Christ's crucifixion is the traditional Western icon. Self-sacrificial death and crucifixion are external analeptic crisis events that haunt both narratives:[6] "The Dead" reserves its climax for Michael Furey's self-immolation under a symbolic tree (the cross) in Gretta Conway's garden, while the man who died reflects back on the injustice, the savage cruelty, as well as the false motivations that fuelled the sacrificial death he endured.

Both Joyce's and Lawrence's stories repudiate one particular version of sacrifice—the Christian doctrine of sacrifice. Based on a purely economic transaction, it constitutes the system of precalculated credits and debts upon which their repudiation is founded. It forms the pivot around which the major encounters in parts 1 of both stories revolve, in which short-term losses and gains, both financial and psychological, are the dominant outcomes. As such, a narrow and restrictive economy aims to secure a return for investment—an aim always fraught with uncertainty. Parts 2 of each story, by contrast, stage an economy of sacrifice without reserve, without hope of reward or return that transcends all economic accounting.[7]

As the main protagonist, Gabriel Conway is at the center of a sequence of events that dislocate his expectations, and from which the reward he had anticipated is lacking. He is caught up in situations that promise an appreciated return but that bring only loss and diminishment. Part 1 of "The Man Who Died" goes even further, exposing the "self-importance" (*EC* 136) and self-deception that fuelled the man's missionary drive—his demand for a return on his sacrifice through his disciples' belief in his destiny as messianic redeemer. In part 2 of each story, a single climactic event shatters the restricted sacrificial economy that part 1 carefully cultivated. In their different ways, both Furey and the man who died enact a sacrifice without reserve beyond retribution or recompense.

WITH THE BUSINESS of close comparative readings of both stories, strategic problems arise. Though part 1 of each story shares with the other a common denominator in an economy of sacrifice, based on the give-and-take of financial and psychological profit and loss, their specific contexts differ so radically as to make side-by-side comparisons difficult. Thus the contemporary social, political, and ecclesiastical contexts of "The Dead" contrast sharply with those of "The Man Who Died," which are mainly tabular and relate to the past. Therefore I shall explore the former first and the latter second, isolating in both those critical encounters fuelled by a common sacrificial economy, reserving a closer comparative analysis for part 2 of both stories.

"The Dead" highlights sacrificial scenarios throughout part 1, which are also nodes of embarrassing tensions, humiliations, and silences that reverberate throughout the rest of the narrative. Critics have been assiduous in uncovering the class, cultural, and imperialistic nuances in Gabriel's initial encounter with Lily, the housemaid. In a perceptive essay, for example, John Paul Riquelme notes a sacrificial gesture without naming it as such: Gabriel offers Lily a "gift of money as if he felt the money would make up" for his earlier gaffe (127). Riquelme also notes that Gabriel's "gestures of generosity [. . .] are self-serving rather than self-sacrificing" (136). Here, however, the use of the term "self-sacrifice" in its untheorized, commonplace sense largely disables its hermeneutic potential, which is a major concern of the present essay, which demonstrates this potential in action.

The encounter opens with Gabriel's *en haut au bas* comment, when he realizes that Lily is no longer the immature schoolgirl he mistook her for: "I suppose we'll be going to your wedding one of these fine days with your young man, eh?" (*D* 178). This remark fulfills one of sacrifice's least recognized functions—that of securing male ascendency by keeping the female in her proper place. Theories of sacrifice, including, of course, economic theories, as Nancy Jay puts it, "commonly exhibit notions of gender ranging from taken-for-granted male domination to explicit misogyny" (128). The hidden victims of cultures of sacrifice, such as Ireland's, are the women, who for complex reasons are largely excluded from the religious, political, and social rituals that men alone practice.[9] Gabriel compounds his social gaffe by treating Lily as a child and gets a rude reply in return—one that cleverly reflects on the male sex in general, and more obliquely on the obtuseness of Gabriel's own tactless palaver in asking such a question: "The men that is now is only all palaver and what they can get out of you" (*D* 178).[10] Clearly Lily is already aware of the sexism endemic to sacrificial cultures that identifies the female with the passive victim of male exploitation. With Gabriel's attempt to compensate for his "mistake" (*D* 178), the sacrificial ethos insinuates itself through a classic economic maneuver—the basic gift-logic of the Latin formula, *do ut des* (I give so that you may give).[11] Each economic sacrifice anticipates in the giving the particular return it solicits. Thus Gabriel's offer of a gold coin at once reestablishes the superior male status Lily undermined, while unobtrusively modifying the *do ut des* formula (I give you a gift of gold so that you may return me the recognition I deserve as your class and cultural superior). Using force, he "thrust[s]" the coin into her hands (*D* 178)—the climactic (sacrificial) "cut" that compels Lily to protest her refusal as Gabriel turns his back on her and hurries upstairs. From this petty economic exchange, Gabriel learns something of immediate consequence: he must sacrifice the Browning quote in his speech for fear that his cultural assertiveness—his airing of "his superior education" (*D* 179)—might earn him a further rebuff.

The wound to Gabriel's self-esteem is immediately reopened when Gretta, with his two aunts as witnesses, makes self-defensive fun of him for his tyrannical imposition of niggling economies of sacrifice within his own home. A restrictive domestic regime inflicts present distress on his wife and two children in order to secure their future health and well-being: Tom must wear eye-shades at night and practice the dumb-bells, while Eva must eat stirabout, which she hates (*D* 180). Though Gretta treats Gabriel's obsessive solicitude as a joke (he makes her wear galoshes, which on the present occasion she refuses to do), he ensures his male ascendency through renunciatory rituals that, as he later guiltily recalls, constitute their "dull existence" together (*D* 214).

Sacrifice, however, can extend from the private tyrannies of the domestic into the public sphere, where the spectacle of punishment being actively inflicted before witnesses is of the essence. Such is the case of Miss Ivors' spectacular mortification of Gabriel before a group of fascinated spectators (a public inquisition is its metaphorical subtext). In a humiliating gender-reversal, the male becomes the sacrificed object (traditionally the sacrificer is always male) of an *auto-da-fé* at the female's instigation: Miss Ivors' "cross-examination," as the text calls it, inflames and exasperates him (he flushes red, and his anger incenses him) (*D* 189). Pitching personal gratification against ideological commitment, at stake here are patriotic ideals among which sacrificing one's life for one's country is the apotheosis. Though Gabriel nervously rejects Ivors' accusation of "shame" for writing reviews in the English *Daily Express* (*D* 220), clearly he is not the enthusiastic Irish nationalist she would like him to be. With Ivors' demand that Gabriel visit the Aran Islands to keep in touch with the Irish language, a sacrificial thematic emerges with full force: Gabriel refuses to renounce his continental holidays, violently repudiating her accusation of political heresy for which she condemns him ("I'm sick of my own country, sick of it!") (*D* 189). Employing further techniques of humiliation, she subjects him to a trial of faith in his country, while attracting attention to herself as an accomplished inquisitor who reduces her victim to silence (*D* 190). His retrospective private assessment of her behavior foregrounds his public humiliation as her main motive for instigating the trial ("She had tried to make him ridiculous before people") (*D* 190). Yet Gabriel enacts his own sacrificial expiation, downgrading Miss Ivors to the status of an importunate animal whom he could readily immolate: making aggressive noises in his direction (she "heckl[es] him), she stares at him "with her rabbit's eyes" (*D* 190); she is blind to what it is like to be human. From the narratological perspective, the narrator colludes with Gabriel, refusing access to Miss Ivors' motivations while faithfully recording the nuances of his. Ironically, however, Gabriel is robbed of his ultimate revenge, his public trial of Miss Ivors in his speech, which celebrates precisely those qualities (hospitality, humor, humanity) that he is convinced that she lacks. As if compelled by a secret telepathic communication, she exits the party before the speech gets under way (*D* 194–95).

The final climactic scenario in part 1, the festive dinner, exemplifies the binary logic that undergirds all practice of sacrifice.[12] It functions at once to weld the participants together into a single community, and it wards off those threats that separate and divide them. It represents a perfect model for distinguishing "between integrative, communal aspects of sacrifice and differentiating, expiatory aspects" (Jay xxvii), between a communion that assimilates and an expiation that alienates and estranges. The Morkans' elaborate repast combines these two aspects of sacrifice in a single alimentary ritual. Thus it conjoins all the guests in an harmonious partaking to which Gabriel's speech is the climax at the same time that it unsettles the familial fellowship the meal sets out to establish.

Just before the dinner begins, the first ominous threat of division appears. Aunt Julia's dismissal from the Westland Row church choir highlights the highly sensitive issue of female exclusion in a patriarchal, ecclesiastical culture that cultivates the sacrifice of women as its strategy for preserving male lines of descent without reference to women's reproductive powers or to biological family ties.[13] Sacrificing women, as Jay puts it, "orders relations within and between lines of human fathers and sons, between men and men, at least as effectively as it does relations between men and their divinities" (34). Fuelled by the ecclesiastical profit incentive, the economy of sacrifice requires the periodic purging of women to ensure ritual purity, secure male ascendency, and ensure female subordination through precalculated acts of expulsion. The tense family fracas involving Julia's dismissal after a life service in the choir concentrates all of these issues. Julia, as Kate claims, was the "slave" of a misogynistic clerical regime that "turn[ed] out the women out of the choirs," and put "little whippersnappers of boys over their heads" (D 194). Though Kate works herself "into a passion" (D 194) in defense of her sister, her internalization of an infallible papal authority automatizes her female self-depreciation: as a "stupid old woman," she dare not question the pope's right to exclude women, despite its offense to "politeness and gratitude" (D 176).

Throughout the dinner itself, an economy of sacrificial profit and loss pervades the discussion. Mr. Browne's claim, for example, that "grand old [Italian] operas" are no longer performed in Dublin because they can no longer find voices to sing them (loss) is rebutted by Bartell D'Arcy, who claims excellence for the living Caruso (profit), yet qualified by Aunt Kate, who recalls the great tenor Parkinson, who is even "too far back" for Browne to remember (loss) (D 179–80). Even in the popular world of the opera, the economy of much-appreciated gift-offerings (music) and reciprocated returns (to Dublin) is already deeply disturbed.

Though from the sacrificial perspective, the meal itself is the central "communion" event whose function is to unite all the participants, yet its persistent evocation of "absent referents"[14]—its obsession with death and with thoughts of Dublin's past—also evokes one startling referent (perhaps the most occluded referent in traditional narratives of communal eating) that the text itself refers to only obliquely. Gabriel's strange reference in his speech to the guests as the "victims" (D 182) of his aunts' hospitality has been linked to the supper itself as a "mock-heroic Mass," a sacrificial enactment in which the congregation offers itself as a victim (Quinn 160). It can also be linked to the ubiquitous anthropological designation of the animal as the victim of sacrificial oblations, which becomes the flesh the participants later consume.[15] By far the most immediate referents, however, are also the real victims, who are invisible as such—the pig, goose, and cow, recently immolated to make the festive meal a reality. Though dead animals dominate the dinner table at both ends, they are rendered absent as animals so that the tasty ham, goose-flesh, and "spiced beef" (D 177) may be relished as meat. Because among these three creatures, the pig is conventionally the most abjected, it is also the one most effectively cosmeticized, aestheticized. Stripped of its name (pig) as well as its outer skin, "peppered over with crust-crumbs," it even has a "neat paper fril round its shin" to disguise the naked bone structure beneath (D 177). In what may be an ironic critique of Gabriel's dedication to sacrificial routines (the uncertainty of narrative tone is of the essence), the text informs us that cutting up dead animals is his favorite occupation: "he was an expert carver and liked nothing better than to find himself at the head of a well-laden table" (D 178). Camouflaging the sanguinary violence their reincarnation as meat entails, the text colludes with its own realistic bent in its knowledge of what unsettling events to exclude. The camouflage is most vulnerable to exposure at the linguistic level when Gabriel asks Miss Furlong whether she prefers a "wing or a slice of the breast," forcing her to name an unnamable part (D 178). Carving up his "victims" is thus the source of his sacerdotal authority over the guests, which he is clearly reluctant to relinquish by starting his own meal (D 178).

With its central emphasis on hospitality—the integrative, communal function of sacrifice—Gabriel's is a "communion" speech par excellence, fuelled by his need to unite all the guests through the fact of their still being alive to enjoy it. Yet in its obedience to sacrificial binaries, the speech also demarcates and estranges. As a function of Gabriel's expertise, a sharp sacrificial "cut" excludes a large swathe of Irish society. With Miss Ivors' "discourteous" departure in mind, Gabriel segregates not only her but a complete "new generation" whose less "spacious" mentalities lack the virtues the old generation cultivated (D

183). Indeed their "thought-tormented" condition is the sacrificial price they must pay for a heretical "sceptic[ism]" that corrals them off from those older orthodox values Gabriel's speech celebrates (*D* 183). As figures of beauty, talent, and charm, the Morkan sisters and Mary Jane are the "Three Graces of the Dublin musical world" who, like Aunt Julia's "perennial youth," are safely beyond the time warp that brought the new generation into existence (*D* 184). At the psychological level, the speech may also be read as Gabriel's attempt to heal the raw wounds to his self-esteem the party inflicted—a process with its vivid literal counterpart in "The Man Who Died," to which I now turn.

Though part 1 of "The Man Who Died" has no great communion scenario to ameliorate those abrasive ruptures and cuts that preceded it (the sole substantial meal the man who died eats is a vegetarian one, which he consumes on his own) (*EC* 51–52), it does have a number of striking resonances with "The Dead," which I shall first summarize. Most significant among these is their shared critical preoccupation with sacrifice as an economic transaction, a niggardly calculus of expenditures in anticipation of an anticipated reward. The investment/return equilibrium is insistently highlighted, but, as in "The Dead," deeply disturbed. Second, the same sacrificial binaries split part 1 of both stories into two oppositional realms: Gabriel's historical split between a "less spacious" present and a more "spacious" past is mirrored in the ontological split in "The Man Who Died" between the "little life" of "greedy desire," fuelled by an economy of sacrifice, and a "greater life" that shatters such recursive trade-offs (*EC* 28). Third, at the narratological level, a solitary male figure—the near-exclusive focus of character concentration—moves uneasily among others, encountering mainly small groups from the past, who misrecognize or misunderstand him, and with whom he feels no longer at home. The contexts of these encounters, however, could scarcely be more divergent: the poorly lit, claustrophobic space of the Morkans' "dark gaunt house on Usher's Island" (160), as opposed to the luxuriant open-air expanses of Mediterranean earth, sea, and sky. The most striking (fourth) difference, however, is between the nature and source of the protagonists' injuries, both of which are sacrificial in essence. While Gabriel's wounds are psychic, internal, the result of blade-like snubs to his self-conceit, those of the man who died are the visible scars of a public crucifixion from which he is seeking a cure. Both stories open up into vaster, more expansive worlds—postsacrificial universes—whose resemblances to each other are as remarkable as their formidable differences.

"The Man Who Died" engages much more openly with the economy of sacrifice than does "The Dead," where it is frequently disguised, distanced, and ironized. Part 1 of "The Man Who Died," by contrast, directly confronts sacrifice with its own limitations—its small meannesses, its self-obsessed traffickings, its cruelty toward the body, as well as its baneful effects on its subjects, who assume that everything, including sex, has its price. The man who died's meeting with Madeleine is the sole exception, though even there its limitations are quickly exposed. (In "The Dead," the single triumph of an economy of sacrifice is Malins' unexpected return of the sovereign Gabriel lent him, for which, ironically, Gretta compliments him on being "a very generous person") (*D* 196).

Just awakened from his death-coma into consciousness, the man who died endures "the sickness of unspeakable disillusion" (*EC* 16) with his soteriological mission—"the fight of self-sacrifice," as Lawrence calls it in his 1929 essay "The Risen Lord," that "would end in crucifixion" (*2P* 575). In 1912, Lawrence renounced an economy of sacrifice in favor of the direct assertion of "desire and need," which no longer demand divine propitiation to achieve their fulfillment. Initially the model for such a libidinal assertion is the natural world itself, whose unconstrained and thrusting vitality by contrast with his own emaciated body the man who died registers for the first time. "Glowing with desire and with assertion," the "creatures of spring" issue their "ringing, defiant challenge to all other things existing" (*EC* 21). They are strangers to those laws of renunciation that transform the "fierce and compulsive" destiny of life into the harrowing "destiny of death" he has just endured (*EC* 22). Indeed the cock the man who dies buys from the peasant allegorizes the escape from sacrificial constriction—he is tied by the leg with a cord—as it, too, "adventur[es] out for the first time into the wider phenomenal world" (*EC* 30). *Blake's "Marriage"*

Lawrence conceived of the ideology of sacrificial sex in two distinctive ways: first, as a site of a general conflict between "renunciation and consummation," which the Christian era initiated and which still dominates "our world of Europe" (*TI* 147). Second, an economy of personal sacrifice dictates that one partner surrenders abjectly to the other in a travesty of erotic fulfillment: "when, of the two parties, one yields utterly to the other, this is called sacrifice, and it also means death" (*STH* 174).[16] In the story, the peasant woman offers her "humble body" to the man who died in anticipation of a financial reward. Because, however, "her little soul was hard, and short-sighted, and grasping, her body had its little greed, and no gentle reverence for the return gift" (*EC* 27). Moralized as a kind of avarice, sex is a trade-off between victim and victimizer that diminishes both. At precisely this point, the text distinguishes between the "little [. . .] life of the body," where libido and greed are synonymous terms, and the "greater life of the body" that supersedes such limited satisfactions, opening up erotic vistas hitherto unrealized (*EC* 28). The man who died's purpose in rising from the dead is, as the text puts it, to encounter a woman "not greedy to give, not greedy to take, and with whom he could mingle his body" (*EC* 28). Unless sex is absorbed into the greater life, it remains the expression of the insatiable sacrificial greed that regulates and controls it.

The encounter with the peasant woman's husband that immediately follows underwrites a more specific problem: how to distinguish unreserved desire from its numerous counterfeits. Though the husband offers free hospitality to the man who died ("all I have is yours"), and thus "risk[s] getting no reward," yet his eyes sparkle "with the hope of greater rewards in money later on" (*EC* 28). With each new encounter, the critique of sacrificial transactions intensifies. Thus a hermeneutics of suspicion completely dominates the final encounters with Madeleine. Because the man who died's public mission is over, the life of his "self-importance" is also ended (the "teacher and the saviour are dead in me") (*EC* 24). Like Madeleine in her messianic zeal, "[he] too ran to excess. [H]e gave more than [he] took, and that is woe and vanity" (*EC* 25).[17]

FROM THE SACRIFICIAL PERSPECTIVE, the four central scenarios in part 2 of both stories highlight intriguing similarities and differences. As preludes to the two climactic events that stage unreserved sacrifice in action (Furey's death-gift to Gretta and the man who died's erotic at-one-ment with Isis), two antithetical scenes mark the petty cruelties attendant on conventional economies of sacrifice.[18]

In "The Dead," "The Lass of Aughrim" ballad Bartell D'Arcy sings upstairs as the guests depart and that Gabriel hears downstairs as "distant music" (*D* 188) evokes the catastrophic site of a sexual economy that, in Lawrence's terms, involves the destructive conflict between consummation and renunciation. Lord Gregory's "consummation"—his date rape of the Lass[19]—soon triggers his "renunciation": his refusal of her entry into his house. D'Arcy's performance prompts a subtle train of narrative associations: the scene of pathetic abandonment, evoked by the ballad, elicits the mysterious "shining" (*D* 190) in Gretta's eyes that at once arouses Gabriel (he thinks it is for him) and that sparks the traumatic revelation of the source of the song in Gretta's conviction that Furey died for her sake (*D* 198). The traversal is from a harsh sacrificial scenario (the rape of the Lass) from which she anticipates recompense or atonement to a postsacrificial enactment that defies the dynamics of profit and loss. Through a violent subjugation ("he had his will of her"),[20] Lord Gregory sexually victimizes the Lass while refusing the sacrificial payoff in money or hospitality, which he violates and betrays. D'Arcy's "hoarse voice," made "plaintive by distance" (*D* 189), evokes the *pathos* of the distance between the suffering endured by the Lass and its expiation that Gregory denies her.[21]

Part 2 of "The Man Who Died" opens similarly with a strange sexual scenario that explicitly stages the rape that "The Lass of Aughrim" merely evokes. As in all sacrificial systems, where, as Jay puts it, "femaleness [is] what must be expiated" (28), both scenarios locate the female as the element that must be disowned or got rid of, exposing those systems' inherent cruelty, especially when their energies are deflected into the sexual sphere. "Performing some sacrifice, or working some incantation" (*EC* 36), the two slaves immolate pigeons, letting the drops of blood fall into the sea. When one pigeon escapes, the boy beats the girl, who, "passive and quivering," submits to the subsequent rape, which a Lawrentian chauvinism identifies with "the blind, frightened frenzy of a boy's first passion" (*EC* 37). The rape, in effect, is the climactic intensification of an act that originated in the sanguinary violence toward nonhuman creatures, now directed at the girl.

The difference between the two scenes is equally striking: while the first is a fictionalized staging from a ruthless colonial past, the second is a "real-life" engagement between two local slaves who are absorbed in slitting the throats of live pigeons in preparation of a sacrificial meal for their masters. The supersession of economies of sacrifice, however, is central to both stories, though their modes of breakthrough are radically different. In "The Dead," Gretta's "I think he died for me" (*D* 198) generates a hysterical crisis in Gabriel, far beyond what a boy's narcissistic, romantic death wish might induce. Indeed the nature of Furey's sacrifice and Gabriel's excessive response has sparked much critical debate. Taking "Christ's supremely unselfish crucifixion" as their model, traditional readings, such as Gerard Quinn's, reduce the effect of Furey's sacrifice to the narcissism of Gabriel's own "selfish lust" (159, 163). More recent colonial readings link Furey's death to a precultured, idealized West of Ireland, and to "the futility of sacrifice for Kathleen ni Houlihan" (Cullingford 227). At the moment when he had "hoped to triumph" (*D* 198)—to "overmaster" (*D* 195) Gretta's sexual apathy— the sacrificial edifice, so cautiously constructed over a lifetime, dissolves. Furey's reckless expenditure is beyond a restricted economy. Therefore it is a sacrifice, which in Derrida's terms, "does not even want to maintain itself, collect itself, or collect the profits from itself or from its own risk" ("Restricted" 264).

The gift-offering of death itself—the last and only gift Furey possesses—fu els the rashly impetuous sacrifice he enacts when he lays his life on the line. The "terror" it induces in Gabriel is one consequence of his recognition that his own tame domestic regime (including the galoshes to keep out the rain) has its roots in a strategic and fearful avoidance of death. By standing "under a dripping tree" (*D* 200) in the pouring rain, the consumptive Furey, by contrast, transforms the risk of death into a certainty. Unlike the original Calvary sacrifice, Furey's anticipates neither the triumphant reward of a resurrection nor the fulfillment of a love for which he gift-offered his death. Thus Gretta's most vivid memory is of the moment Furey looked death in the face, and so chose his destiny—of the image of her lover's eyes when he told her that he "did not want to live" (*D* 199). It helps explain her perpetuation of such a vivid image of imminent death throughout the course of her marriage ("I can see his eyes as well as well") (*D* 199).

Gabriel's engagement with the limitations of his own sacrificial past is reflected in the man who died's complementary engagement with his, though his revisions are more fiercely subversive and confrontational. Unlike in part 1, where he uncovers his motives for sacrifice (self-importance, power over others), in part 2 he rehearses the events leading up to his crucifixion, including the last supper, and the Judas-kiss of betrayal, which Lawrence radically revises. It opens with the shock recognition that if he is "naked" enough to respond to Isis' erotic desire, then he has "not died in vain" (*EC* 52). His remembrance of the crucifixion is not of an expiation successfully achieved but of the "agony of injustice and cruelty" of which his own wounds are a bitter reminder (*EC* 54).

In the Lawrentian schema, the crucial self-split is not the traditional one between body and spirit, but between body and desire, which is why self-assertion is vital to well-being. It underwrites both the function of Isis' massage—she restores desire to the body—as well as the man who died's reappraisal of the last supper transactions. With Isis' question—"Did you let [Madeleine] serve you with the corpse of her love?" (*EC* 55)—comes the equally shattering revelation that he, too, offered his disciples only "the corpse of [his] love. This is my body—take and eat—my corpse" (*EC* 55). Their bodies, like his, were bodies without desire—sacrificial victims of a renunciatory imperative and of their own attraction to death.[22]

The man who died's repudiation of an ideology that imbues sacrifice with access to transcendental truth is so complete as to allow him to perceive his own sacrifice as a criminal being executed: "They murdered me, but I lent myself to murder" (*EC* 56). Its sacrificial legitimation withdrawn, what was a sacred event is now subsumed under a purely legal injunction that interprets the killing of humans as murder.[23] In the end, Isis erases not only literal wounds but also the man who died's complicity with his own sacrificial death, his secret desire to be immolated as public proof of his eschatological mission—the triumph of spirit over material flesh. Thus his healing of wounds coincides with the resurgence of desire, and his realization that "his death and his passion of sacrifice were all as nothing to him" now that he knows "the crouching fullness of the woman there, the soft white rock of life" (*EC* 57). The resurgence of Gabriel's desire for Gretta in the Gresham hotel, by contrast, suffers a terminal defeat, as an exhausted sleep overtakes her (*D* 199).

The final release from engagement with the past in both stories opens up new postsacrificial worlds—visions of an otherness, previously foreclosed: Gabriel's access to the world of the dead, where sacrifice itself is redundant, has its counterpart in the man who died's access to an erotic potency that transcends sacrificial conflict, and that surprises even himself. Their striking divergences, however, point back to the rigid sacrificial dichotomies these new states surpass.

While Gabriel enters a disembodied world, doomed soon to its final extinction (the dead's present mode of existence is "wayward and flickering") (*D* 200), the man who died's "marvelous piercing transcendence of desire" (*EC* 57) completes his return to embodied existence. In turn, Gabriel's radical loss of identity—the "dwindling" of his once "solid world" (*D* 200)—has its inverse in the man who died's revelation of a phenomenal world, "great beyond all gods," which "leans around" and enfolds him (*EC* 58). As his desire is aroused for the first time ("Father! why did you hide this from me?") (*EC* 57), he flaunts the visible sign of a potency "I am risen" (*EC* 57), hitherto sacrificially numbed and anaesthetized. Gabriel's dream of a renewed sexual relationship with Gretta, which ends in defeat, is reversed in the man who died's "great atonement, the being in touch" (*EC* 58). (This audacious purging of "atonement" of its traditional sacrificial connotations recenters its meaning on a tactile at-one-ment.)

Unlike Gabriel's "impalpable world" (*D* 200), in which contact by touch is extinguished, the man who died's world is revealed through libidinal touch, semantically linked to its intimate extension—"being in touch" (*EC* 58). Thus an economy of sacrifice, rooted in opposites (especially the Lawrentian consummation/renunciation duo), gives way to a concord ("So he knew her, and was at one with her") that heals the "great scars in his sides"—the last visible signs of a death, now surpassed (*EC* 58). The desire that restores the body to life after its mutilation also "consum[es]" it in the radiance of old wounds, now transformed into "suns" (*EC* 57, 58). Such exotic idealizations of a resurrected potency that consummates sexual contact stand in sharp contrast to Gabriel's wary acceptance of his vision of death.

Finally, in the most unexpected convergence of all, both protagonists decide on a "journey westward" (*D* 200), away from the sacrificial entanglements that previously bound them. "The Dead" buries under thick snowdrifts the three instruments of torture—the cross, the spear, and the thorns—the ultimate farewell to sacrifice toward which the text repeatedly gestured. Likewise with the man who died: his contact with Isis is finally "perfected and fulfilled" (*EC* 59); he too moves westward, following the course of the sun and ensuring his escape from those who seek sacrificial revenge on the male factor who gave Roman justice the slip.

The journeys the protagonists initiate cross unfamiliar landscapes that lead them away from the closed sacrificial worlds they inhabited: for Gabriel, from the claustrophobic enclosure of the Morkans' annual dance, across the dark central plain to the churchyard where Michael Furey lies buried (*D* 200–201); for the man who died, from the east beyond Damascus to the west, "as the road goes" (*EC* 44). Gabriel's move westward is the source of much critical speculation: is it a journey toward death, or a movement toward liberation (or both),[24] or away from an oppressive sacrificial bondage, as my present reading suggests?[25] With "departure" now "in the air" (*EC* 59), the man who died escapes the ever-menacing threat of a second crucifixion.[26] Unlike Gabriel, however, he anticipates a return ("The suns come back in their seasons; and I shall come again") (*EC* 61) with the spring sun as lodestar and guide.

In the context of Abraham's intended sacrifice of his son (Genesis 22.1–19), Derrida is eloquent in *The Gift of Death*: "without calculating, without investing, beyond any perspective of recuperating the loss," this sacrifice without reserve is also "beyond recompense or retribution [. . .] without any hope of remuneration" (*Gift* 95). Derrida reserves the term "absolute" for this "infinite and dissymmetrical economy" of the gift of death (*Gift* 107, 113).[27] The two climactic scenarios, by contrast, enact the supersession of those petty sacrificial constraints that part 1 of each story engaged with. Abolishing those sacrificial binary oppositions—life/death, communion/expiation, victimizer/victimized—both stage the sacrifice of sacrifice itself, shattering the limits regulating the economic exchange. The difference between the two scenarios may also be summed up as a difference in style: between Joyce's metaphysical realism that combines nonhuman perspectives (Gabriel's vision of the dead) with acute attention to detail, and Lawrence's tabular narrative that balances a mythological remoteness with vivid sensuous images.[28] Such transcendence of restrictive economies opens up uncanny new worlds, previously foreclosed, where sacrifice no longer functions as a regulatory ideal. In "The Dead," spectral, disembodied presences—"the vast hosts of the dead" (*D* 200)—are precisely those whose achieved passage through death makes further sacrifice redundant.[29] For the man who died, a new potent cosmos, reflecting the potency of his own erect body, relegates sacrifice to the "little life" of the Roman masters and slaves, who desire to crucify him for a second time.

What both Joyce's and Lawrence's stories have strikingly in common is their repudiation of one particular version of sacrifice—the Christian doctrine of sacrifice that "subtly worked its way into the very heart of [. . .] numerous nineteenth-century and early twentieth-century theories of sacrifice" (Keenan 10). Based on a purely economic transaction, it constitutes the system of precalculated credits and debts upon which their repudiation is founded. It forms the pivot around which the major encounters in part 1 of both stories revolve, in which short-term losses and gains, both financial and psychological, are the dominant outcomes. Part 2 of each story, by contrast, stages an economy of sacrifice without reserve, without hope of reward or return that transcends all economic accounting.

Notes

1. In a 1904 letter to Nora Barnacle, Joyce states that he left the Catholic Church in 1898, "hating it most fervently" (*SL* 25). For Lawrence's engagement with Congregationalism, see Masson 53–68.

2. Although the title character is deliberately never named, Lawrence intended the man who died to be the posthumous Christ, risen from the grave, with all of the connotation of the crucifixion experience, which is referred to throughout the text.

3. By "economies of sacrifice," I mean exchanges that have financial negotiation as their metaphorical model. As Dennis Keenan puts it: "Most theories of sacrifice are predicated on an economy of debts and credits in which one gets a return on one's sacrificial investment" (10). In "Money and Other Rates of Exchange," an interesting essay on Joyce's short story "Counterparts," Schloss examines the ways in which economic discourse structures the story, though she makes no connection between economic exchange and dynamics of sacrifice.

4. In the same 1904 letter to Nora, Joyce uses the term "victim" to characterize his mother's life of sacrificial renunciation: "When I looked on her face as she lay in her coffin—a face grey and wasted with cancer—I understood that I was looking on the face of a victim and I cursed the system that had made her a victim" (*Letters II* 48).

5. In a sequence of essays, I have explored the role of sacrifice, among other subjects, in *The Trespasser, Sons and Lovers, The Rainbow,* and *Women in Love.*

6. External analeptic events are those that precede the start of the main narrative.

7. "The Dead," part 1, though not marked as such, ends with the departure of the guests from the Morkan party. In "The Man Who Died," parts 1 and 2 are specifically marked.

8. A feminist theory of sacrifice, Jay maintains, "must recognize the historically contingent nature of gender relations of different traditions, seeing them neither as universal nor as biologically determined, but as historical products" (133).

9. In the context of women's exclusion from the Roman Catholic priesthood, Luce Irigaray suggests that "the hidden sacrifice is in fact this extradition, this ban on women's participation in religious practice, and their consequent exile from the ultimate source of social decision making" (92).

10. As John Paul Riquelme notes, the word "palaver" was often used as verb or noun to describe in a condescending way native habits of talking. Palaver was predicated of the Indians, the Africans, "and, of course, those loquacious Irish" (128). Interestingly, money itself has a sacrificial origin. As Keenan notes, "the oldest Greek measure of value was the sacred sacrificial ox, the tribute that was paid to the deity" (11).

11. For Hubert and Mauss' discussion of this gift-logic, see their highly influential book *Sacrifice* (101). For an anthology of essays on sacrifice, ranging from such nineteenth-century anthropologists as E. B. Tylor and James G. Frazer, whom Lawrence read, to modern theorists of sacrifice such as René Girard, Nancy Jay, and Walter Burkert, see Carter, ed., *Understanding Religious Sacrifice: A Reader.*

12. For excellent discussions of these binary oppositions, see Jay, *Throughout Your Generations Forever,* 17–29; and Kearns' *The Virgin Mary, Monotheism, and Sacrifice,* 27–31.

13. For the historical and ecclesiastical background to the papal interdiction on female participation in Catholic choirs, see Morgan's "Queer Choirs."

14. This is Carol Adams' term for the rhetorical strategy by means of which animals "in name and body are made absent *as animals* for meat to exist" (51).

15. To take just one example: in her discussion of Hubert and Mauss', Girard's, and Burkert's theories of sacrifice, Kathryn McClymond notes that "all three approaches emphasize the destruction of the animal victim and find in that activity the defining point of sacrifice" (16).

16. Ironically, Gretta's "yielding" to Gabriel in the Gresham hotel—"she had fallen to him so easily" (196)—exemplifies Lawrentian sacrificial sex where one partner (in this case Gabriel) assumes absolute mastery. Gabriel's dream of "overmastery" (195) of course turns out to be an illusion.

17. It is important to distinguish this new concept of excess from an earlier, better-known Lawrentian one, which signifies exactly the opposite. In the *Study of Thomas Hardy* (1914), for example, excess connotes an ontological exuberance, a prodigal self-

expenditure, a sacrifice without reserve that wastes itself without counting the cost. In "The Man Who Died," excess is also a form of extravagance, whose meaning, however, has radically altered. Tied to a moralistic concept of greed, it connotes a precalculated return for expenditure—the overriding demand for too much (or too little) from the other.

18. In *On the Genealogy of Morals*, Friedrich Nietzsche repeatedly stresses the connection between the compulsion to sacrifice and sadism: "the kind of pleasure the selfless, the self-denying, the self-sacrificing man feels from the outset [. . .] belongs to cruelty" (68).

19. See especially Bauerle's essay, which quotes a stanza from "The Lass of Aughrim" describing Lord Gregory as "hav[ing] [his] will" of the Lass (124–25).

20. From "The Lass of Aughrim," qtd. in Bauerle 124–25.

21. By expiation, I mean the possibility of ridding herself of the suffering her seduction by Gregory has caused her.

22. Earlier commentators read this scene (and others) in mythological terms: "the mother Goddess [. . .] restores life to the dead god, and then accepts his renewed vitality in the renewal of her own womb" (LeDoux 137). They also record numerous other rewritings of the Christian myth before Lawrence's time—by Oscar Wilde, Frank Harris, and George Moore among others (Thompson 19–39).

23. Such an injunction, however, leaves open a sacrificial space for the noncriminal putting to death of animals (Wolfe 100–101).

24. Elizabeth Cullingford succinctly summarizes both these positions (228).

25. Seamus Deane characterizes the celebrated end of "The Dead" as the conversion of "something solid into something spectral"—an aesthetic movement where "everything is dissolved into writing" (6). My present reading makes its range of reference more concrete and brings it closer to home. The uneasy tension between its sedating rhythms and its evocative power camouflages those disturbing details. Indeed the mapping of the journey itself is far from spectral: it includes its own meticulous signpostings—the central plain, the "treeless hills," the "mutinous Shannon waves," and the "lonely churchyard on the hill" (*D* 200–201). With its glimpse of the "last end" of "all the living and the dead" (*D* 201), their final passage through death renders sacrifice itself anachronistic.

26. At the same time he completed part 2 of "The Man Who Died" (summer 1929), Lawrence wrote to his friend Dorothy Warren concerning the threat to thirteen of his paintings, on exhibition in London, which the authorities wanted to burn: "To admit that my pictures should be burned, in order to change an English law, would be to admit that sacrifice of life to circumstance which I most strongly disbelieve in. [. . .] No more crucifixions, no more martyrdoms, no more *autos da fé*, as long as time lasts, if I can prevent it" (*4L* 369).

27. As Derrida, however, shrewdly notes, God's decision to return Isaac to Abraham "reinscribe[s] sacrifice within an economy by means of what thenceforth comes to resemble a reward" (*Gift* 96).

28. For a perceptive analysis of the fabular mode in "The Man Who Died," see Padhi 207–11.

29. With its emphasis on purgation and purification, the Roman Catholic doctrine of Purgatory—a place of temporary punishment—may be read as an attempt to reinstall sacrifice in a life after death.

Works Cited

Adams, Carol. *The Sexual Politics of Meat: A Feminist-Vegetarian Critical Theory*. New York: Continuum, 2004.

Bauerle, Ruth. "Date Rape, Mate Rape: A Liturgical Interpretation of 'The Dead.'" *New Alliances in Joyce Studies*. Ed. Bonnie Kime Scott. Newark: U of Delaware P, 1988. 113–35.

Carter, Jeffrey. Ed. *Understanding Religious Sacrifice: A Reader*. London: Continuum, 2003.

Cullingford, Elizabeth. "Phoenician Genealogies and Oriental Geographies: Joyce, Language, and Race." *Semi-Colonial Joyce*. Ed. Derek Attridge and Marjorie Howes. Cambridge: Cambridge UP, 2000. 219–39.

Deane, Seamus. "Dead Ends: Joyce's Finest Moments." *Semi-Colonial Joyce*. Ed. Derek Attridge and Marjorie Howes. Cambridge: Cambridge UP, 2000. 21–36.

Delany, Paul. "'A Would-Be-Dirty Mind': D. H. Lawrence as an Enemy of Joyce." *Joyce in the Hibernian Metropolis*. Ed. Morris Beja and David Norris. Columbus: Ohio State UP, 1996. 76–82.

Derrida, Jacques. "From Restricted to General Economy." *Writing and Difference*. Trans. Alan Bass. London: Routledge and Kegan Paul, 1978. 251–77.

———. *The Gift of Death*. Trans. David Wills. Chicago: U of Chicago P, 1995.

Doherty, Gerald. "D. H. Lawrence's *Sons and Lovers* and the Culture of Sacrifice." *D. H. Lawrence Review* 34–35 (2010): 5–24.

———. "Farewell to Romantic Ontologies: Sex, Sacrifice and the Animal Body in D. H. Lawrence's *The Trespasser*." *Etudes Lawrenciennes* 39 (2009): 87–110.

———. "Violent Immolations: Species Discourse, Sacrifice, and the Lure of Transcendence in D. H. Lawrence's *The Rainbow*." *Modern Fiction Studies* 57.1 (2011): 47–74.

———. "*Women in Love*: Sacrifice, Sadism and the Discourse of *Species*." *Windows to the Sun: D. H. Lawrence's "Thought-Adventures."* Ed. Earl Ingersoll and Virginia Hyde. Madison, NJ: Fairleigh Dickinson UP, 2009. 68–98.

Girard, René. *Violence and the Sacred*. Trans. Patrick Gregory. Baltimore: Johns Hopkins UP, 1977.

Hubert, Henri, and Marcel Mauss. *Sacrifice: Its Nature and Function*. Trans. W. D. Halls. Chicago: U of Chicago P, 1964.

Ingersoll, Earl. *Engendered Trope in Joyce's Dubliners*. Carbondale: Southern Illinois UP, 1996.

Irigaray, Luce. "Women, the Sacred, Money." *Sexes and Genealogies.* Trans. Gillian Gill. New York: Columbia UP, 1993. 73–88.

Jay, Nancy. *Throughout Your Generations Forever: Sacrifice, Religion, and Paternity.* Chicago: U of Chicago P, 1992.

Kearns, Cleo McNelly. *The Virgin Mary, Monotheism, and Sacrifice.* Cambridge: Cambridge UP, 2008.

Keenan, Dennis King. *The Question of Sacrifice.* Bloomington: Indiana UP, 2005.

LeDoux, Larry V. "Christ and Isis: The Function of the Dying and Reviving God in 'The Man Who Died.'" *D. H. Lawrence Review* 5.2 (1972) 132–48.

MacDonald, Robert H. "The Union of Fire and Water: An Examination of the Imagery of 'The Man Who Died.'" *D. H. Lawrence Review* 10.1 (1977): 34–51.

Masson, Margaret J. "D. H. Lawrence's Congregational Inheritance." *D. H. Lawrence Review* 22.1 (1990): 53–68.

McClymond, Kathryn. *Beyond Sacred Violence: A Comparative Study of Sacrifice.* Baltimore: Johns Hopkins UP, 2008.

Morgan, Jack. "Queer Choirs: Sacred Music, Joyce's "The Dead," and the Sexual Politics of Victorian Aestheticism." *James Joyce Quarterly* 37.1/2 (1999/2000): 127–51.

Nietzsche, Friedrich. *On the Genealogy of Morals.* Trans. Douglas Smith. Oxford: Oxford UP, 2008.

Padhi, Bibhu. *D. H. Lawrence: Modes of Fictional Style.* New York: Whitston, 1989.

Quinn, Gerard. "Joyce and Tenebrae: The Ironic Passion and Death of Gabriel Conroy." *James Joyce Quarterly* 37.1/2 (1999–2000): 153–66.

Riquelme, John Paul. "Joyce's 'The Dead': The Dissolution of the Self and the Police." *ReJoycing: New Readings of Dubliners.* Ed. Rosa M. Bollettieri Bosinelli and Harold F. Mosher. Lexington: UP of Kentucky, 1998. 123–41.

Schloss, Carol. "Money and Other Rates of Exchange: Commercial Relations and 'Counterparts.'" *European Joyce Studies 7: New Perspectives on* Dubliners. Ed. Mary Power and Ulrich Schneider. Amsterdam: Rodopi, 1997. 181–94.

Singleton, Mark. "Lure of the Fallen Seraphim: Sovereignty and Sacrifice in James Joyce and Georges Bataille." *James Joyce Quarterly* 44.2 (2007): 303–23.

Thompson, Leslie M. "The Christ Who Didn't Die: Analogues to D. H. Lawrence's 'The Man Who Died.'" *D. H. Lawrence Review* 8.1 (1975): 19–30.

Wolfe, Cary. *Animal Rites: American Culture, the Discourse of Species, and Posthumanist Theory.* Chicago: U of Chicago P, 2003.

5

Reader - response (handwritten)
redux (handwritten)

The Isis Effect

How Joyce and Lawrence Revitalize Christianity through Foreignization

MARTIN BRICK

In November 1922, Lord Carnarvon and Howard Carter opened Tutankhamen's tomb, and in 1923 E. A. Wallis Budge published an assessment of their discoveries. An understandable fascination with all things Egyptian overtook the United Kingdom. Not surprisingly, Egyptian mythology made its way into the writing of several modernist authors, James Joyce and D. H. Lawrence among them. Late in his short life, Lawrence retells Christ's resurrection in *The Escaped Cock (The Man Who Died)* (1929), a work featuring a brief sexual affair between Christ and a priestess of Isis. Joyce, as well, includes the Isis/Osiris myth in his story of death and resurrection, *Finnegans Wake* (1939). An examination of how Egyptian myth functions in each author's works provides a compelling case study for the status of Christianity in the early twentieth century. As traditional religious authority was challenged by scientific discoveries and Victorian rationalism, many modernist authors responded with literature that appeared to further threaten conventional faith. Traditional Christian narratives were often treated in a profane manner, or alternately, augmented or appended to pagan religions. Rather than entirely diminishing Christianity, however, such treatments can be seen to revitalize religion.

This essay examines how Joyce and Lawrence each produce works of literature that revive or rejuvenate Christianity in the modernist period through their use of "foreignization," or the intentional estrangement of the familiar. Each author takes common Christian narratives or themes and juxtaposes them with those of other religions—in this examination the Egyptian myth of Isis and Osiris. Both *The Escaped Cock* and *Finnegans Wake* address the resurrection of Christ, the event at the heart of Christian belief. By asking readers

Left: No head (handwritten marginal note)

to reimagine this event, these authors ask readers to reimagine Christianity's core concepts: sin, death, judgment, and how individuals define or understand their relationship with God.

Joyce and Lawrence prove particularly interesting examples, and not only due to their common use of the Isis/Osiris myth to reexamine the Christian notion of resurrection. Each author also displays a complicated, controversial relationship with religion. While the scope of this essay does not allow a thorough examination of either author's religious agenda, it is worthwhile to note that each writer appears drawn to religion but troubled by the Church as an institution. Many scholars contend that Joyce disavowed the Church but remained devoted to the "mystery" of Catholicism and fascinated with ritual; as Umberto Eco puts it, "Joyce abandons the faith but not religious obsession" (3). One of the more amusing anecdotes illustrating Joyce's estrangement from the Church tells of Nora, frustrated by her husband's drinking and debt, threatening to have the children baptized (McCourt 126). Alternately, as evidence of his preoccupation with Catholic ritual, Joyce's fascination with the symbolic rites reportedly drew him to Good Friday and Holy Saturday Mass each year (Schlossman 85). Mary Colum notes that she had never known anyone "on whom the Church, its ceremonies, symbols, and theological declarations had made such an impress" (qtd. in Fargnoli 1).

Similarly, Lawrence shows a strong spirituality that disregards the formal dogma of the Church. His view of religion as a natural, almost unconscious but still powerful state is reflected in *Sons and Lovers*. Paul explains that a crow is religious in its flight, but "not religious to be religious. [. . .] it only does it because it feels itself carried to where it's going, not because it thinks it is being eternal" (*SL* 291). Critics often read Lawrence's religion as a frustration with the limits of the Church's understanding. Evelyn Hinz and John Teunissen point out that across his career, "Lawrence's quarrel with Christianity was that the traditional Christ was too mild, that the Christian love ethic failed to accommodate the power and violence which are an essential object of religious reverence" (285) Lawrence's fascination with a faith that explored the most powerful of human emotions and Joyce's fascination with sacrament, ceremony, and religious mystery, then, display a common need—for humans to experience religion in an individual and psychologically charged way.

Modernity called for exactly this sort of revitalization. Paul Delany sets his examination of a rivalry of sorts between Joyce and Lawrence within the context of a social structure longing for a mysterious, nonrationalistic imagination: "Modernism might even be considered a religious revival, challenging the Victorian idea that religion would wither away and be replaced by science" (80). Michael Levenson expresses similar thoughts in his book *A Genealogy of Modernism*. As the title suggests, he traces modernism's roots, noting that Matthew Arnold initiated a program of "revis[ing] Christianity in order to retain it" (10). As the Victorian scientific worldview only valued experimentation, things directly perceptible, Arnold responded by shifting the understanding of religion from miracle and revealed Truth to personal experience. Levenson explains that Arnold offered a "redefinition" of religion to focus upon "an immediate perception of primary religious categories: 'Eternal,' 'Righteousness,' 'not ourselves'" (11). These categories are exactly the issues that surround Lawrence's man who died and Joyce's HCE.[2] While connections between these characters and the Christian resurrection narrative seemingly promote heresy and sacrilege, they concurrently promote the individual experience with mystery, with the irrational, with the inexplicable. Lawrence and Joyce finesse this balance between sacred and profane religious perception by offering narratives that at once resemble traditional religious texts and depart from them, contradict them, or augment them with narratives from alternate religious or mythological traditions.

Both Lawrence and Joyce schooled themselves in alternative religions, particularly ancient pagan traditions. John B. Vickery notes, in separate venues, each author's use of James Frazer's *The Golden Bough* as a resource for exploring the concept of resurrection. Vickery observes that "Frazer's drama of the dying and reviving god and his wife-mother-lover" makes frequent appearances in Lawrence's stories and constitutes "one of Lawrence's major *leit-motivs*" ("Myth" 65). The same drama and leitmotifs permeate *Finnegans Wake* and its two central characters. Still, within Vickery's examination of each author's debt to Frazer, distinct differences emerge. While both authors are drawn to themes of death, sex, and resurrection, Lawrence uses such material in order to celebrate vitality and concrete sensation, whereas Joyce turns to more abstract notions of creativity via language. Lawrence ritualizes "[d]eath, marriage, fornication, initiation, dancing, sacrifice, departure, and arrival," so that "[t]he very manner of their performance testifies to their connection with the sacred existence, that is, the order in which the mysterious potency of life itself resides" (Vickery, "Myth" 67–68). Joyce, on the other hand, links death and resurrection with vegetative growth, and also with language. In reference to the portmanteau word "mistletropes" (*FW* 9.19), Vickery observes that "by identifying it with the verbal realm as well as the natural world of objects, he suggests that, in a century assured of the unreality of magical powers or supernatural properties in things, the metamorphic power to encompass life as well as death lies in language" ("Finnegans" 217).

This distinction between an emphasis on performance versus language is more directly noted in Delany's assessment of the authors. He argues that Lawrence should have approved of the idea of *Ulysses* given the similarity between the novel's topic—a lusty woman, her lover, and her impotent husband—and the themes of Lawrence's own fiction (Delany 79). But letters reveal that the Englishman found Joyce's writing far too abstract or "too mental" and therefore running counter to the vitality of lived experience (*6L* 548). So while both authors handle the topic of sex as regenerative, they diverge in how intercourse ought to be depicted in literature. Delany writes, "Lawrence found that treatment [of sexuality in nineteenth-century realism] a deliberate narrowing of human potential; whereas Joyce accepts realism's fundamental project of documenting, without moral preconceptions, people's everyday behavior" (79). Each author's use of Isis further illuminates Delany's assessment. In *The Escaped Cock*, the sexual relationship between Isis and Christ challenges a perceived narrowing of human potential by Christianity, while Joyce blends ALP with Isis (among other sacred and secular figures) and HCE with Osiris (and many others); more importantly, Joyce displays a fascination with *The Book of the Dead*, a set of incantations, hymns, and "power words" used to guide individuals through the underworld. Therefore, Joyce emphasizes the individual's participation in otherworldly acts, which comes via language.

Foreignization

The term "foreignization" is borrowed from Juliette Taylor's article "Foreign Music: Linguistic Estrangement in 'Proteus' and 'Sirens,'" in which she asserts that "rejuvenation" is made possible by inspiring feelings of estrangement in the reader (409). She challenges those modernist critics like F. R. Leavis who disdain Joyce's prose for calling too much attention to itself, for concerning itself too deeply with form. In Leavis' own words, *Ulysses* is a "dead end," a point further proven by the "disintegration" of structure in *Finnegans Wake* (39). It is exactly this disintegration, this lack of stability in structure and signification, that allows the very organic principle of the reader providing order and wholeness as he or she becomes unsettled and thus approaches even those words and phrases in one's native language as if they were foreign. Taylor asserts that "multilingualism makes us step outside any single language, including our "own," and view it from a different perspective" (409). In a similar sense, the juxtaposition of Christianity with the Isis/Osiris myth (and others) produces an experience of estrangement for the reader, by which even religious traditions familiar to the reader are viewed from a new, polyglossic perspective to produce a new form of signification.

While the idea of estrangement or foreignization strengthening religion may seem counterintuitive, its success lies in the reader's active role. Taylor uses Bakhtin to argue that linguistic estrangement overcomes the arbitrariness of the sign, leading to heightened awareness of the material presence. The juxtaposition of religious allusions allows the reader to reconsider the metaphorical and metonymic underpinnings of religious narratives. Readers become estranged from otherwise familiar religious characters, narratives, and symbols by their conflation with other traditions. On the most basic level, Lawrence's novel displays this process of reconsideration by asking readers to recast their conception of Christ by not explicitly naming him. The story contains enough clues to inform readers that Lawrence is building upon the late chapters of the four canonical Gospels, but the Christ figure is always referred to as "the man who died," as if advising us not to fall into lazy patterns and preconceived ideas.

Such a process distances the reader from traditional interpretations of the religious material and thus allows the reader to examine the spiritual messages in a less schematized manner. The reader is prompted to ponder why certain actions and objects (e.g., the cross itself) symbolize certain relationships with divinity. Just as foreignization of language allows a heightened attention to the material presence of words, foreignization of religious allusions allows a heightened sensitivity to components of religious narrative.

Lawrence's Foreignization

"Now I am not myself. I am something new . . ."

D. H. Lawrence, *The Escaped Cock* (*The Man Who Died*)

Lawrence performs two scandalous maneuvers in *The Escaped Cock*. He creates a character, rather clearly Christ, who experiences a sexual awakening after his resurrection. Second, this sex occurs with a priestess of a pagan religion. While a reader's initial response might be to regard these items as a rejection of Christian beliefs and standards while embracing paganism, even hedonism, a more nuanced reading may recognize the inherent power of the resurrection narrative with a shifted emphasis. No longer does the cross function as Christianity's central symbol, but rather, the risen Christ himself does.

Even before Lawrence introduces the priestess of Isis, he makes the text appear foreign by presenting events that both borrow and depart from the Gospel accounts of Jesus' resurrection. This aids readers in accepting the "man who died" as Christ, a necessary step since part 2 does not follow any preexisting narrative. Part 1, then, familiarizes readers with a character who is like Jesus, but different from any Jesus they have read about before.[3]

Upon reviving, the man who died "was alone; and having died, was even beyond loneliness" (*EC* 16). This attitude calls to mind Christ's cry on the cross: "My God, my God, why hast thou forsaken me?" (Mark 15:34). Lawrence's description of the actual resurrection and its subsequent events corresponds to the Gospels in some respects. No one, for example, witnesses Christ's actual rising. Each of the four Gospels records women arriving to find an empty tomb, and in Lawrence's narrative the man who dies slips away unnoticed. Upon first meeting someone after leaving the tomb, the man who died says, "Do not be afraid" (*EC* 16). The Gospel accounts use nearly the exact phrase: "Do not be afraid" (Matt 28:10) and "Do not be terrified" (Mark 16:16). When the man who died returns to the garden and finds Madeleine, he says to her, "Don't touch me. [. . .] Not yet! I am not healed and in touch with men" (*EC* 24). In the Gospel of John he meets Mary Magdalene and tells her, "Do not touch me, for I have not yet ascended to my Father" (John 20:17). The former assumes a long-term return to life, while the latter suggests only a short stay prior to his ascension. These and other small details allow readers to feel at once familiar with yet disassociated from the resurrection story in Lawrence's work.

A more significant departure from the Gospels emerges in the earthly, unsensational explanation of the resurrection. Twice the man who died explains his resurrection in physical terms: "They took me down too soon" (*EC* 18, 24). Rather than presenting his resurrection as a glorious return to life, Lawrence depicts a seriously injured man. He is "numb and cold," wincing as he uses his "scarred feet" to "climb painfully" (*EC* 15, 17, 18). The peasant who takes him in notes "with terror the livid wounds on the thin, waxy hands and the thin feet of the stranger" (*EC* 19). Still, even as he is depicted in a very concrete manner, a tone of mystery and otherworldliness envelops him. He is described as "still cold and remote in the region of death, with perfumes coming from his transparent body as if from some strange flower" (*EC* 19). While his translucent body and the comparison of him to a "strange" flower may invite supernatural interpretations, readers are also presented with the coldness of his death. They must wonder if he really died or merely came close. While phrases like "For I have died, and now I know my own limits" (*EC* 24) seem rather direct, others like "region of death" as well as "had been killed from out of [the world of things]" are more cryptic but hint at incompleteness (*EC* 19, 18). Declarations like "So I have risen up" immediately follow "They took me down too soon" (*EC* 18), leading readers to wonder if all talk of death is merely metaphorical. We receive a "yes and no" answer to this dilemma in his encounter with Madeleine: "Yet his eyes were open. And she looked at him again, and she saw that it was not the Messiah. The Messiah had not risen. This was just a man. The enthusiasm and the burning purity were gone, and the rapt youth. His youth was dead" (*EC* 26). It is as if the divine part of Jesus has died, and what remains is the purely human. Reference to his "open eyes" reminds us of Genesis: "And the eyes of them both were opened: and [. . .] they perceived themselves to be naked" (Gen 3:7). The man who died acquires knowledge and understanding. And just as in Genesis, knowledge after the fall is quickly associated with sex: "And Adam knew Eve his wife" (Gen 4:1). Lawrence's book, as well, links knowledge to both pleasure and pain of mortality.

Part 2 of *The Escaped Cock* most directly "foreignizes" the Christian resurrection narrative since, apart from a few echoes of Gospel events like the washing of feet, this half of the book does not build upon an existing narrative. Christ is depicted in a radically different manner from that to which most readers are accustomed, but this sensation of foreignization is modeled in the main character, who, like readers, conditionally accepts this disorientation. In a conversation with Madeleine he admits to being unsure of his immediate plans, aspirations, or desires, feeling open to possibility: "'I do not know what I shall do,' he said. 'When I am healed I shall know better'" (*EC* 24). The man who died attempts to find new purpose, since "[he has] outlived [his] mission and know[s] no more of it" (*EC* 24). There is a great deal of musing on his part, and this musing in turn invites readers to reconsider or reframe their conception of what the resurrection means.

It may be easy to view *The Escaped Cock* as Lawrence's rejection of the past, a denial of the teaching of Christianity. Within the narrative, the man who died does speak despairingly of his own past practices, declaring "The Word is but the midge that bites at evening" and "What a pity I preached to them" (*EC* 30, 31). But it is the emphasis rather than the thesis of his teachings that the man who died reconsiders. It is not that he denies "the Word" but that he recognizes its limited application: "But beyond the tomb [words] cannot go" (*EC* 30). In these statements Lawrence demonstrates his disdain for the abstract, for conceptions bound up in language that so fascinates Joyce.

Readers who flinch at this character's reconceived notion of purpose, perhaps regarding it as self-indulgent and even hedonistic, will not be alone, as Madeleine also questions the philosophy of the man who died. "Have you risen for yourself alone?" she asks (*EC* 25). His response displays what many scholars see as the crux of Lawrence's spiritual position. Within Christianity, too much attention is awarded to death and not enough to the return of life. The man who died responds, "I have not risen from the dead to seek death again" (*EC* 25). This is likely the kind of thinking Kingley Widmer has in mind when he notes that "Lawrence insists upon the 'joy' of resurrection into life as far more important than the 'agony' of crucifixion into salvation" (200). In other words, he emphasizes lived experience over the more abstract eschatological understanding of reward. Joyce Carol Oates suggests that Lawrence rejects theological dogma of original sin and replaces it with a psychological dogma that recognizes a split between "mind" and "blood-consciousness" (99). While at first blush this may appear hedonistic, as Madeleine's accusation suggests, Lawrence, in *Reflections on the Death of a Porcupine*, outlines the nuances and personal responsibilities of such an outlook. He writes, "Living consists in doing what you really, vitally want to do: what the *life* in you wants to do, not what your ego imagines you want to do. And to find out *how* the life in you wants to be lived, and to live it, is terribly difficult" (*RDP* 323). This is the heart of Lawrence's idea of "vitalism"—not simply to do as one feels but to find the purpose of one's actions.

The distinction between self-indulgent hedonism and vitality is illustrated through the man who died's sexual encounter in part 2. On a conscious level, the man who died expresses considerable trepidation before experiencing sex. "I am almost more afraid of this touch than I was of death. For I am more nakedly exposed to it," he observes (*EC* 52). In addition to expressing fear, his actions are marked by passivity. The priestess of Isis takes the lead in his healing and reeducation. She must convince him to disrobe, as he is hesitant. Furthermore, she imposes an identity upon him, a role he plays, though he does not fully accept it: "'You are Osiris, aren't you?' she said naively. 'If you will,' he said" (*EC* 53). But as this scenario progresses, fear transfers to the priestess and as the man who died comes to realize the potential of this new blood consciousness, he takes a more active role. He recognizes the potential of life, while simultaneously the priestess recognizes the bleakness of death. She feels "the shadow of the grey, grisly wind of death triumphant" (*EC* 54), reflecting Lawrence's frustration with a Church that fixates on death. In a book review, he once wrote: "I worship Christ, I worship Jehovah, I worship Pan, I worship Aphrodite. But I do not worship hands nailed and running with blood upon a cross, nor licentiousness, nor lust" (*1P* 307). Lawrence's interest lies in shifting attention from what he perceived to be undue attention to the Passion of Christ, to a celebration of the physical joy of life.

Often the case in Lawrence's fiction, vitality in *The Escaped Cock* is expressed through sex. Larry V. LeDoux explains the significance of sex in Lawrence's interpretation of the resurrection, since sex demonstrates "Christ learning how to love, in the only way man is truly able to love—vitally, with his body" (140). This learning is demonstrated both through sudden revelation as the man who died declares, "[W]hy did you hide this from me?" and "[T]his is beyond prayer" at their first touch (*EC* 57). But this education also emerges through a reassessment of his former philosophy. The priestess refers to disciples in his past as serving him with "the corpse of [their] love" (*EC* 55). The man who died's contemplation of her remark expresses Lawrence's disdain not only for the Church's fascination with both death and abstractness. "Perhaps he loved me in the flesh," he ruminates on Judas, "and I willed that he should love me bodilessly" (*EC* 55). A love that is conceptual and not rooted in the actual experience of living is a dead love to Lawrence.

Sex provides an avenue to self-discovery and an adequately "foreignized" Christ and could in this sense deliver Lawrence's message of revitalization. But the Christian resurrection narrative is further displaced since his sexual partner is a priestess of a foreign and ancient religion. Further, the connection to Isis augments this revitalized Christian view with something mythic and therefore authoritative. In fact, it may be that Lawrence held greater faith in myth than in individual humans. Oates makes the observation, comparing *The Escaped Cock* to Lawrence's other fiction, that "[o]nly in parable, in myth, can tragedy be transcended" (107). Myth works against the constraints of the world, especially the dehumanizing mechanization of modernity. By turning to Isis, as opposed to Madeleine or any secular human, Lawrence allows readers to view the resurrection as a recapturing of something lost as opposed to a simple rejection of theological dogma. Widmer draws our attention to Lawrence's own reflections on primitive mythology's power over rationality, as it is myth, not reason, "which reaches the deep emotional centres every time" (202).

While his affair with an Egyptian priestess might lead readers to view *The Escaped Cock* as a rejection of Christianity in favor of paganism, close reading reveals a resistance to this notion. While the man who died rejects his former methodology, preaching in particular, he never rescinds his teachings. And though he discovers the vitality of his body through his encounter with the priestess, the man who died never embraces the Isis/Osiris myth. On several occasions the priestess identifies him as Osiris, but the man who died always dodges the identification. When she says "Stay! I am sure you are Osiris!" he replies "Not yet!" (*EC* 46). Soon after, he appears to play along, accepting it disingenuously in order to receive what he needs: "Yea, if thou wilt heal me!" (*EC* 47). Still other places echo the Gospels, as Pilate asks Christ if he was "King of the Jews," and Christ responds, "You say so" (Mark 15:2). The man who died answers the query, "You are Osiris, aren't you?" with "If you will" (*EC* 53).

Beyond his reluctance to definitively accept the name, the man who died appears indifferent to the substance of the role the priestess thrusts upon him. He proclaims his interest in the immediate, visceral qualities of life, nothing deeper or dogmatic. He declares, "I shall be warm again like the morning. I shall be a man. It doesn't need understanding" (*EC* 56). A number of critics remark that across Lawrence's oeuvre, sex represents creativity and often the only portal to personal fulfillment. Paul Poplawski, for example, writes: "It is his measure for authenticity of experience and being, and it is also the means by which the individual can explore and extend the limits of identity and achieve full self-knowledge" (120–21). In the man who died's resistance to the Osiris mantle, readers are reminded of the importance of self-knowledge and identity. A reversion to an ancient religious system is simply not useful or relevant as it replaces one dogma with another. Rather, Lawrence makes Christ foreign, presenting him questioning his own identity, seeking something richer or more purposeful, thereby modeling for readers the notion of a religious reawakening, a metaphorical death and reawakening.

Joyce's Foreignization and the Persistent Underworld

the doom of the balk of the deaf

James Joyce, *Finnegans Wake*

Joyce's use of the Isis/Osiris myth differs significantly from Lawrence's, as his process of foreignization takes on a much different form. Like Lawrence, Joyce recognizes and exploits the thematic parallel between the death and resurrection of Christ and the dismemberment and reconstitution of Osiris. But rather than blending the two figures, Joyce features Osiris as just one piece of the vast mosaic that comprises Humphrey Chimpden Earwicker. Thus the foreignization that the reader experiences in *Finnegans Wake* is not simply a matter of reframing his or her perception of Christianity through its juxtaposition with another myth; rather, it is a redefining of Christianity as it is situated among a few millennia of religion, mythology, folk traditions, history, and literature, both sacred and secular.

A number of scholars have commented on the religious identity of *Finnegans Wake,* many seeing the book as a hybrid faith of sorts. Bernard Benstock, for example, suggests that "Joyce fuses the material of [various religious] texts, arrives at his own version of a common denominator of mythical prototypes, and creates his synthetic 'bible' of twentieth-century civilization" (179). Despite such claims, it is difficult to argue against Christianity's prominent role in the book. Allusions to Christian figures and Bible passages are common, so much so that Harry Burrell claims that "that is *all* it is about. Virtually every page has the Bible story as its basic level of communication" (7). Each of these two viewpoints, however—that *Finnegans Wake* is a new, collective bible, or is essentially the retelling of an old story—limit the extent to which readers process or contemplate religion. The former idea offers no real interpretation of what religion does (it is there, in myriad forms), while the latter presents a rather strict interpretation of what it does (it does more or less what the old story did).

James Atherton's assessment better accounts for the foreignizing effect of the interplay of religions. His *Books at the* Wake naturally acknowledges Joyce's cataloging technique, stating that the *Wake* "contain[s] within itself all the [other] sacred books" (169). Despite this collective effort, Atherton believes, "the basic religion is Christianity" (171). To consider Joyce's text as reshaping the Christian narrative, asking readers to reconsider their understanding of it, acknowledges the fact that Judeo-Christian references are among the most common type in the book and that for many readers of Joyce, these would be references most readily spotted. At the same time, it values the contributions made by the inclusion of other religions and myths. It recognizes something more concrete than a simple amalgam of religions. Atherton's label, "a new sacred book" (169), grants the text its own religious authority. It is not a commentary on religion nor an anthology of religions but rather a scripture in and of itself.

The theme of rebirth in *Finnegans Wake* plays out not only through allusions to narratives of renewal (Noah's flood, Tim Finnegan, the phoenix, and so on) but also through the structure of Joyce's narrative, which juxtaposes these myths and stories. The Judeo-Christian influence on the book is seen almost instantly in the opening line: "riverrun, past Eve and Adam's" (*FW* 3.1). The importance of the Genesis narrative is emphasized again as "the fall" is introduced, but more so, the story "is retaled early in bed and later on life down through all christian minstrelsy" (*FW* 3.15, 17–18). The fall of Eve and Adam (notably inverted from their more familiar order) resonates through generations of Christian ministry; also, rather than being retold, is "retaled." Shifting from the verb "tell" to the noun form "tale" suggests the very substance of the story changes, not just the time and place of telling.

Of course this retaling, in Joyce's hands, is highly inclusive. On the *Wake*'s first page the biblical fall is mixed with more literal falls. Humpty Dumpty appears in the "great fall of the offwall" and "the humptyhillhead of himself" (*FW* 3.18–20). With the inclusion of Humpty, the stage is set for the Osiris cycle. The egg breaks, and like Osiris' dismemberment by Set, inspires a quest to reconstitute his body: "prumptly sends an unquiring one well to the west in quest of his tumptytumtoes" (*FW* 3.20–21). Allusion to Isis appears soon after as the search goes west, "bedoneen the jebel and the jypsian sea" (*FW* 5.22–23). An unnamed female "has the gift of seek on site" (*FW* 5.25), second sight, or the seeker of a site between Jebel and the Egyptian sea. Mark L. Troy notes that Bahn-el-Jebel means "mountain river" or the upper Nile, the area of Isis' search for the fourteen parts of her husband's body (44). Dozens of other facets of HCE's identity are established in the first pages, referencing the Old Testament, Islam, Hinduism, Norse mythology, and nonreligious narratives as well, such as the legends surrounding Sir Tristram, Finn MacCool, and Tim Finnegan. But the Humpty Dumpty and Egyptian stories create a compelling complication of the traditional Judeo-Christian concepts of the fall and redemption. On the one hand, the text displays a fascination with fluidity and timelessness, a "vicus of recirculation" (*FW* 3.2). But at the same time, the text highlights fragmentation. The king's horse and men never put Humpty back together, and though Isis does restore Osiris, his genitals are forever lost. Through these themes, as well as Joyce's shattering and reconstitution of language itself, the reader experiences a foreignized text, one that resembles the familiar original, but one that also requires assembly. With assembly comes fresh interpretation.

An aspect of foreignization common to Joyce and Lawrence is their movement away from the supernatural elements of the Christian resurrection. Lawrence offers a literal explanation of events by having the man who died taken off the cross too soon (*EC* 18, 23). Joyce's conflation of Christ with Tim Finnegan also downplays the literalness, or at least the sanctity, of Christ's death through the comic rejuvenation of Tim by a splash of whiskey. Neither author utterly denies the mystery of Christianity, but each shifts emphasis. As noted above, Lawrence pushes against the conventional understanding of the resurrection by emphasizing "vitality," drawing attention to "blood-consciousness." His critique of "the corpse of love" denies love that lacks concrete expression. Joyce, on the other hand, also wants to challenge a conventional understanding of the resurrection, but his approach dwells on death. His text appears to relish the "corpse." He is fascinated by mystery and therefore wants to prolong the underworld experience. While Lawrence's reframing of Christianity emphasizes actuality, Joyce's emphasizes potentiality, the artist's perspective of being able to create understanding out of raw material.

In the last pages of the first chapter of *Finnegans Wake,* the Christian perspective is again made prominent but at the same time scrutinized. The proclamation "O foenix culprit!" (*FW* 23.16) references both Augustine's "fortunate fall" and the phoenix, reinforcing the tone of rebirth. But the text also paints the phoenix as a culprit, establishing it as an agency of offense. The idea that resurrection is unwelcome is echoed a page later when the mourners of the now roused Tim Finnegan attempt to coax him back into the coffin. "Now be aisy, good Mr Finnimore, sir," they tell him. "And take your laysure like a god on pension" (*FW* 24.16–17). Egyptian allusions complement the desire to keep Finnegan in the grave. The mourners promise to visit his grave, "bringing you presents," but in particular they promise to bring nice things, "Not shabbty little imagettes" (*FW* 24.36, 25.2). In ancient Egypt, however, shabti figures were tiny statues placed in the tomb, carved with incantations and hymns that would animate the figure so it could aid the deceased in the afterlife (Budge 53n1). A few lines later the mourners declare, "peace to his great limbs," suggesting an unwillingness to seek out and reconstitute Osiris' body (*FW* 25.25). Between the felix culpa, Tim Finnegan, and Egyptian references, our figure becomes an Adam/Christ type who has fallen but is denied the ability to reconcile. Furthermore, his conflation with Osiris paints the eventual resurrection not as a divine act that benefits all followers but rather as the passage of one individual aided by language.

The theme of death and a deferred resurrection is introduced in the first chapter of the *Wake* and establishes the overall concept of the book. Joyce wrote to Harriet Shaw Weaver of his "experiment in interpreting 'the dark night of the soul'" (*Letters I* 258). Debates over whether the book is really a dream or not aside, the scrutiny given to HCE's "sin" throughout the book resonates a theme of final judgment. Further, allusions such as the "felix culpa" noted above and similar Christian references call to mind Christ's time spent in Hell prior to his resurrection. Taking place over the span of an evening, the story suggests the Egyptian concept of the afterlife: death with sunset, the night spent in the underworld, and sunrise coinciding with resurrection (Rose 1). Using both

Christianity and Egyptian mythology as models, Joyce's text ruminates on the time spent prior to resurrection. As a revision of Christian theology, the text can be seen as Ignatian in tone, but rather than envisioning Christ's passion, the spiritual exercises address his time spent in the underworld.

Joyce differs significantly from Lawrence, then, in that his interest appears to lie more in *The Book of the Dead* as document than in Isis and Osiris as characters. And indeed, Joyce does more than simply blend or juxtapose the characters of Christianity and Egyptian mythology. *The Book of the Dead* becomes a character itself and is conflated with other texts. In the first chapter of *Finnegans Wake* it is counterposed with annals of Irish history. Here "the leaves of the living in the boke of the deeds, annals of themselves timing the cycles of events grand and national, bring fassilwise to pass how" (*FW* 13.30–31). Readers of these leaves might learn how to pass easily (fassilwise) into the Egyptian afterlife or might come across an account of the Jewish Passover (the Greek "Passah" or Passover [McHugh 13]). Both interpretations involve instructions, but one is directed at a single deceased individual while the other concerns an entire race.

The notion of a book of "deeds" pulls this curious text in two directions as well. On the one hand, it could be a descriptive record of a person's actions to be reviewed upon death. Or it could be a prescriptive manual of the acts/ deeds to be performed in order to pass into the afterlife. Their identification as historical "annals" might undercut any religious significance, but then again, the "timing of the cycles" adds a cosmic tone. As these divergent notions come together in a single collection of leaves, the reader is left to reconsider his or her conception of apocalypse.

Joyce juxtaposes *The Book of the Dead* with other texts in many places, always blurring the line between sacred and secular. At the beginning of II.iii, Joyce writes of "the doom of the balk of the deaf" (*FW* 309.3), meshing it with the doombook, a Saxon lawbook compiled by Alfred the Great in 893 CE, or possibly with William the Conqueror's Domesday Book, his census of 1086. Both possibilities address authority, but these legal documents deal with the earthly realm, while the Egyptian text addresses something otherworldly. Since Alfred's doom book uses the Ten Commandments as its base, one text links behavior to morality in life, while the other provides postlife instructions not particularly linked to personal decency. The overall connection between morality and judgment is obfuscated.

Later, as *Finnegans Wake* begins to wind down, ALP, speaking as "Leafy," reflects on the stranger things that have happened in the "badst pageans of unthowsent and wonst nice or in eddas and oddes bokes of tomb" (*FW* 597.6–7). References to the best (or baddest) pages of *A Thousand and One Nights*, the Icelandic Eddas recording Nordic mythology, and *The Book of the Dead* suggest an unclear line between what has been recorded as history and what as fiction. A connection to *A Thousand and One Nights* undercuts the authority of the religious texts, insinuating that they might be mere fabrications, tales spun to preserve the life of the teller. At the same time, however, this juxtaposition allows religious/mythological texts to be endlessly generative, not static or coldly authoritative texts. Joyce goes on to weave other religious texts into this passage, including "alkovan" (alcoran or Koran [see McHugh 597]). Also present is the declaration "graced be Gad [. . .] in whose words were the beginnings" (*FW* 597.9–10). This phrasing offers a different nuance than the line that begins the Gospel of John: "In the beginning the Word was." The Word, in Joyce's text, is no longer an independent, preexisting entity but rather a product of God's agency, not necessarily constant. The words mark the beginnings, but an implication that things will change hovers. Such juxtaposition invokes both the creative power of words (or the Word) and also the agency of the individual.

Leafy's monologue brings a sense of conclusion to this book that famously does not end. But morning does arrive in *Finnegans Wake*, and so in the Egyptian tradition, the afterlife is reached. In the Christian tradition, the New Covenant is formed. But in each case, the tone of Joyce's narrative differs from the source narratives. By and large, Leafy's message is one of forgiveness and acceptance. She describes her laissez-faire attitude: "I'll wait. And I'll wait. And then if all goes. What will be is. Is is. But let them" (*FW* 620.31–32). Here a simple space dissects Isis into "Is is" and allows Joyce to play with the paradox of her name. The very active agent of Osiris' resurrection in Egyptian mythology is here viewed as a patient receptor of what simply "is." The Christian narrative enters into this passage through references to the nativity. Leafy speaks of "The child we all love to place our hope in" (*FW* 621.31–32) and decrees, "Pax Goodmens will" (*FW* 621.35), which resembles the familiar Bible passage, "and on earth, peace among men of good will" (Luke 2:14). The implication of Christ's arrival, however, is unclear. The sins of humankind are brought up: "Be the time they've come to the weight of old fletch" (*FW* 621.32–33). But the response, "We'll lave it" (*FW* 621.33), is unclear. Is she suggesting they leave the old flesh? Or wash it clean (Latin, *lavare*)? All of the situations throughout this passage involve renewal, but the language obscures the nature of the renewal.

A message of flexibility emerges in which the text calls for renewal but not necessarily replication. This is allowed through stories, finished and begun again, but always reenvisioned the second time through. In her acceptance of events, of what will be, Leafy declares, "the book of the depth is. Closed" (*FW* 621.3). Throughout Leafy's monologue Joyce makes frequent use of full stops where standard syntax needs no punctuation, often creating paradoxical readings. Here, the tone of acceptance and conclusion resonating throughout the passage makes the reading "*The Book of the Dead* has been closed" a sensible interpretation. Exiting the underworld, its purpose has now passed. On the other hand, the punctuation emphasizes its basic existence. This alone can be read multiple ways. If *The Book of the Dead* simply "is," does that dismiss its authority (It exists. What of it?)? Or does it lend the book a cosmic authority (perhaps akin to John's "The Word is . . .")? In this interpretation the "Closed" that follows might mean the issue is closed, no room for debate. Soon after this reference, *The Book of the Dead* is again connected to other texts, and the attitude leans toward dismissing old narratives in favor of new. Leafy states, "I won't take our laddy's lampern. For them four old windbags of Gustsofairy to be blowing at" (*FW* 621.5–6). She will not take Aladdin's lamp, dismissing *A Thousand and One Nights*, and further, the Gospel's four evangelists are full of air.

What Leafy can take, then, is her own "retaling" of myth, a myth that presents its Christian elements fairly prominently but skews them and juxtaposes them with other myths. We have a man who falls or sins and is metaphorically linked to death in several ways throughout the tale; thus on a relatively accessible level, the story follows the typology of Christianity. Joyce's narrative invites the reader to reconsider it, but unlike Lawrence, he does not want the individual to reconsider how he physically lives; rather, Joyce wants the reader to reconsider how he encounters the myth—through narrative. Egyptology is particularly useful to Joyce due to the power it grants to words, language, and incantations, a quality that meshes with the rites and rituals of Joyce's Catholicism.

Joyce's revitalization of Christianity lies in the spiritual empowerment of the reader. Sheldon Brivic argues that Joyce's narrative style allows the reader to experience the "mind of God" (75). Brivic finds that the text's power emerges through identity, or more precisely, self-alienation. "The more readings a passage sustains," Brivic writes, "and the further from the surface, the more spiritually powerful that passage is" (41). In essence, readers lose themselves in a book with too many possibilities, and the responsibility and power of creation are thrust upon them in the process. These moments demand an internalization of language, through which readers take ownership of these words with myriad meanings and so are granted an ultimate sort of authority through which mystery, life, creation, and all those concepts of Christianity demand reconsideration.

Lawrence would likely protest, finding any experience thinking about the meanings of words a pitiful substitute for lived experiences. Interestingly, considering their different perspectives on what constitutes a spiritual experience, both Joyce and Lawrence associate artistic creation with divinity. One of the most-quoted passages in *A Portrait of the Artist as a Young Man* is Stephen's assessment that the artist, "like the God of his creation, remains within or behind or beyond or above his handiwork" (*P1* 215). Here Joyce at once links the artist to his or her creation but at the same time releases authoritative bounds. Readers or viewers of art are never fully aware of the artist and thus are forced to shape experiences on their own. Lawrence's take does not exactly align the artist with God, as Joyce's does, but nevertheless poses creation as a religious experience. In a letter, Lawrence writes: "I often think one ought to be able to pray, before one works—and then leave it to the Lord. Isn't it hard, hard work to come to real grips with one's imagination—throw everything overboard. I always feel as if I stood naked for the fire of Almighty God to go through me—and it's rather an awful feeling. One has to be so terribly religious, to be an artist" (*1L* 519). Perhaps the significant difference here is that Lawrence views writing as a surrender to something larger, while Joyce considers it actually becoming that something larger. This schism leads us back to the two artists' differing views of spirituality itself. Lawrence sees religion as fiery, grand, and awe-striking. Joyce, on the other hand, sees it as contemplative, individual, and mysterious.

Still, each author shows a firm upper lip to the conditions of modernity. As religion is threatened by science, rationality, and a diminished sense of the human's place in the universe, both of these writers make a case for otherworldly experience, for a sense of cosmic significance, without looking entirely to otherworldliness. They look inside our experience with the physical world, and look inside our experience with the verbal world, and there find mystery.

Notes

1. For readers unfamiliar with the myth of Isis and Osiris, I offer this summary, condensed from James Frazer's *Golden Bough*, which both authors used as a source. Osiris is the illegitimate son of the goddess Nut, wife of the sun god Ra. Among his siblings are a sister Isis, whom he marries, and Set, a brother who murders him. Set and a group of conspirators create a richly decorated coffer, crafted to Osiris' body size.

During merrymaking, Set promises to give the coffer to whomever it fits. After every-one else, Osiris steps into the coffer and the conspirators quickly seal it shut and send it down the Nile. The coffer comes aground in Byblus (often identified as Phoenicia, or present-day Lebanon). When it lands, an Erica tree sprouts, its trunk enclosing Osiris. The King of Byblus makes this tree into a pillar of his house. Isis begins seeking Osiris up and down the Nile, and eventually she finds and reclaims the pillar containing him. She hides the coffer, but Set finds it while hunting and chops the body into fourteen pieces. Isis then seeks these pieces. Supposedly she recovers and buries each piece, so graves of Osiris are found all over Egypt. But it is alternately believed that she faked burial to mislead Set after she had collected all the parts of Osiris' body except his geni-tals, which were eaten by fish. Her lamentations lead Ra to send the jackal-headed god Anubus, who pieces Osiris together again. He is finally revived as Isis fans her wings, and Osiris goes on to rule the underworld, judging the dead by weighing their hearts. Osiris' reconstitution makes him the first mummy, and belief spreads that survival in the afterlife is dependent upon friends attending to the body as Isis and Anubus did Osiris (see Frazer 420–27).

2. Throughout this essay, Lawrence's main character, following the author's practice, is identified in lowercase as "the man who died."

3. This analysis examines how readers interpret the full text of *The Escaped Cock*. Lawrence wrote each part at separate times, first publishing part 1 under the title *The Escaped Cock* and only later publishing the two-part *The Man Who Died*. Readers in-terested in Lawrence's composition process and its biographical context should consult Viinikka, "The Men Who Died," in which she argues that in the early 1920s Lawrence is primarily concerned with rebirth while later in the decade his interests turn to the afterlife, as reflected in the Isis-Osiris myth.

Works Cited

Atherton, James S. *Books at the* Wake: *A Study of Literary Allusions in James Joyce's* Finnegans Wake. London: Faber and Faber, 1959.

Benstock, Bernard. *Joyce-Again's Wake: An Analysis of* Finnegans Wake. Seattle: U of Washington P, 1965.

Brivic, Sheldon. *Joyce the Creator.* Madison: U of Wisconsin P, 1985.

Budge, E. A. Wallis. *The Egyptian Book of the Dead.* Introd. John Romer. New York: Penguin, 2008.

Burrell, Harry. *Narrative Design in* Finnegans Wake: *The Wake Lock Picked.* Gainesville: UP of Florida, 1996.

Delany, Paul. "'A Would-Be-Dirty Mind': D. H. Lawrence as an Enemy of Joyce." *Joyce in the Hibernian Metropolis: Essays.* Ed. Morris Beja and David Norris. Columbus: Ohio State UP, 1996. 76–82.

Eco, Umberto. *The Aesthetics of Chaosmos: The Middle Ages of James Joyce*. Trans. Ellen Esrock and David Robey. Cambridge: Harvard UP, 1989.

Fargnoli, A. Nicholas. *James Joyce's Catholic Moments*. Dublin: National Library of Ireland, 2004.

Frazer, James. *The Golden Bough: A Study in Magic and Religion*. New York: MacMillan, 1951.

Hinz, Evelyn J., and John J. Teunissen. "Savior and Cock: Allusion and Icon in Lawrence's *The Man Who Died*." *Journal of Modern Literature* 5.2 (1976): 279–96.

Leavis, F. R. *The Great Tradition*. Garden City, NY: Doubleday, 1954.

LeDoux, Larry V. "Christ and Isis: The Function of the Dying and Reviving God in *The Man Who Died*." *D. H. Lawrence Review* 5 (1972): 132–47.

Levenson, Michael H. *A Genealogy of Modernism: A Study of English Literary Doctrine 1908–1922*. New York: Cambridge UP, 1984.

McCourt, John. *The Years of Bloom: James Joyce in Trieste 1904–1920*. Dublin: Lilliput, 2000.

McHugh, Roland. *Annotations to* Finnegans Wake. Rev. ed. Baltimore: Johns Hopkins UP, 1991.

Oates, Joyce Carol. "Lawrence's Götterdämmerung: The Apocalyptic Vision of *Women in Love*." *Critical Essays on D. H. Lawrence*. Ed. Dennis Jackson and Fleda Brown Jackson. Boston: G. K. Hall, 1988. 92–110.

Poplawski, Paul. *Promptings of Desire: Creativity and the Religious Impulse in the Works of D. H. Lawrence*. Westport, CT: Greenwood, 1993.

Rose, Danis. *Chapters of Coming Forth by Day*. Colchester, UK: Wake Newslitter Press, 1982.

Schlossman, Beryl. *Joyce's Catholic Comedy of Language*. Madison: U of Wisconsin P, 1985.

St. Joseph New Catholic Edition of the Holy Bible. New York: Catholic Book Publishing, 1962.

Taylor, Juliette. "Foreign Music: Linguistic Estrangement in 'Proteus' and 'Sirens.'" *James Joyce Quarterly* 41.3 (Spring 2004): 407–19.

Troy, Mark L. "Mummeries of Resurrection: The Cycle of Osiris in *Finnegans Wake*." Diss. Uppsala University, 1976. Stockholm: Almqvist and Wiksell International, 1976.

Vickery, John B. "*Finnegans Wake* and Sexual Metamorphosis." *Contemporary Literature* 13.2 (Spring 1972): 213–42.

———. "Myth and Ritual in the Shorter Fiction of D. H. Lawrence." *Modern Fiction Studies* 5 (1959): 65–82.

Viinikka, Anja. "'The Man Who Died': D. H. Lawrence's Phallic Vision of the Restored Body." *Journal of the D. H. Lawrence Society* (1994–95): 39–46.

Widmer, Kingsley. *The Art of Perversity: D. H. Lawrence's Shorter Fictions*. Seattle: U of Washington P, 1962.

6

"In Europe They Usually Mention Us Together"

Joyce, Lawrence, and the Little Magazines

LOUISE KANE

In November 1922, D. H. Lawrence wrote to F. Wubberhorst, an acquaintance of his publisher Thomas Seltzer, declaring *Ulysses* to be somewhat tedious: "I am sorry, but I am one of the people who can't read *Ulysses.* Only bits" (4L 340). However, he admitted, "I am glad I have seen the book, since in Europe they usually mention us together—James Joyce and D. H. Lawrence" (4L 340). This casual observation attests to the fact that by the early 1920s, D. H. Lawrence and James Joyce were, as F. R. Leavis has claimed, "pre-eminently the testing, the crucial authors" (10) of prose fiction. Against this backdrop, it is perhaps inevitable that critical comparisons of the two writers have alluded to and constructed something of a Joyce/Lawrence dichotomy. The two writers, largely on account of their perceived divergent stylistic methods and personalities, have been polarized as binary opposites whose work inspired a reception characterized by mutual exclusivity: "if you took Joyce for a major creative writer, then [. . .] you had no use for Lawrence, and if you judged Lawrence a great writer [. . .] you could hardly take a sustained interest in Joyce" (Leavis 10). As a result, Lawrence and Joyce have been viewed as "eternal opposites" who stand "in curious and uneasy juxtaposition" (Allen 439). Lawrence's observation challenges the idea that this juxtaposition is one of unease. While both writers occupied and competed in the same literary space, Lawrence's recognition that critics and readers "mention us together" implies that there may be many convergences and areas of comparison, and not just points of contrast, between the two writers.

The pages of modernist little magazines are spaces in which these convergences become particularly evident. That both Lawrence and Joyce published within little magazines is well known. The serialization of *Ulysses* (1922) in the *Little Review* from March 1918 to December 1920 and Lawrence's affiliation with periodicals such as the *English Review* and the *Blue Review* have received significant critical attention.[1] Furthermore, many critics have noted the place of little magazines within a multifarious and interwoven network that characterized the production and publication histories of modernist texts. As Aaron Jaffe has recognized, little magazines exist as a microcosm of this overarching system of modernist production, comprising "a complex constellation of institutions that gave precarious modernist cultures a small but influential foothold on both sides of the Atlantic" (867–68). Yet a comparison of Lawrence's and Joyce's publications within these little magazines has not yet been undertaken. In a period in which most modernist writers used little magazines as a springboard to attain their first publications, it would be a mistake to see the fact that both writers published within little magazines as a particularly startling area of congruence. However, the ways in which their careers develop via little magazines, when coupled with the similarities in the content of both writers' periodical contributions, suggest strong areas of congruence between Joyce and Lawrence.

These areas of congruence are apparent in three main lines of convergence. Firstly, both writers' periodical publications follow a similar pattern; beginning with pieces in niche, British "little" magazines and newspapers, both writers expand into a wider pool of continental or American magazines that blur the distinction between modernism and commercial culture, such as *Vanity Fair*. Secondly, both writers gained their most significant publications at the instigation of Ezra Pound. For both Joyce and Lawrence, Pound was the point of contact between themselves and the little magazines and was responsible for gaining publications for both men within the *Egoist*, *Poetry: A Magazine of Verse*, and the *Smart Set*. Despite their different writing styles and personalities, Pound viewed both writers as important figures in the development of literary modernism. By securing publications for both writers within the same periodicals, Pound at once constructed a literary scene in which Joyce and Lawrence were the key players and, as a result, inadvertently set up the earliest form of the Joyce/Lawrence dichotomy in which the two writers, competing for literary success, became each other's "arch rival" (Scherr 6). Thirdly, comparing the actual content of their periodical publications shows how both Joyce and Lawrence were, despite their alleged differences, working within and reacting to a similar framework of concerns. As Robert Scholes and Cliff Wulfman assert, "the three decades leading up to 1922 constitute a period of intense experimentation and debate about the proper mode of artistic response to modernity. This debate was conducted mainly in periodicals" (36). Joyce and Lawrence, through their periodical publications, both participate in this debate. While the type of magazine in which each writer published does determine the type of modernism with which they became associated, in their periodical contributions Lawrence and Joyce demonstrate shared artistic techniques and similar treatments of themes such as love, the Great War, and religion, challenging the idea that the two writers exemplify two separate and polarized types of Georgian and "high" modernism.

An Outline

Prior to embarking on an exploration of the specific similarities between the content of Joyce's and Lawrence's periodical contributions, an outline of these contributions is necessary, as well as a definition of the little magazine. In their now seminal text *The Little Magazine: A History and a Bibliography* (1946), Frederick John Hoffman, Charles Albert Allen, and Carolyn F. Ulrich define the little magazine as "a magazine designed to print artistic work which for reasons of commercial expediency is not acceptable to the money-minded periodicals or presses" (2). The difference between a little magazine and "the big 'quality' magazines" lies in the fact that while "big" magazines will accept only "commercially profitable writers," little magazines are "non-commercial by intent" (Hoffman, Allen, and Ulrich 2–3) and have, through this noncommercial emphasis, "introduced and sponsored every noteworthy literary movement or school" (Hoffman, Allen, and Ulrich 1–2). Finally, the term "little," they argue, "did not refer to the size of the magazines, nor to their literary contents. [. . .] What the word designated above everything else was a limited group of intelligent readers" (3). More recently, Suzanne Churchill and Adam McKible echo Hoffman, Allen, and Ulrich's definition of the little magazine as a noncommercial venue for artistic experimentation: "little magazines are non-commercial enterprises founded by individuals or small groups intent upon publishing the experimental works or radical opinions of untried, unpopular, or under-represented writers" (3). In their preference for experimentation, little magazines "appeal to small, sometimes elite (or elitist) readerships willing to exercise their minds to comprehend aesthetic movements such as Futurism, Imagism, and Dada" and are "integral, rather than incidental, to the development of modernism" (Churchill and McKible 4–5).

However, recent critical attempts to reconsider these easy systems of categorization through which little magazines are seen as entirely removed from the worlds of commercialism (and accordingly commercial "big" magazines) have implications for the study of any apparently modernist writer's involvement with these magazines. As Mark Morrisson has argued, the easy polarization of "little magazines" and commercial "mass market periodicals" as mutually exclusive, diametrically opposed organs is misleading as it implies that modernism and commercialism are not in any way connected to one another (4). While it may be expected that Joyce and Lawrence, two writers at the forefront of literary experiment, might publish in accordingly modernist and noncommercial magazines, their engagement with periodicals betrays the fact that both writers wrote for commercial gain. In fact, both Joyce and Lawrence engage with a wide variety of periodicals, some big, some little, some literary, and some distinctly modernist, and it is this eclectic engagement that forms a particularly strong line of convergence between the two authors.

Joyce's first published pieces of prose fiction appeared in an agricultural farming magazine. "The Sisters," "Eveline," and "After the Race," all of which would later appear in a revised form as parts of *Dubliners* (1914), were published in the *Irish Homestead* between August and December 1904. Despite this marking the first publication of his fiction, at this point Joyce already had some twenty-five reviews published, twenty-one of which appeared in the *Daily Express*. His first periodical publication was a review of Ibsen's *When We Dead Awaken* (1899). Entitled "Ibsen's New Drama," this review appeared in the *Fortnightly Review* on 1 April 1900. Joyce also already had three poems published prior to the publication of his short stories. His first poetry publication was "Silently She's Coming," published in the *Saturday Review* on 14 May 1904, followed by "O Sweetheart" in *Speaker* on 30 July 1904 and "Song" in the August 1904 issue of *Dana*, a Dublin-based monthly magazine that published poetry by other Irish writers like Yeats along with sociopolitical articles.[2] These three poems would later form parts XXIV, XVIII, and VII of *Chamber Music* (1907).

Between 1907 and his death in January 1941, more than sixty articles by Joyce, including extracts of prose, poetry, reviews, and letters, appeared in various periodicals, ranging from newspapers like the Trieste based *Il Piccolo della Sera*[3] to Harriet Monroe's Chicago-based *Poetry*, the British little magazine the *Egoist*, and Margaret Anderson's anarchic American magazine the *Little Review*.[4] The *Egoist* serialized Joyce's *A Portrait of the Artist as a Young Man* (1916) from 2 February 1914–1 September 1915.[5] Parts of *Ulysses* appeared in Margaret Anderson's the *Little Review* from March 1918 to December 1920. In February 1921, serialization of the novel was stopped after court action brought by the Society for the Suppression of Vice.[6] The *Egoist* also serialized extracts from *Ulysses* from January to December 1919, the month in which it ceased publication.

From 1920 to 1923, Joyce's output to little magazines was somewhat minimal. Despite publishing many reviews in his early career (1900–1914), after Joyce gained his first serialization of *Portrait* in 1914 his periodical contributions centered almost entirely on prose fiction and a few poetry contributions. In August 1919 he published "Bahnhofstrasse" in the *Anglo-French Review*, and in April 1920 "A Memory of the Players in a Mirror at Midnight" appeared in *Poesia*, a Milan-based poetry magazine. The same poem was republished in the *Dial* in July 1920.

Joyce's next major periodical contribution was the serialization of *Finnegans Wake* (1939). A nine-page extract of the novel originally appeared in *transatlantic review*—the Paris-based literary monthly edited by Ford Madox Ford—in April 1924, and intermittently in *transition*, another Paris-based magazine that specialized in the publication of modernist, surrealist, and Dadaist art and writing, between April 1927 and April/May 1938.[7] Several other magazines also published extracts from what would later become *Finnegans Wake*. T. S. Eliot's *Criterion* published a "Fragment of an Unpublished Work" in July 1925 and the continental magazines *This Quarter* (Milan) and *Navire d'Argent* (France) published extracts from the as yet untitled "Work in Progress" in October 1925 and Autumn/Winter 1925 respectively.[8] After the publication of parts of *Finnegans Wake*, Joyce made no more contributions of prose fiction to literary magazines.

Instead, from 1924, the year in which *Finnegans Wake* was first serialized in *the transatlantic review*, until January 1941, the month in which he died, Joyce's contributions to periodicals were mainly in the form of various letters and translations. Joyce contributed "Ecce Puer" to the New York magazine the *New Republic* in November 1932, but his last publication within a periodical was a letter to Ettore Settanni, the cotranslator of *Anna Livia Plurabelle* into Italian. This letter was dated 16 March 1940 and reprinted in *Prospettive* (an Italian magazine) as "Una Lettera di Joyce" in March 1940.[9] Surprisingly, the serialized extracts of his novels *Dubliners*, *Portrait*, *Ulysses*, and *Finnegans Wake* constitute Joyce's only prose fiction contributions to periodicals. "A Boarding House" and "A Little Cloud" appeared in the May 1915 issue of *Smart Set: A Magazine of Cleverness*, but these were reprints of parts of *Dubliners*.

While Joyce's contributions to little magazines are fairly sporadic (he sometimes went for several years without publishing through them), D. H. Lawrence published profusely within many different periodicals and used them as vehicles for the publication of more than two hundred poems, short stories, and nonfiction articles between 1907 and 1930, the year of his death. This figure is particularly remarkable considering that Joyce's periodical publishing history spanned forty years (his first publication appearing in 1900 and his last in 1940), almost double the length of Lawrence's; Lawrence fitted almost double the amount of contributions into half the amount of time. Whereas Joyce used the literary magazine as a vehicle for gaining publication of increasingly controversial novels, Lawrence never serialized any of his novels through little magazines. Parts of *The Fox* (1923) appeared in *Hutchinson's Story Magazine* (November 1920) and the *Dial* (May and June 1922) and another novella, *The Escaped Cock* (1929), was originally printed in *Forum* (February 1928), but for Lawrence literary magazines were mainly a venue through which he practiced and refined a particular genre, the short story, as well as developing his poetics and political viewpoints through essays and reviews.

Lawrence's periodical publication began in 1907, when he won the *Nottinghamshire Guardian*'s Christmas story competition. Lawrence submitted three entries, "The Prelude," "Ruby Glass," and "The White Stocking," and the winning entry, "The Prelude," appeared in the December 1907 issue of the newspaper (*EY* 189–90). Lawrence also gained the first publication of his poetry via periodicals. "A Still Afternoon," a sequence of five poems, appeared in the December 1909 issue of Ford Madox Ford's *English Review*. In February 1910 Ford also published Lawrence's short story "Goose Fair," followed by "Night Songs," another poetry sequence, in April 1910. Lawrence's affiliation with the *English Review* lasted many years. From 1909 to 1923, the little magazine published more than thirty pieces of Lawrence's prose fiction, poems, and essays, including "Odour of Chrysanthemums" (June 1911), "England, My England" (October 1915), the *Studies in Classic American Literature* series (November 1918–April 1919), and installments of "The Reality of Peace" (May–August 1917).[10] The *Nation* published some of Lawrence's poetry ("Lightning" and "Violets") in November 1911, and throughout 1912, the year his first novel, *The White Peacock*, was published, Lawrence continued to publish poetry, prose, and reviews in the *Nation*, the *English Review*, and the *Saturday Westminster Gazette*.[11] Throughout 1912–13, Lawrence's periodical publications took something of a more political turn, with many short stories and essays of a distinctly sociopolitical nature appearing in more conservative monthly reviews like the *New Statesman* and the liberal London-based newspaper, the *Westminster Gazette*.[12]

While his initial periodical publications suggest Lawrence stuck to a small set of magazines, in March 1913 he soon gained his first American publication when "The Soiled Rose" appeared in the New York little magazine *Forum*. In 1913, Lawrence also appeared in two little magazines whose existence exemplifies Lucy Delap's notion of "periodical communities" (235): *Rhythm* and the

Blue Review. The "first of the English little magazines," *Rhythm* was established in the summer of 1911 by John Middleton Murry and his Oxford University companion Michael Sadleir (Bradbury 423). Originally issued as a quarterly, the magazine aimed to represent "the ideal of a new art [. . .] an art that strikes deeper [. . .] that passes outside the bounds of a narrow aestheticism" and "to provide art, be it drawing, literature, or criticism [. . .] which shall have its roots below the surface, and be the rhythmical echo of the life with which it is in touch" (Murry, "Aims and Ideals" 36). The result was a magazine that "stressed Paris, Post-Impressionism, the more romantic aspect of Bergson" (Bradbury 423). Its contributors included Picasso, J. D. Fergusson, and Katherine Mansfield. After *Rhythm* folded in March 1913, Murry and Mansfield (who had been working as assistant editor at *Rhythm*) established the *Blue Review*, a monthly magazine of "Literature, Drama, Art, Music" that ran from May to July 1913.[13] Delap has defined a "periodical community" as "the material, cultural, or intellectual milieu of a periodical or group of periodicals" (235). *Rhythm* and the *Blue Review*, in their shared contributors, editors, and ethos, are part of the same periodical community, a community with which Lawrence was very much involved. Due to his personal friendships with both Murry and Mansfield, Lawrence was a frequent contributor to both periodicals. Among his contributions are a review of an anthology of Georgian poetry in the March 1913 issue of *Rhythm* and a short story, "The Soiled Rose," reprinted from *Forum* in the July 1913 issue of the *Blue Review*. In 1915, Lawrence formed his own little magazine, the *Signature*, with Murry, but it folded after just three numbers.

Between 1914 and 1922, Lawrence published a considerable amount of poetry in literary magazines. Much of this poetry centered on the Great War. "War-Baby" appeared in the *English Review* (June 1918); Thomas Moult's short-lived little magazine *Voices* published "Rondeau of a Conscientious Objector" (July 1919); and *Poetry* published two sequences of war poetry that included poems such as "Tommies in the Train" (February 1919) and "War Films" (July 1919). While continuing to contribute to the *English Review* and *Poetry*, like Joyce, Lawrence also began to publish in the *Smart Set*, the *Egoist,* and *Dial,* and from 1923 he began contributing to the *Adelphi*, John Middleton Murry's new literary weekly. Lawrence published profusely in the *Dial* throughout the 1920s; in total twenty-six poems and short stories appeared between 1920 and 1929, including "Sea and Sardinia" (October–November 1921), "The Woman who Rode Away" (July–August 1925), and "The Man Who Loved Islands" (July 1927).

The impression of Lawrence's publication history within literary magazines in the 1920s is one of breadth and variety. While publishing short stories in the *Dial*, he simultaneously published essays such as "Art and Morality" (November 1925) and "Morality and the Novel" (December 1925) in Desmond MacCarthy's Bloomsbury review the *Calendar of Modern Letters*. As Lawrence travelled more extensively, his experiences gained documentation through periodical publication. In the mid- to late 1920s, Lawrence published many pieces of travel writing in various magazines, including "The Hopi Snake Dance," an article in *Theatre Arts Monthly* (December 1924), and "The Wind-swept Strong Hold of Volterra" in *Travel* (February 1928). The *Laughing Horse* even published a special D. H. Lawrence issue of the magazine that printed several of his travel pieces, including the poem "Mediterranean in January" and a drawing entitled *Pueblo Indian Dancers* (April 1926). Unlike Joyce, Lawrence continued actively contributing to periodicals until the end of his life. During these last years he began to publish less prose fiction and more essays in newspapers including the *Evening News*, the *Sunday Dispatch*, the *Daily Chronicle*, and other, larger, more "commercial" periodicals like *Vogue* and *Vanity Fair*.[14] Although several periodicals continued to publish Lawrence's work well after his death in March 1930, the last article Lawrence intentionally contributed to a periodical was a review of V. V. Rozanov's *Fallen Leaves* that appeared in *Everyman* on 23 January 1930.

Patterns: Communities and Commerce

At surface level, the periodical publication histories of Joyce and Lawrence appear as somewhat divergent. While Joyce began with reviews and moved on to novel serializations, translations, and letters, Lawrence's periodical contributions seem to occur in reverse, beginning with publications of poetry and short stories and developing toward the nonfiction genres of travel writing and the literature review toward the end of his life. However, comparing their contributions demonstrates that despite Lawrence having entered the periodical scene somewhat later than Joyce, both writers partook in similar periodical communities, a participation that exemplifies Jaffe's idea of a network of modernist magazines. Both Joyce and Lawrence appeared in the *Egoist*, the *Smart Set*, *Poetry*, *Dial*, and *This Quarter*, yet, surprisingly, were only published simultaneously in the same periodical once—the 1 April 1914 issue of the *Egoist*. While these magazines form sites of convergence for Joyce and Lawrence, the fact that both writers published within a wide variety of magazines outside of this small selection points to several other, more implicit, patterns of similarity between the pair.

Both writers, in engaging with such a vast set of periodicals, interacted not only with what are now recognized as quintessentially modernist little magazines, such as the *Little Review* or *Rhythm*, but also with newspapers, literary magazines, foreign and continental periodicals, and magazines that were the organ of recognized institutions (such as the *Irish Homestead*). This demonstrates that as much as there are overlaps between Lawrence and Joyce, there are also artistic overlaps between the periodicals themselves, challenging the ways in which we distinguish between little magazines, literary reviews, commercial "big" magazines, and newspapers. If the *Irish Homestead* and the *Little Review* have both championed Joyce, then does that make the *Irish Homestead* an early venue of modernist writing? Equally, that Lawrence could be published within a newspaper like the *Saturday Westminster Gazette*, along with a magazine that is, to a degree, the epitome of high modernism, *Dial*, implies that the apparent chasm between everyday culture and the cultures of modernism was narrower and less obvious to contemporary readers than we may imagine. If critics define the little magazine on account of its publication of experimental work by "unknown or relatively unknown writers" (Hoffmann, Allen, and Ulrich 2), then in theory the *Saturday Westminster Gazette* or *Il Piccolo Serra* could be classed as little magazines.

Furthermore, Joyce's and Lawrence's engagement with periodicals and little magazines demonstrates a shared participation in a particular form of everyday culture that critics have held to be the antithesis of modernism: the culture of commerce. Both Joyce's and Lawrence's career trajectories reflect a similar pattern in which both writers gained their first creative publications in small magazines and local newspapers (Lawrence in the *Nottinghamshire Guardian*, Joyce in the *Irish Homestead*) but, as their careers progressed, gradually began to participate in a transnational engagement with various literary magazines that are both "big" and "little," commercial and noncommercial. Andreas Huyssen may have argued that modernism and modernist writers epitomize an "anxiety of contamination by [. . .] mass culture" (vii), but the way in which Joyce and Lawrence eagerly interacted with periodicals and actively sought publication through them, not purely out of a desire to gain publication but to gain the financial rewards that went with it, complicates the idea of a "Great Divide" between modernism and commerce (viii). By publishing several articles in *Vanity Fair*, a magazine that was by no means "little" but occupied "a middle space, located between the author-centered production model of the avant-garde magazines and the market-driven arena of the daily paper and mass circulation weeklies" (Hammill 128), and the *Southwest Review* ("Pan in

America," January 1926), Lawrence openly embraced the larger, "big 'quality' magazines" that Hoffmann, Allen, and Ulrich saw as the antithesis to little magazines (3). Indeed, he marveled at the prospect of getting "$50 extra" than he had expected for an article published in *Vanity Fair* (*7L* 118). Similarly, Joyce may have started his publication history within a "pig's paper," his nickname for the *Irish Homestead* (*JJII* 170), but he soon began engaging with periodicals like *Dial*, which by the early 1920s was earning $73,000 per annum in patronage (an amount that dwarfs the *Little Review's* figure of $2,350), had paid out $2,000 for Eliot's *The Waste Land* (1922), and had a circulation of 9,500 (Rainey, *Institutions* 98), compared, for example, to the *Egoist*, which at one point had just two hundred subscribers (Brooker and Thacker 67).

Despite the fact that "little" magazines were not large-scale commercial institutions, often having barely enough money to pay contributors, their editors were aware that their magazines were, with their numerous transactions between contributors, publishers, and advertisers, microcosms of larger commercial companies and organizations. Reflecting on his stint as coeditor (with John Middleton Murry) of the short-lived the *Signature* between October and November 1915, Lawrence described the problems involved in the little magazine's business model. Proving that modernists were eager to immerse themselves in the culture of commerce, for Lawrence, the problem with little magazines was, quite simply, that they did not (or could not) venture far enough into this culture; they did not make enough money. While publication through large publishing houses ("in the ordinary way") offered a more steady income for both editors and writers, contributing to or editing a little magazine meant relying on subscribers ("the few who sent their half-crowns") for revenue, a practice derided by Lawrence as "ridiculous" and financially unviable (Murry, *Reminiscences of D. H. Lawrence* 145).

As John Xiros Cooper has maintained, "it is a mistake to think that the radical poetics of modernism were 'co-opted' by market society" (217). On the contrary, modernist writers like Joyce and Lawrence actively participated in the cultures of commerce and trade. Far from propagating the "myth of the artist" (Wexler xii) as a solitary, poor figure unaware and indifferent to commerce and money, Joyce's and Lawrence's relationships with little magazines demonstrate that both writers deliberately capitalized on the better opportunities that their developing careers afforded them. The fact that both writers' career paths show a deliberate and sustained attempt to gain publications within such a wide range of different periodicals, papers, and little magazines reminds us that little magazines are not the sole venues of modernist literature and, moreover, that little magazines are not immune to the temptations and rewards of commercialization. The *Adelphi*, for instance, the magazine to which Lawrence frequently contributed, placed advertisements for a wide range of heteroclite and fashionably "modern" goods such as the Remington portable typewriter and the latest "Hand Made Lingerie" from Debenhams within its pages.

Convergences: Prose and Poetry

Both writers would engage with the increasing sense of an encroaching modernity through their later prose. However, comparing Joyce's first prose publications within the *Irish Homestead* in 1904 against Lawrence's first piece of published prose fiction, "The Prelude," published in the *Nottinghamshire Guardian* in 1907, demonstrates that their early writing style evinces a similar engagement not with ideas of newness but with ideas of tradition. Their work displays a distinct interest in the small-scale realism of everyday life. This interest continued to inform their later prose. *Ulysses* (1922) famously charts one seemingly noneventful day in the busy city of Dublin, while *Sons and Lovers* (1913) utilizes the bildungsroman genre—just as Joyce would with *Portrait*—to explore the nuances of Paul Morel's emotional and intellectual development. Both Lawrence and Joyce were somewhat unwilling to send their earliest works to magazines. Joyce may have already published several reviews by 1904, but it was only after George Russell, the editor of the *Irish Homestead*, approached Joyce and personally requested that he send "anything simple, rural? livemaking? pathos?" (*Letters II* 43) to the paper that Joyce submitted "The Sisters," "Eveline," and "After the Race." Similarly, on account of his "reluctance to submit his writing to magazines" (*EY* 214), it was Jessie Chambers who submitted Lawrence's first poems to Ford Madox Ford, editor of the *English Review* (Wulfman 235).

The first sentences of Joyce's "Eveline" and Lawrence's "A Prelude" are strikingly similar. Both engage in an ekphrastic representation of a sole female protagonist positioned in a familiar and homely scene:

> She sat at the window watching the evening invade the avenue. Her head was leaned against the window-curtain, and in her nostrils was the odour of dusty cretonne. She was tired. Few people passed. (Joyce, "Eveline" 761)

> In the kitchen of a small farm a little woman sat cutting bread and butter. The glow of the clear, ruddy fire was on her shining cheek and white apron; but grey hair will not take the warm caress of firelight. She skill-

fully spread the softened butter, and cut off great slices from the floury
loaf in her lap. Already two plates were piled, but she continued to cut.
Outside the naked ropes of the creeper tapped and lashed at the window.
(Chambers, "Prelude" 17)[15]

Through this particular staging that emphasizes small details like "the window-
curtain," "the odour of dusty cretonne," "the glow" of the fire, and the "white
apron," Joyce and Lawrence immediately locate their protagonists within interior settings but allude to the exterior world. By juxtaposing the interior
scene against the outside scenes beyond the window ("few people passed," "the
creeper tapped") both writers foreground a tension between the two that informs the events of their stories. "Eveline" depicts the tale of a young girl due
to leave the confines of the family home, in secret, and marry, whereas "A
Prelude" depicts a romance between Fred, the working-class son of the woman
cutting bread, and Nellie, a wealthy young woman who lives on the outskirts
of the village. In both stories, home becomes the location of familiarity and a
symbol of identity. For Eveline, the eponymous protagonist, home is a place of
"shelter and food," and the idea of leaving "those whom she had known all her
life" and escaping to "her new home in a distant, unknown country" appears
as a daunting but exciting prospect (761). Similarly, for Fred, the farmhouse is a
representation of his class difference from Nellie. Significantly, Nellie's decision
to join Fred on Christmas Eve at the farm marks the point at which this difference is overcome; the story ends with the line "[a]lready she was at home" (17).

In their geographical settings (Joyce's story is set in Dublin and would later
form part of *Dubliners* and Lawrence's in a small town in Nottinghamshire),
the stories show that both writers wrote from what they knew. Both stories
depict the everyday lives of ordinary people and attempt to engage with the
interiority of their main characters. Joyce's story contains just two lines of dialogue, uttered by Frank (her fiancé) right at the end of the story: "Come!" and
"Eveline! Evvy!" (761). Instead of relying on dialogue, Joyce employs free indirect discourse long before it was recognized as a familiar staple of modernist
narrative: "She had consented to go away—to leave her home. Was it wise—was
it honourable? She tried to weigh each side of the question in her mind. [. . .]
What would they think of her in the Stores when they discovered she had gone
away?" ("Eveline" 761).

Lawrence, too, utilizes a similar narrative technique in "A Prelude": "how
could he have asked her; she must think he wanted badly to become master of
Ramsley Mill. What a fool he had been to go—what a fool!" (17). Yet it is the

realism of both stories that renders them so similar. "Eveline" and "A Prelude" both engage with characters experiencing romantic dilemmas that result in a questioning of self-identity through the frame of ordinary life. Just as Lawrence sets Fred's dilemma against the backdrop of mundane household events and routines (bread cutting, "lifting potatoes to the fire," the "clinking scrape of iron shod boots" announcing the arrival home of family members after a hard day's work [17]), Joyce also situates his protagonist within the context of routine, daily events of others ("[t]he man out of the last house passed on his way home; she heard his footsteps clacking along the pavement" [761]), creating a more powerful divide between the realms of this exteriority and her own internal thoughts. In this way, both Joyce's and Lawrence's first examples of prose fiction reflect the nineteenth-century realism of writers like George Eliot, while evincing the earliest forms of a modernist focus on interiority.

Just as their early prose bears similarities, the two writers also demonstrate a shared style of early poetics that places a premium on the qualities Lawrence would later describe as the key qualities of Georgian poetry. Writing in *Rhythm*, Lawrence praised the poems in the latest *Georgian Anthology* (1913): "every poem in the book is romantic, tinged with a love of the marvellous, a joy of natural things" ("The Georgian Renaissance" xix). However, while Lawrence has been accepted as a participant in this Georgian poetics (his poetry appeared in all but one of the Georgian anthologies), Joyce's early works have instead been viewed as "harbingers of the 'high' modernism of the 1920s" (Lewis 120). This polarization does not account for the similarities between poems like Joyce's "Song," published in *Dana* in 1904, and Lawrence's "Snap-Dragon," published in the *English Review* in June 1912.

Both poems depict a woman in a garden seen through the male gaze of her lover. While Joyce's poem consists of three quatrains written in common meter, Lawrence's is a longer verse experimenting with different uses of rhyme and meter. Yet, both poets use the same natural imagery to create a vivid representation of the garden. In Joyce's "Song," the sky is metaphorically presented as "a pale blue cup" (11), while in Lawrence's "Snap-Dragon," the "sunlight stood as in a cup / Between the old grey walls" (2–3). The details of the girl's dress are highlighted by both poets: "I followed [. . .] the swing of her white dress" ("Snap-Dragon" 8); "My love goes lightly, holding up / Her dress with dainty hand" ("Song" 11–12), and both use the word "laughing" as an adjective ("laughing land" ["Song" 10]; "laughing voice" ["Snap-Dragon" 7]), framing the scene with a sense of joy.

However, just as the poets share a Georgian love of nature, other poems published within little magazines demonstrate how both Joyce and Lawrence were experimenting with some of the ideas we now equate with modernist writing. In "Workaday Evenings" (the first poem of the "Night Songs" sequence published in the *English Review* in April 1910), a speaker stands inside his house and gazes up at the sky:

> Still there is left us
> The golden grained night aflower across the sky.
>   Shall we lament for what is bereft us
> While the street lamp censers swinging high
>   Stream golden smoke—?
> ("Workaday Evenings" 8–12)

A poem Joyce published in *Poetry* in November 1917 distinctly echoes Lawrence's "Workaday Evenings." In "Alone," the speaker sits in a garden watching how

> The moon's soft golden meshes make
> All night a veil;
> The shore-lamps in the sleeping lake
> Laburnum tendrils trail. (1–4)

The images of "golden meshes," "Laburnum" and "shore-lamps," paint a similar scene to that of "Workaday Evenings" with its "velvet flowers" (1), "golden grained night" (9), "golden smoke" (12), and "river-lamps" (13). However, it is not the fact that both writers use natural imagery that is strikingly similar, but the ways in which both use it to foreground a sense of foreboding and subtly hint at modernity as a threat that may intrude upon the beauty of their scenes.

In "Workaday Evenings," Lawrence creates a tension between the quietness of the house and the garden over which the speaker looks out and the ever-encroaching city life outside. As the speaker contemplates the night, a "dark narcotic of weariness" (27) and the moon "a reddening lantern" (28), these images serve as a catalyst for a deeper contemplation of the routines of daily city life that takes place beyond the walls of the house. In language that anticipates Eliot's *The Waste Land* (1922), the speaker ponders the "—Endless whisper of passing feet / And wash of voices along the street / Where the ebb of life slips by" (21–23). The stream of "passing feet" is compared to the endless ebb and flow of the tide, "how / The waves ran laughing up the shore / When the tide was high" (18–20). Similarly, Joyce's "Nightpiece," published in Harriet Monroe's Chicago-based fifteen-cent monthly *Poetry* in May 1917, invokes the image of the night sky, which becomes a focal point through which the speaker contemplates the world in a state of disillusionment: "To night's nave upsoaring / A star-knell tolls" (13–15). The speaker sits watching the sky, full of "Ghost fires" (4), and ponders how he, along with his fellow star-gazers, are nothing but a "Waste of souls" (24). Joyce had originally used this technique in "I Hear an Army," a poem published in *Glebe*, a New York–based little magazine, in February 1914. Here Joyce uses the natural imagery of the sea as an analogy to the threat of modern warfare. The army is described through the semantic field of the sea: its soldiers "come shaking in triumph their long / Green hair" (9) and with "foam about their knees" (1–2). Through this conflation of sea and warfare Joyce engages in a peculiar clash of imagery that foreshadows the nature/machine organic/inorganic dichotomies that would become crucial concerns within modernist poetry.

While the poems Joyce published in *Poetry*, through their references to "fear, descending / Darkness of fear above" ("On the Beach at Fontana" 9–10) and the "star-knell" tolling and the "Waste of souls" ("Nightpiece"), vaguely hinted at the ongoing Great War, the poems Lawrence published in the same magazine are a specific and explicit response to modern warfare. "Tommies in the Train" uses natural images to foreground the threat of war. The poem depicts a band of privates travelling across the continent by train. The world beyond the train window is beautiful with its "coltsfoot flowers" (2), "purplish elms" (6), daffodils that "Sparkle beneath" (7), and "luminous hills" (7), but Lawrence undercuts this beauty with the speaker's realization that due to impending battle it may be the last time the tommies sit in the train: "the train [. . .] falls like a meteorite [. . .] to alight / Never again" (25–28), and the conclusion is accordingly bleak: "We are lost, since we fall apart / Forever, forever depart / From each other" (34–36).

"Pound's Pound of Commission": *Poetry*, the *Egoist*, and the *Smart Set*

That Lawrence and Joyce both published within *Poetry* is not a coincidence, but the result of their mutual friendship with Ezra Pound. Pound was the foreign editor for *Poetry* from 1912 to 1914 (Rainey, *Anthology* 39) and had written to Joyce in late 1913: "'Poetry' wants top notch poetry [. . .] they pay 2 bob a line and get the best people" (*Letters II* 326). Equally, it was Pound's editorial sway and praise of Lawrence in *Poetry* that resulted in Lawrence's poems being published in the magazine in January 1914. Indeed, such was Lawrence's relationship with Pound that Pound offered to give Lawrence the commission he had been paid for handling Lawrence's works, prompting an amused response from Lawrence: "I didn't want Pound's pound of commission!" (*2L* 132). [These relationships—between Joyce and Pound, Lawrence and Pound, and Pound and the little magazines *Poetry*, the *Egoist*, and the *Smart Set: A Magazine of Cleverness*—form a particular area of convergence between Joyce and Lawrence as both men advanced on a trajectory engaging with the same people and periodicals.]

Pound's first negotiations with Joyce occurred in late 1913 and culminated in the serialization of *Portrait* in the *Egoist*.[16] After being told about Joyce by W. B. Yeats, Pound had sent a letter to Joyce asking if he had any material that might be suitable for any of the journals with which Pound was involved (Rainey, *Anthology* 211). In February 1914, Joyce "delivered [. . .] to Mr Pound" the manuscript of the novel he was working on, *Portrait* (*Letters I* 81). Pound first sent "cuttings of the first 15 or 20 instalments" of the novel to H. L. Mencken, editor of the *Smart Set*, who, in April 1915, declined to serialize the novel: "the story, unfortunately, is too long and diffuse for the Smart Set" (*Letters I* 79).

However, Pound then turned to another magazine with which he was closely associated. The *Egoist* began life as the *Freewoman: A Weekly Feminist Review* in November 1911. Established and edited by Dora Marsden, the magazine dealt with contemporary debates, many of which centered on feminist causes, and also printed poetry, fiction, and drama. By June 1913, Marsden had changed the title to the *New Freewoman*, and in January 1914 the *New Freewoman* became the *Egoist*. Although Marsden continued to edit the magazine until mid-1914, the arrival of Harriet Shaw Weaver as assistant editor (and chief financial backer) in mid-1913 channeled the magazine toward a new direction, focusing on "egoist" philosophy and taking a more serious and sustained interest in literary affairs.[17] Although Pound never had an official title at the *Egoist*, he was, as James Boulton avers, "closely associated with the editors and tended to adopt a proprietal attitude" toward the periodical (*2L* 131). Indeed, Pound's editorial sway with Marsden and Weaver was such that contemporaries like the Irish poet James Stephens complained about the chumminess of the magazine: "There is a superficial and ephemeral air about the paper. Most persons appear to know the gang who are running it. [. . .] It is getting a stale affair this business of writing each other up., Hueffer-Pound, Pound-Hueffer, Pound-Aldington, Aldington-Pound [. . .]" (Clarke, "D. H. Lawrence" 67).

It was this chumminess that gained Joyce his first novel serialization via a periodical. When Pound showed the first chapter of *Portrait* to Marsden, she "at once agreed" to serialize the novel through the *Egoist*, and the first installment appeared on 2 February 1914 (*JJII* 353). As Stuart Gilbert recognizes, "there is no question of the importance of the part played by Mr Pound—and by *The Egoist* magazine with which he was so closely and dynamically associated—in bringing Joyce to the notice of the more literate public" (*Letters I* 23). *A Portrait* had been "refused by nearly all the publishers in London" before the "courageous review *The Egoist* decided to publish it" (*Letters I* 132), and Pound had, through his links with periodicals, provided Joyce with a small, but nonetheless valuable, audience of some two hundred subscribers.

The publication of "A Curious History" in the 15 January 1914 issue of the *Egoist* represents an interesting tactic through which Pound at once introduced Joyce to this audience, and subtly hinted at the importance of giving writers like him publication venues. "A Curious History" is a series of letters by Joyce, introduced by Pound, which recalls the difficulties Joyce experienced in trying to find a publisher for *Dubliners*. Pound introduced the letters as those of "an author of known and notable talents" and explained how he "considered it more appropriate to print his communication entire than to indulge in my usual biweekly comment about books published during the fortnight" ("Curious History" 26). The printing of the letters is almost polemical; by printing a series of letters lamenting the state of the British publishing industry and what Joyce termed "the present conditions of authorship in England and Ireland" ("Curious History" 26), Pound implicitly set up the idea that the failure of British publishers to notice or publish writers like Joyce is a dilemma that the *Egoist* is willing and able to rectify. In "A Curious History," Joyce explains how Grant Richards had initially agreed to publish *Dubliners* "six years ago," but after Joyce had refused "to omit one of the stories," the MS "was returned to me, the publisher refusing to publish, notwithstanding his pledged printed word, the contract remaining in my possession" ("Curious History" 26).[18] The subsequent beginning of the serialization of *Portrait* in the very next issue of the *Egoist* appears as a brave publishing step that challenges these practices of censorship and contract-breaking that were becoming routine within anxious publishing and printing houses.

Yet the *Egoist* was not immune to the pressures of censorship. The magazine's own press (Egoist Press) published *Portrait* in book form in 1917, but the publication was beset by problems relating to the work's perceived incendiary content: "[N]ot one printing works in the whole UK could be found to consent to print it," Joyce reflected (*Letters I* 132), an assertion supported by Harriet Shaw Weaver's exasperated letter to Joyce on 31 March 1914 informing him that she was "experiencing difficulty in securing a printer willing to print without deletions" (*Letters I* 90). Pound's literary associations and influence within the realm of little magazines had provided Joyce with a valuable opportunity that furthered his early career, but it was not just Joyce to whom Pound was offering this privilege. Lawrence's correspondence shows that, at the end of 1913, Pound was also actively seeking to publish work by Lawrence within the *Egoist*. Of course, at this point the magazine was still the *New Freewoman*, hence Lawrence's perplexity at Pound's mention of the magazine in a letter of 26 December 1913: "I don't know [...] what is *The Egoist*. [...] Is the *Egoist* then, French-English, or what?" (*2L* 131–32). Lawrence had first met Pound in November 1909 at a dinner party held by Ford Madox Ford (then Hueffer), the editor of the *English Review*. Ford had just published Lawrence's "A Still Afternoon" in the November issue of his magazine, and Lawrence wrote excitedly to Louie Burrows that he had been introduced to "Pound [...] a well-known American poet" and a "genius" (*2L* 144–45).

While correspondence between the two men from 1909 to 1912 is somewhat intermittent, by 1913 Pound had begun to champion his contemporary within the pages of *Poetry*. In July 1913, Pound used his book review section to praise Lawrence's *Love Poems* (1913) and declared, "If this book does not receive the Polignac prize a year from this November there will be due cause for scandal" ("Review" 150). The Polignac Prize was awarded annually by the British academic committee for creative work and was, scandalously, awarded to John Masefield, rather than Lawrence, the following year. In particular, Pound praised "Violets," a poem that had already appeared in the *Nation* prior to its collection in the volume, as "great art" ("Review" 151). Pound reiterated this praise in another review of *Love Poems* for the *New Freewoman* in September 1913: "Mr. Lawrence's book is the most important book of poems of the season," he declared ("In Metre" 113).

Pound's championing of Lawrence in *Poetry* led to Lawrence gaining several publications in the magazine in 1914.[19] For Lawrence, Pound's influence in gaining these periodical publications for him was much welcomed, enabling him to concentrate on writing rather than selling his work: "[T]his transacting of literary business makes me sick. [...] It is a sickening business. [...] [T]he literary world seems a particularly hateful yet powerful one" (*2L* 161–62). Lawrence's naiveté and disinclination to enter into this "literary business" manifests itself in a letter he sent to Arthur McLeod in January 1914: "There is an American magazine, or review, called *Poetry*. It is published in Chicago. I don't know whether you have ever seen it—I never have. But this month—January—it contains some of my work—at least they've sent me a cheque for £20. [. . .] I have no idea what these people have put in their paper—of mine—only they have paid me fabulously" (2L 138–39). By early 1914, Pound had also secured publication of some of Lawrence's poetry within the *Egoist*. Lawrence's description of this transaction again demonstrates the extent to which Pound had become something of an unofficial literary agent for an ever-confused Lawrence: "I think there will be some of my poems in a paper called *The Egoist*. I don't know anything about it. Ezra Pound took some verses and sent me £3.3—Try to get a copy. [. . .] I absolutely don't know what they have published" (2L 155–56). The *Egoist* had in fact published five of his poems—"A Winter's Tale," "Song," "Early Spring," "Honeymoon," and "Fooled"—in the 1 April 1914 issue.

It is in this issue of *The Egoist* that the only literal convergence between D. H. Lawrence and James Joyce occurs, a convergence that had been brought about by Pound. By simultaneously soliciting *Portrait* from Joyce and poetry from Lawrence, Pound was able to publish Lawrence and Joyce alongside each other for the first time. An extract of *Portrait* appeared over three pages toward the middle of the issue, and Lawrence's "A Winter's Tale" began on the last page on which Joyce's extract is printed.

Although the extract of chapter 1 of Joyce's *Portrait* and Lawrence's poetry are hardly similar in content—one narrating the incident in which Stephen Dedalus is caned in the classroom by the sadistic prefect of studies and the other a collection of verse depicting scenes between lovers—the striking similarity between Joyce's and Lawrence's work at this point is their realism. Whereas *Ulysses* evinces all of the stylistic and structural criteria of the quintessential modernist text, the extract from the opening of *Portrait*, as it appears in the *Egoist*, is distinctly unmodern. In book form, other chapters of *Portrait* exemplify several early modernist stylistic impulses, such as the subject/object, ideas/reality, interiority/exteriority, and private/public dichotomies that are explored through its distinctive narrative technique. The opening of chapter 1 is typically modernist in its use of stream of consciousness: "Once upon a time and a very good time it was there was a moocow coming down along the road" (P2 5). As Jeri Johnson has argued, "from the opening page of *Portrait*, the narrative proceeds in Stephen's idiom: Joyce uses language, style, idiolect not to embellish an identificative authorial signature [. . .] but instead as markers of character" (P2 xxi–xxii). However, the particular extract Pound chose to reprint in the *Egoist* begins midway through chapter 1, omitting the most modernist parts of the chapter. The extract contains free indirect discourse:

Was that a sin for Father Arnall to be in a wax or was he allowed to get
into a wax when the boys were idle because that made them study better
or was he only letting on to be in a wax? It was because he was allowed
because a priest would know what a sin was and would not do it. But
if he did it one time by mistake what would he do to go to confession?
Perhaps he would go to confession to the minister. And if the minister
did it he would go to the rector: and the rector to the provincial: and the
provincial to the general of the jesuits. (*P2* 40)

Yet, overall, the extract largely pertains to the genre of realism, Joyce's narrative
style appearing as naturalistic and teleological in its depiction of Fleming and
Stephen receiving the "pandybat" (*P2* 40).

Similarly, Lawrence's poetry published in this same issue of the *Egoist* is not
modernist in the sense of later "high" modernist work by poets such as Pound
and Eliot; nor does it exemplify the Imagist tradition with which Amy Lowell
would later identify Lawrence.[20] Instead, it harks back to traditions of romanticism and folklore. In their experimental rhyme patterns and verse forms, the
five poems are characteristic of the early phase of Lawrence's poetics, a phase
marked "by an attempt to emulate conventional rhyming forms and a growing
awareness of the limitations of such forms" (Poplawski 237). "Early Spring" invokes the quasi-romantic tone and emphasis on natural imagery used in earlier
poems like "Workaday Evenings" in its depiction of the "yellow crocuses" (1):
"deep in the golden wine of their chalices / Sway the live pearls their flowering
pledges" (3–4). "A Winter's Tale" depicts a young woman walking through the
snow to meet her lover while, unknown to her, he is about to break things off:
"She is only the nearer to the inevitable farewell" (Lawrence, "Winter's Tale"
10). The use of a fixed rhyme scheme coupled with pathetic fallacy as Lawrence
depicts a bleak winter scene ("scattered snow" [1], "the hill's white verge" [4],
"mist's pale scarf" [5], and "dull orange sky" [6]) imbues the poem with a story-
like realism that renders it more in keeping with the conventions of narrative,
rather than modernist, poetry. The five poems published in the 1 April issue
of the *Egoist* were all later collected in *New Poems* (1916). Other poems in this
volume are more modern; the depictions of cityscapes in "Hyde Park at Night,
Before the War" and "Piccadilly Circus" anticipate the modernist preoccupation with city life and the nature of war. It is only when the five poems in the
Egoist are placed against the other poems like "Piccadilly Circus" in the *New
Poems* volume that it becomes apparent they are part of Lawrence's emerging
and increasingly modernist aesthetic.

⌈This demonstrates how the material context in which a work appears affects its reception.⌉ Recently, many critics have noted the value of McGann's notion of "bibliographical codes" to the study of modernist texts, particularly to the study of little magazines. These codes are features operating at the "material (and apparently least 'signifying' or significant) levels of the text," which "are not regularly studied" and include "typefaces, bindings, book prices, page format, and all those textual phenomena usually regarded as (at best) peripheral to the text" (McGann 12–13). Brooker and Thacker have developed the idea of *periodical codes*, "a particular subset" of bibliographical codes "at play in any magazine" incorporating "a whole range of features [. . .] page layout, typefaces, price, size of volume" (6).

However, George Bornstein's identification of a particular bibliographic code helps to illuminate why the extract from the first chapter of *Portrait* in the *Egoist* appears as less modernist than the entire chapter as it appears in book form. Analyzing the printed version of Marianne Moore's poem "The Fish" in the August 1918 issue of the *Egoist*, Bornstein argues that "the precise placement of the poem" is a specific bibliographical code that serves to intensify the poem's apparently antiwar sentiments. Placing "The Fish" immediately after a column entitled "Fighting Paris" highlights the militaristic language and "submerged warlike imagery in Moore's poem" that might have gone unnoticed (Bornstein 95).

This argument can be applied to the placement of Joyce's chapter and Lawrence's poetry in the 1 April issue of the *Egoist*. The extract of Joyce's first chapter of *Portrait*, when taken out of context and placed within the pages of the *Egoist*, is literally disjointed from the rest of the text (the other chapters) and thus removed from its modernist context. Lawrence's poems, not wholly representative of the overall stylistic impulse of *New Poems*, appear in the *Egoist* as rather archaic, lyrical pieces that, like Joyce's extract, are fairly straightforward and "un-modernist" in terms of their thematic content, use of fixed form, rhyme schemes, unified voice, and naturalistic syntax. Just as Moore's poetry appears as more politicized when placed against the "Fighting Paris" column, the five poems by Lawrence in the 1 April issue of the *Egoist* appear as more modernist when they are read as part of the *New Poems* volume. Similarly, the extract of the first chapter of *Portrait*, when read in book format rather than as it is printed in the *Egoist*, appears not as a small piece of prose found in a magazine, but as part of an interactive text. This first chapter interacts with all of the other chapters of the text—chapters that, in their accumulative experimentalism, combine to produce an obvious and undeniably modernist novel.

Devoid of these contexts, the printed versions of Joyce's and Lawrence's texts in the *Egoist* only serve to reinforce each other's naturalism. The physical placement of Lawrence's poetry on the very same page as the last few paragraphs of Joyce's extract ensure that Lawrence's poems are read within the realist context (albeit unconsciously) of Joyce's text. While we cannot prove that selection of these particular extracts and their juxtaposition next to one another was a deliberate editorial ploy designed to showcase the writers' similar talent for realism, it should be noted that it was the naturalistic quality of both Joyce's and Lawrence's writing that Pound admired most. For Pound, Joyce's "most engaging merit" is that "he is a realist" (Pound, "Dubliners" 267), and Lawrence's greatest strength lay in his ability to write "low life narrative" ("Review" 149): "he has attempted realism and he has attained it" (151).

However, Pound's influence extended beyond the realm of the *Egoist*. In June 1913, Lawrence wrote to Edward Garnett to tell him that Ezra Pound had been in touch and "asked me for some stories" (*2L* 26). Evidently pleased at Pound's request, Lawrence declared that he "should be glad to have some stories in magazines" and set about preparing a few pieces (*2L* 27). Pound, at this point the literary agent in England for the American little magazine the *Smart Set*, gained six publications for Lawrence within the magazine between 1913 and 1914, despite William Wright, the magazine's editor at the time, complaining that some of Lawrence's stories were "too hot" (*2L* 67). One of these stories was "The Christening," published in the *Smart Set* in February 1914.

The *Smart Set* was an American little magazine whose subtitle "A Magazine of Cleverness" hinted at the subtle elitism that ran through its pages. Its contributors included F. Scott Fitzgerald, Eugene O'Neill, and Ezra Pound. After first publishing Lawrence's work in November 1913 (a poem entitled "The Mowers"), in May 1915, the *Smart Set* also published work by Joyce. H. L. Mencken, the *Smart Set's* editor (he had replaced William Wright as editor in August 1914), may not have been prepared to serialize *Portrait* on account of its length, but he was happy to print Joyce's short stories and even wrote to Joyce to congratulate him: "two of your stories [. . .] are in the May *Smart Set*. [. . .] [K]eep the *Smart Set* in mind" (*Letters I* 79). These two stories were "A Boarding House" and "A Little Cloud."

Comparing Joyce's "A Boarding House" to Lawrence's contribution, "The Christening" demonstrates how, within the *Smart Set*, both writers utilize a similar prose style, continuing the realism they had employed in their earliest prose pieces. In terms of content, both stories deal with similar subject matter. "A Boarding House" concerns the illegitimate pregnancy of a young girl living in her mother's bed-and-breakfast lodgings. The father of the child is one of the tenants, but the reader is not given this crucial piece of information immediately. Similarly, in Lawrence's "The Christening," a baby has been born out of wedlock to a single young mother. The fact that "the father of the baby was the baker's man at Berryman's" (Lawrence, "Christening" 85) is revealed as a climactic twist; Lawrence had earlier shown one of his characters, Hilda Rowbotham, the young mother's sister, visiting the bakery and ordering several cakes. Similarly, in Joyce's tale the paternity of the unborn child is revealed as a shocking climax: "the priest had drawn out every detail of the affair. [. . .] What could he do now but marry her or run away?" ("Boarding House" 95).

Even before the publication of their most controversial novels, Joyce and Lawrence were both engaging with narratives that were somewhat risqué, especially considering the rather upmarket nature of the *Smart Set*. Wright (the magazine's former editor) had, after all, complained that Lawrence's stories were "too hot," and both Lawrence and Joyce's prose pieces are provocative. In his description of Polly (the pregnant girl) as a "perverse Madonna" and "a little vulgar" ("Boarding House" 93, 95), Joyce painted a portrait of a coquettish young woman with dubious moral integrity, but, crucially, he did not comment on this integrity and chose instead to present the situation objectively. Tellingly, Lawrence also adopted this technique in his story. Emma's (the young mother) sister Hilda may flush "with shame" ("Christening" 82) in the baker's shop (the reader is not told why until the end of the story), but Lawrence appears to sidestep any moral questions. The priest arrives and christens the child, seemingly sanctifying the situation: "But what does the man matter? [. . .] Lord, what father has a man but Thee?" ("Christening" 85). Here, within the pages of the *Smart Set*, Joyce and Lawrence played out moral dilemmas without entering into debates on morality; in their shared refusal to pass judgment on their protagonists, both writers pave the way for their later, even more provocative prose styles that would become a defining hallmark of their careers.

"The Two Strongest Prose Writers among *Les Jeunes*"

Evidence that both writers were becoming recognized as the two foremost prose writers of their era comes in the form of a letter from Pound to Amy Lowell. Joyce and Lawrence, he argued, were "the two strongest prose writers" of their generation (Pound, *Letters* 34). Their contributions to periodicals demonstrate that before the end of the 1910s and throughout the 1920s both writers were using increasingly idiosyncratic writing styles in order to advance particularly controversial viewpoints relating to key aspects of modern life. "The Reality of Peace," the essay Lawrence serialized in the *English Review* from May to August 1917, and "Nestor," published in the *Little Review* in April 1918, show the similar ways in which Lawrence and Joyce consider the issue of war.

The opening scene of "Nestor" in the *Little Review* posits war, and by implication the Great War that was still raging, within a cyclical view of history:

—There was a battle, sir.
—Very good. Where? . . .
—I forget the place, sir. 279 B.C.
—Asculum, Stephen said, glancing at the name and year in the gorescarred book.
—Yes, sir. And he said: *Another victory like that and we are done for.*
That phrase the world had remembered. A dull ease of the mind. From a hill above a corpsestrewn plain a general, speaking to his officers, leaned upon his spear. Any general to any officers. (Joyce, "Nestor" 32)

The fact that the pupil cannot remember the place of the battle, and that even Stephen has to look it up, coupled with the reference to the "gorescarred book," a symbol of older times, implies that the war of 279 BC is in some way irrelevant. The phrase "Any general to any officers" reiterates this, and the imagined rendering of the "corpsestrewn plain" telescopes events backwards onto an unfamiliar, distant, and in some way detached realm. War is presented as part of history—a few sentences in an old book—and in evincing this existential view of world events (a view that the entire structure of *Ulysses* reflects), Joyce trivializes the life cycle.

Lawrence's essay displays a strangely similar philosophy. By 1917, the year the essay appeared in the *English Review*, Lawrence had grown confident in expounding his own unique philosophies via the medium of nonfictional prose. He had established the *Signature* with the sole purpose of disseminating his philosophical essay "The Crown" (1915), and "The Reality of Peace" appears as a similar expression of his own personal philosophy. It is a particularly personal reflection on the nature of peace that, like Joyce's "Nestor," places war within the context of a cyclical view of history. The opening of the essay illustrates this viewpoint: "There is a great diastole of the universe. It has no why or wherefore, no aim or purpose" (Lawrence, "The Reality of Peace" 415). Within this context war and peace are a dialectic, part of the "mechanical round" (417) of life that continues interminably. Lawrence also invoked older battles as a means of illustrating this philosophy; just as "Red Indians of America" showed "courage of death" (418), so too will many other men engaged in many other battles: accepting this, Lawrence argues, is the only way toward finding peace.

While not a direct comment on the Great War, the publication of these two pieces of prose within a time of war appears as somewhat political, especially considering the pacifist stance of the *Little Review*. As David Weir recognizes, it was under the Espionage Act (1917) and Trading-with-the-Enemy Act (1918) that the U.S. Post Office enacted a partial suppression of the January 1919 issue (containing the "Lestrygonians" episode of *Ulysses*) of the *Little Review* (391). Pound would later reflect how "[t]he censorship was very much troubled by it [the serialization of *Ulysses*] during the war. Thought it was all code" (Weir 391). This supports Robert Spoo's idea that, despite the fact that few critics have "suggested that the war influenced Joyce's narrative," there are "remarkable traces" of its presence within *Ulysses* and specifically "Nestor" (Spoo 138).

Both Joyce and Lawrence extend this cyclical view of history through their later prose fiction. In *Finnegans Wake* this cyclicality manifests itself in the physical, material form of the narrative itself. The novel appears the archetypal nonlinear text. The first few sentences of its "Opening Pages" printed in *transition* (Eugene and Maria Jolas' expatriate Parisian magazine) in April 1927 signify that Joyce had begun to extend the experimental possibilities of modernist prose to extremes, disrupting any sense of a linear, teleological narrative: "riverrun brings us back to Howth Castle and Environs" (Joyce, "Opening Pages of a Work in Progress" 9). It is not just the linear framework of a teleological narrative that Joyce is challenging but the framework of language itself. However, perhaps the most controversial part of *Finnegans Wake* is the fact that Joyce parodies not only the idea of a linear narrative, or a linear sense of history, but a particular event that, in a Christian narrative of history serves as the defining event of human life: the resurrection. In "Opening Pages of a Work in Progress" the promise that Finnegan, after his death ("The great falle of the offwall entailed [. . .] the schute of Finnegan" [Joyce, "Opening Pages" 9]) will be resurrected appears as a blasphemous parody of the original events of the Bible.

Lawrence read parts of *transition*'s serialization of *Finnegans Wake* and infamously declared his contempt for Joyce's prose style: "Somebody sent me *Transition*—American number—that Paris modernissimo periodical, James Joyce and Gertrude Stein etc. What a stupid *olla podrida* of the Bible and so forth James Joyce: is just stewed-up fragments of quotation" (*6L* 507). Part of Lawrence's now infamous critique of Joyce may have related to the latter's "*olla podrida* of the Bible," but a remarkable line of convergence between both writers is the fact that Lawrence, at roughly the same time as Joyce, was embarking on his own refashioning of biblical narrative—a refashioning that saw him, just as Joyce had, questioning the idea of the resurrection.

Whereas Joyce had implied that the resurrection could happen to an ordinary man, in "The Escaped Cock," published in *Forum* in February 1928, Lawrence posited the resurrection as a means through which the actual Christ was transformed into an ordinary man. Upon his resurrection, Christ loses his divinity and marvels at things he had never noticed prior to his death: "They came forth these creatures of spring, glowing with desire and with assertion" (*EC* 288). However, Lawrence's most controversial act is to place Christ as a subject of this desire. By depicting Christ, "the man who died" (*EC* 287), gaining union with a woman, Lawrence challenges the fundamental basis of Christ's divinity as well as the whole biblical narrative of the event he has reconstructed. Lawrence's story may possess a linear narrative, but the implication is that the very narrative on which all history is based is flawed. Both Joyce and Lawrence deconstruct the fundamental narrative of the Bible and replace it with their own Fall narratives. The fact that they do so via publications first published within little magazines shows how both writers were actively engaging with the same narrative experiments and the same specific theme within a year of each other. This experimentation bears no similarity to the original focus on realism and linearity that both writers initially favored in their earliest periodical publications.

Tracing their publication history from these earliest examples to those from their later careers enables us to chart the various experimental phases and engagements with modernism and modernity that Joyce and Lawrence made throughout their writing careers. In some ways, the little magazines and other periodicals in which both writers were published serve as the most concise reflection of their developing careers. These magazines offer small snapshots into a particular moment in time that their larger pieces of prose fiction (published in book form and divested of their original material conditions of production) do not. By actively returning to the original sites and venues in which Joyce and Lawrence received their publications, we are reminded that these little magazines and periodicals are as much, if not more, a part of both writers' oeuvres as the books (their novels and collected works) we can find in libraries.

This shows us that the literary modernism of Joyce and Lawrence does not begin in the pages of their published texts (some of which were published several years after extracts of these texts had first appeared in little magazines) but in the little magazines in which the earliest forms of these texts appeared, demanding further study of little magazines and periodicals. The continuing development of online databases dedicated to the digitization of little magazines such as the Modernist Journals Project (a joint project of Brown University and the University of Tulsa) is beginning to make this further study possible. Moreover, these online libraries of little magazines make exploring the convergences between not only Joyce and Lawrence, but the whole host of writers and institutions who define our conception of the "modernist" era, an easier task. Against this wider backdrop of cooperation and convergence, it is perhaps not surprising that Lawrence was able to tell Wubberhorst that "in Europe they usually mention us together—James Joyce and D. H. Lawrence" (4L 340). Yet what is surprising is that Lawrence did not object to or attempt to challenge this dual identification. We can only assume that he had already recognized and accepted the lines of convergence between himself and James Joyce that modern critics are only just beginning to examine in greater detail.

Notes

1. On Joyce and little magazines, see Mullin 374–89. On *Ulysses'* serialization, see *Ulysses* 740–52. On Lawrence and the *English Review,* see Wulfman 234–35. On Lawrence and the *Blue Review,* see Bradbury 423–24.

2. On *Dana*, see Davis 170–75.

3. Between March 1907 and September 1912, this Trieste-based newspaper published eight nonfiction articles by Joyce. These articles, printed in Italian, mostly focused on contemporary political debates, but Joyce also wrote pieces of literary criticism on George Bernard Shaw and Oscar Wilde. See Joyce "L'Irlanda alla Sbarra," *Il Piccolo della Sera* 26 (16 September 1907): 1; "La Battaglia fra Bernard Shaw e la Censura," *Il Piccolo della Sera* 28 (5 September 1909): 1; "La Cometa dell 'Home Rule,'" *Il Piccolo della Sera* 29 (22 December 1910): 1; "Oscar Wilde: Il Poeta di Salome," *Il Piccolo della Sera* 28 (24 March 1909): 1. These articles mark the main bulk of Joyce's periodical publications between the publication of his first *Dubliners* stories in the *Irish Homestead* in 1904 and the appearance of *Portrait* in the *Egoist* ten years later.

4. See Slocum and Cahoon, "Contributions to Periodicals" 91–106.

5. The *Egoist* serialized *Portrait* in twenty-five installments between vol. 1, no. 3 (2 February 1914) and vol. 2, no. 9 (1 September 1915). A hiatus in serialization occurred from vol. 1, no. 18 (15 September 1914) to vol. 1, no. 22 (16 November 1914) as "Joyce was unable to send the manuscript from Trieste to London," and an installment could not appear in vol. 2, no. 5 (1 May 1915) as this issue was the special *Imagist* number (Slocum and Cahoon 95). On the *Egoist's* serialization of *Portrait*, see Clarke, "Scientism," 119–31; and *JJI* 351–56.

6. The *Little Review* serialized twenty-three extracts of *Ulysses* from 4.11 (March 1918) to 7.3 (December 1920). This serialization was controversial; in January 1919, the United States Post Office confiscated copies of the *Little Review* on account of the presence of Joyce's "Lestrygonians" episode within its pages. In May 1919, "the *Little Review* suppressions began in earnest" (Weir 389). In February 1921, the New York Court of Special Sessions found the "Nausicaa" installment in the July–August 1920 issue "obscene" (Weir 390), and the *Little Review* was forbidden to publish any more extracts of *Ulysses* (Weir 400). The *Egoist* also serialized *Ulysses*: extracts from around "three and a half" episodes appeared in the following volumes: 1.1 (January–February 1919), 1.2 (March–April 1919), 1.3 (July 1919), 1.4 (September 1919), and 1.5 (December 1919) (see Slocum and Cahoon 98).

7. The *transatlantic review* was a short-lived magazine of only twelve published issues that appeared monthly throughout 1924. It was Ford who gave the then unfinished *Finnegans Wake* its title "Work in Progress" (see *transatlantic review* 1.4 [April 1924]: 215–23). The twenty-two pages of "Opening Pages of a Work in Progress" first appeared in the April 1927 issue of *transition* and then continued from May to November 1927 and in February and March 1928 in monthly extracts of approximately twenty pages, each under the title "Continuation of a Work in Progress." Another extract of twenty-eight pages appeared in the summer 1928 issue, and further extracts appeared in the following issues: February 1929, November 1929, and February 1933. More extracts appeared in July 1935 and February 1937 under the title "Work in Progress." The final extracts, entitled "Fragment from a Work in Progress," appeared in the April–May 1938 issue. While the February 1929 serial was particularly long, at forty-four pages, the latter extracts returned to the typical twenty-page length (see Slocum and Cahoon 101).

8. Furthermore, between September 1925 and September 1926, under the title of "A New Unnamed Work," a New York quarterly entitled *Two Worlds* published several unauthorized reprints of the extracts of *Finnegans Wake* originally printed in *Navire d'Argent*, *This Quarter*, and the *transatlantic review* (see Slocum and Cahoon 99–100). See also "Work in Progress," *Contempo* 3.13 (15 February 1934): 14; and "A Phoenix Park Nocturne," *Verve* 1.2 (March–June 1938): 26.

9. A paragraph from a letter to Carlo Linati was printed in the same magazine in December 1940 under the title "Il Romanzaccione," but this letter was written more than twenty years earlier (it is dated 10 October 1920) (see Slocum and Cahoon 104).

10. For a more detailed bibliography of Lawrence's periodical publications, see Roberts and Poplawski, "Contributions to Periodicals" 449–513. It seems likely that the departure of Austin Harrison, Ford's successor, as the editor of the *English Review* in 1923 was a contributing factor in Lawrence's sudden disappearance from within its pages. Furthermore, 1923 was also the year in which Lawrence's close friend John Middleton Murry founded the *Adelphi*. For Lawrence, the *Adelphi* formed almost a replacement venue for the *English Review,* and Lawrence began to publish frequently within its pages.

11. The *Saturday Westminster Gazette* published the "Schoolmaster" series of poems

from May to June 1912. These poems were "derived from Lawrence's teaching experience" (Roberts and Poplawski 454–55).

12. In August 1912, the *Westminster Gazette* published "German Impressions: I. French Sons of Germany" and "German Impressions: II. Hail in the Rhineland." The paper also published several other articles throughout 1913 including "Christs in the Tyrol," an essay recalling Lawrence and Frieda's walking trip through the Tirol (March 1913), "Strike-Pay I, Her Turn" (September 1913), and "Strike-Pay II, Ephraim's Half Sovereign" (September 1913). The *New Statesman* published the short stories "The Fly in the Ointment" (August 1913), "A Sick Collier" (September 1913), and the poem "Service of all the Dead" (November 1913) (see Roberts and Poplawski 455–58).

13. See the front cover of the *Blue Review* 1 (May 1913).

14. See, for example, "On Being a Man," *Vanity Fair* June 1924: 33–34.

15. As Lawrence submitted the story in Jessie Chambers' name, Jessie Chambers is listed as the author in the *Nottinghamshire Guardian*.

16. In 1913, Ezra Pound was the agent in England for the *Smart Set* (*Letters I* 26).

17. For more on Pound's association with the *Egoist*, see Clarke, "D. H. Lawrence" 65–76.

18. Although "A Curious History" contains letters written by Joyce, the article is credited to Pound on the contents page of the *Egoist*, hence Pound's name rather than Joyce's appears in the bibliographical reference to this article.

19. In *Poetry* 3.4 (January 1914): 115–25, see, for example, "Green," "All of Roses," "Fireflies in the Corn," "A Woman and her Dead Husband," "The Wind the Rascal," "The Mother of Sons," "Illicit," and "Birthday." In *Poetry* 5.3 (December 1914): 102–6, see "Grief," "Memories," "Weariness," "Service of all the Dead," "Don Juan," and "Song."

20. In 1915, Lowell, an American poet and sometime acquaintance of Pound, included Lawrence within her anthology *Some Imagist Poets* (1915).

Works Cited

Allen, Walter. *The English Novel.* New York: Dutton, 1954.

Bornstein, George. *Material Modernism.* Cambridge: Cambridge UP, 2001.

Bradbury, Malcolm. "'Rhythm' and 'The Blue Review.'" *Times Literary Supplement* 25 April 1968: 423–24.

Brooker, Peter, and Andrew Thacker, eds. *The Oxford Critical and Cultural History of Modernist Magazines.* Vol. 1, *Britain and Ireland: 1880–1955.* Oxford: Oxford UP, 2009.

Brown, Richard, ed. *A Companion to James Joyce.* Oxford: Blackwell, 2008.

Chambers, Jessie. "A Prelude." *Nottinghamshire Guardian* 17 (December 1907): 17.

Churchill, Suzanne, and Adam McKible. "Introduction." *Little Magazines and Modernism: An Introduction.* Ed. Suzanne Churchill and Adam McKible. Spec. issue of *American Periodicals: A Journal of History, Criticism, and Bibliography* 15.1 (2005): 1–5.

Clarke, Bruce. "D. H. Lawrence and the *Egoist* Group." *Journal of Modern Literature* 18.1 (1992): 65–76.

——. "Suffragism, Imagism, and the 'Cosmic Poet': Scientism and Spirituality in *The Freewoman* and *The Egoist.*" *Little Magazines and Modernism: New Approaches.* Ed. Suzanne Churchill and Adam McKible. Hampshire, UK: Ashgate, 2007. 119–31.

Cooper, John Xiros. *Modernism and the Culture of Market Society.* Cambridge: Cambridge UP, 2004.

Davis, Alex. "Yeats and the Celtic Revival: *Beltaine* (1899–1900), *Samhain* (1901–8), *Dana* (1904–5), and *The Arrow* (1906–9)." *The Oxford Critical and Cultural History of Modernist Magazines.* Vol. 1, *Britain and Ireland: 1880–1955.* Ed. Peter Brooker and Andrew Thacker. Oxford: Oxford UP, 2009. 152–75.

Delap, Lucy. "*The Freewoman*, Periodical Communities, and Feminist Reading Public." *Princeton University Library Chronicle* 61.2 (2000): 233–76.

Ellmann, Richard. *James Joyce.* New York: Oxford UP, 1983.

Haiti Trust Digital Library. *The Smart Set.* Accessed 21 July 2011. http://catalog.hathitrust.org/Record/008881616.

Hammill, Faye. "In Good Company: Modernism, Celebrity, and Sophistication in *Vanity Fair*, 1914–1936." *Modernist Star Maps.* Ed. Jonathan Goldman and Aaron Jaffe. Surrey, UK: Ashgate, 2010. 123–36.

Hoffman, Frederick J., Charles Albert Allen, and Carolyn F. Ulrich, eds. *The Little Magazine: A History and a Bibliography.* Princeton, NJ: Princeton UP, 1946.

Huyssen, Andreas. *After the Great Divide: Modernism, Mass Culture, Postmodernism.* Basingstoke, UK: Macmillan, 1986.

Jaffe, Aaron. "General Introduction." *The Year's Work in English Studies* 88 (2009): 867–78.

Joyce, James. "Alone." *Poetry* 11.2 (November 1917): 70–71.

——. "A Boarding House." *Smart Set* 46.1 (May 1915): 93–98.

——. "Eveline." *Irish Homestead* 10 September 1904: 17.

——. "I Hear an Army." *Glebe* (February 1914): 40.

——. "Nestor." *Little Review* 4.12 (April 1918): 32–45.

——. "Nightpiece." *Poetry* 10.2 (May 1917): 74–75.

——. "On the Beach at Fontana." *Poetry* 11.2 (November 1917): 70.

——. "Opening Pages of a Work in Progress." *transition* 1 (April 1927): 9–30.

——. *A Portrait of the Artist as a Young Man.* Ed. Jeri Johnson. Oxford: Oxford UP, 2008.

——. "A Portrait of the Artist as a Young Man." *Egoist* 1.7 (1 April 1914): 132–34.

——. "Song." *Dana* 4 (August 1904): 124.

——. *Ulysses.* Ed. Jeri Johnson. Oxford: Oxford UP, 2011.

Lawrence, D. H. "The Christening." *Smart Set* 42.2 (February 1914): 81–85.

——. "Early Spring." *Egoist* 1.7 (1 April 1914): 134.

——. "The Escaped Cock." *Forum* 79 (February 1928): 286–96.

——. "The Georgian Renaissance." *Rhythm* (Literary Supplement) 2.14 (March 1913): xvii–xx.

———. "The Reality of Peace (i)." *English Review* 24 (May 1917): 415–22.

———. "Snap-Dragon." *English Review* 11 (June 1912): 345–48.

———. "Tommies in the Train." *Poetry* 13.5 (February 1919): 258–59.

———. "Violets." *Nation* 4 November 1911: 204.

———. "A Winter's Tale." *Egoist* 1.7 (1 April 1914): 134.

———. "Workaday Evenings." *English Review* 4 (April 1910): 4–6.

Leavis, F. R. *D. H. Lawrence: Novelist.* London: Chatto and Windus, 1955.

Lewis, Pericles. *The Cambridge Introduction to Modernism.* Cambridge: Cambridge UP, 2007.

McGann, Jerome. *The Textual Condition.* Princeton, NJ: Princeton UP, 1991.

Modernist Journals Project. Accessed 19 August 2011. http://dl.lib.brown.edu/mjp/.

Morrisson, Mark S. *The Public Face of Modernism: Little Magazines, Audiences, and Reception 1905–1920.* Madison: U of Wisconsin P, 2001.

Mullin, Katherine. "Joyce through the Little Magazine." *A Companion to James Joyce.* Ed. Richard Brown. Oxford, UK: Blackwell, 2008. 374–89.

Murry, John Middleton. "Aims and Ideals." *Rhythm* 1.1 (Summer 1911): 36.

———. *Reminiscences of D. H. Lawrence.* New York: Holt, 1933.

Poplawski, Paul, ed. *Encyclopedia of Literary Modernism.* London: Greenwood, 2003.

Pound, Ezra. "A Curious History." *Egoist* 1.2 (15 January 1914): 26–27.

———. "Dubliners and Mr. James Joyce." *Egoist* 1.14 (15 July 1914): 267.

———. "In Metre." *New Freewoman* 1.6 (September 1913): 113.

———. *The Letters of Ezra Pound.* Ed. D. D. Paige. New York: Harcourt, Brace, 1950.

———. "Review: *Love Poems and Others.*" *Poetry* 2.4 (July 1913): 149–51.

Rainey, Lawrence. *Institutions of Modernism: Literary Elites and Public Culture.* New Haven: Yale UP, 1998.

———. *Modernism: An Anthology.* Ed. Lawrence Rainey. Oxford, UK: Wiley-Blackwell, 2005.

Roberts, Warren, and Paul Poplawski. "Contributions to Periodicals." *A Bibliography of D. H. Lawrence.* 3rd ed. Cambridge: Cambridge UP, 2011.

Sagar, Keith. *D. H. Lawrence: A Calendar of His Works.* Manchester, UK: Manchester UP, 1979.

Scherr, Barry J. *D. H. Lawrence Today: Literature, Culture, Politics.* New York: Peter Lang, 2004.

Scholes, Robert, and Clifford Wulfman. *Modernism in the Magazines.* New Haven: Yale UP, 2010.

Slocum, John J., and Herbert Cahoon. "Contributions to Periodicals." *A Bibliography of James Joyce, 1822–1941.* London: Hart Davis, 1953. 91–106.

Spoo, Robert. "'Nestor' and the Nightmare: The Presence of the Great War in *Ulysses.*" *Twentieth Century Literature* 32.2 (1986): 137–54.

Weir, David. "What Did He Know, and When Did He Know It: *The Little Review,* Joyce, and *Ulysses.*" *James Joyce Quarterly* 37.3/4 (2000): 389–412.

Wexler, Joyce Piell. *Who Paid for Modernism? Art, Money, and the Fiction of Conrad, Joyce, and Lawrence.* Fayetteville: Arkansas UP, 1997.

Wulfman, Clifford. "Ford Madox Ford and *The English Review* (1908–37)." *The Oxford Critical and Cultural History of Modernist Magazines.* Vol. 1, *Britain and Ireland: 1880–1955.* Ed. Peter Brooker and Andrew Thacker. Oxford: Oxford UP, 2009. 226–39.

7

Lawrence and Joyce in T. S. Eliot's Criterion Miscellany Series

ELENI LOUKOPOULOU

> *I am glad I have seen the book [Ulysses]. [. . .] I feel I ought to know in what company I creep to immortality. I guess Joyce would look as much askance on me as I on him. We make a choice of Paola and Francesca floating down the winds of hell.*

D. H. Lawrence to F. Wubbenhorst, 14 November 1922

> *Joyce on "Lady Chatterbox's Lover": "I read the first 2 pages of the usual sloppy English."*

Richard Ellmann, *James Joyce* (1982)

Letters and biographical accounts have offered substantial evidence about the extent to which James Joyce and D. H. Lawrence disapproved of each other's art. Critical explorations have focused on the great divide between them mainly for two reasons: F. R. Leavis' championing of Lawrence to the detriment of Joyce; and the impact that this dichotomy had on English studies.[1] But that divide, this essay argues, is much narrower when we consider their work in the context of the mechanisms of London's literary marketplace—through which both authors relaunched their careers in England in the late 1920s in the aftermath of the scandalous reception of *Ulysses* (1922) and *Lady Chatterley's Lover* (1927). Both authors' work circulated and was read within similar publishing and cultural contexts. In some cases, they dealt with the same publishers (Faber and Faber) and the same agents (Pinker). This essay contextualizes a particular moment in their literary lives—the publication background and dissemination of the pamphlets by Lawrence and Joyce in T. S. Eliot's successful publishing venture, the Criterion Miscellany series (1929–36). For this series of pamphlets, Lawrence was invited to publish his essay on censorship, *Pornography and Obscenity* (1929, No. 5), and the collection of poems *Nettles* (1930, No. 11). For the same series, Joyce contributed two sections from *Work in Progress*, the early name for *Finnegans Wake* (1939): *Anna Livia Plurabelle: Fragment of* Work in Progress (1930, No. 15) and *Haveth Childers Everywhere* (1931, No. 26).

By locating Lawrence and Joyce in the Criterion Miscellany series and by relating them to Eliot's role as their publisher, this essay explores a significant shift in their careers. Although they had become associated with scandal and censorship, their new writings became widely available in the pages of a respected series, and they were read by the political and literary establishment. Eliot, the catalyst for this process, used his knowledge of the rules of London's publishing industry to promote both writers. In 1929, while a director at Faber and Faber, Eliot initiated a side project to the journal the *Criterion* (1922–39), which he named the Criterion Miscellany series. A significant number of distinguished figures in public life as well as Eliot's "phalanx," his collaborators in the journal, became contributors to the series as writers of pamphlets (Nourie 64). For Lawrence and Joyce—both stigmatized as "banned" writers—the Criterion Miscellany series constituted a crucial publication outlet enabling them to reach new and diverse audiences.

By the late 1920s, both authors had acquired the status of "celebrities" because of scandalous texts published outside the United Kingdom: the private editions of *Lady Chatterley's Lover* (Florence) and *Ulysses* (Paris), which were banned in England. The appearance of their work in the pages of a Criterion Miscellany pamphlet marks a clear shift toward their cultural valorization within the context of Eliot's programmatic interventions in the literary scene. One of Eliot's strategies was to place these two authors in dialogue with the exemplification of Puritan England, William Joynson-Hicks (home secretary from 1924 to 1929). He was popularly referred to as "Jix," and after the general election of May 1929, when the Labour government came into power, and he relinquished his post, he used his new title, Viscount Brentford. In the late 1920s, the divide between Joyce and Lawrence narrowed thanks to the fertile conditions the cultural field of the Criterion Miscellany series offered. This essay will first outline the history of this series of pamphlets and its significance in relation to Eliot's cultural interventions against censorship, then focus on the works that Joyce and Lawrence contributed and how these specific publications impacted their careers and reputations.

Eliot's Pamphleteers

The Criterion Miscellany series of pamphlets grew in parallel with the development of the journal the *Criterion,* with which Eliot's work as an editor is most often associated. The issues covered within the pamphlets were wide-ranging, topical, and often provocative. Promoting pluralism and diversity—and in this, he followed the same policies as in the *Criterion,* that is, to "remain open to all political perspectives" (Ayers, *1920s* 111)—Eliot sought new approaches to diverse topics and forms (literary prose, essay, manifesto). The series featured both original literary works and essays on contemporary sociopolitical matters and artistic movements. The pamphlets can be grouped in the following categories: literature (a great number of which dealt with the Great War), visual culture (ranging from Persian art to caricatures and surrealism), economics, politics, and social matters: from censorship to obscenity and from imperial defense to birth control. The forty-three pamphlets of the series featured a wide variety of authors; in addition to Joyce and Lawrence, they included, among others, Herbert Read, Naomi Mitchison, André Breton, and George Grosz.

Eliot's work as editor, publisher, and influential figure of the interwar period has recently become recognized as worthy of study. For instance, in 2009, the British Library in London organized the exhibition *In a Bloomsbury Square: T. S. Eliot the Publisher.* It was dedicated to Eliot's work as a director at Faber and Faber and foregrounded the wider cultural impact the author of *The Waste Land* had on the development and consolidation of modernist literature and aesthetics in the publishing market.

Similarly, Eliot's role as key cultural commentator in the *Criterion* has been examined in critical studies. David Ayers has analyzed Eliot's skillful manipulation of the field of modernist magazines, taking as example the debates around romanticism and classicism that ensued in the pages of the *Criterion* and the *Adelphi.* As he notes, such struggle "was not wholly one-sided. John Middleton Murry's *The Adelphi* provided a convenient foil to *The Criterion*'s polemics, and Murry rose to Eliot's challenge with articles printed in both journals" (Ayers, *1920s* 114). Drawing on this line of inquiry, Jason Harding has suggested that "Eliot carefully selected Murry as an antagonist in order to advance and develop his editorial goals," characterizing the romanticism/classicism clash as "an important means of providing good copy for both periodicals. [. . .] Descending from the intellectual high ground into the imbroglio of literary journalism unearths a complex exchange of viewpoints occurring both within and across the *Criterion*—a discourse in which Eliot's trenchant and timely editorial interventions could be decisive" (25–26).

The above analysis about the ways Eliot and Murry operated is a useful point of entry to understand the mechanics and strategic preoccupations that underpinned the production and promotion of the pamphlets that featured in the Criterion Miscellany series on which there is scant research. Alan R. Nourie, in his article "The *Criterion Miscellany*: A Lost Series," expressed surprise about the paucity of informed accounts of the series. There is evidently a bias for the journal the *Criterion*, leaving the Criterion Miscellany series underexplored. One reason is perhaps that the study of a publisher's series as a cultural phenomenon presents methodological challenges. Nonetheless, its study is emerging as a new field of research. Such is the case of Max Saunders' project on the highly influential booklet series To-day and To-morrow (1923–31). It was edited by C. K. Ogden, and his rationale for the series "was to combine the popularization of expert knowledge with futurology" (Saunders and Hurwitz 3). In 2008, Routledge republished the greatest part of the 104 titles in the series, and as Saunders and Hurwitz observe, the reissuing of the series rightly suggests "that it has a more enduring interest" (4). This is because a publisher's series can shed light on its time even though this publishing phenomenon "has generally been neglected by all but a few scholars working on individual publishing houses or specific series" (Spiers 5). The editor, John Spiers, and the contributors to the two-volume study *The Culture of the Publisher's Series* offer useful methodological tools to demonstrate the need for a holistic approach to a publisher's series, especially in relation to wider changes in cultural production *and* within specific sociopolitical and geographical contexts. A series of books or pamphlets can thus play the role of both "actor and mirror" (Spiers 1). Arguably, Spiers' observations concur with recent developments in the methodologies of the New Modernist Studies, the research program that advocates a reassessment and revision of the set agendas of modernist studies and addresses "the relations between not merely individual authors and artists, but among various aspects of culture."[2]

The shift of focus is evident in studies that privilege microhistories and consider in detail the political economy of the literary marketplace and the persistent engagement of writers and editors in shaping literary taste and influencing cultural and sociopolitical developments. To achieve this, modernist writers cultivated an image of indifference or even developed mechanisms such as the construct of the snob, as Sean Latham has persuasively demonstrated, to challenge "directly the structuralist organization of aesthetic production [. . .]

[to map their] own position within the chaos of the expanding literary marketplace and [articulate their] resistance to its organizational logic" (Latham 121–22). In their own ways, nonetheless, they were enmeshed in the politics of the marketplace through diverse networks of influence and collaboration.

As Aaron Jaffe has pointed out, (these networks (both major and minor) need to be explored so that theorizing on the radical aesthetics of modernism can be firmly and historically grounded in sites of "literary labor." Jaffe has called this form of labor "downstream" work. It involves "criticism, reviewing, introducing, editing, anthologizing, even blurb-writing" (Jaffe 102). Modernist writers were engaged in this type of activity alongside creative, or "upstream," work because, as Jaffe notes, "the work of editing and introducing operates *between* contemporaries, fixing one established singular artist/solitary genius to another would-be singular artist/solitary genius. [. . .] [M]odernist careerists like Ezra Pound and T. S. Eliot had a stake in offering their literary durable goods as the embodiment of representative distinction: it was their means to economize and thus monopolize the plentitude of the literary firmament" (102). By inviting Lawrence and Joyce to contribute to the Criterion Miscellany series, Eliot and the publishers Faber and Faber further cultivated the reputation of these writers while also relying on the merit of their literary work and reputation to further promote their own publishing series. Indeed, according to Nourie's account of the Criterion Miscellany, "the best-sellers of the series were numbers" by Joyce and Lawrence (64).[3] When it came to the series, Eliot aimed at commercial success. As he reportedly explained to Stephen Spender in 1938, "in order to justify the production of a pamphlet a sale of ten thousand copies would have to be guaranteed" (Nourie 64).

The originality and appeal of the pamphlets by Joyce and Lawrence were further accentuated by the fact that they were presented to their prospective readerships through a distinctive medium in the modernist literary marketplace. The pamphlet as a format is worth considering here. As a genre, a pamphlet is expected to provoke debates about current sociopolitical matters and instigate change, especially if we consider that, beginning in the 1880s, the format was widely used by the Fabian Society to disseminate their proposals for political and social improvement. It is through such referential frameworks that, in November 1929, Eliot described the purposes of the Criterion Miscellany series. He invited James Maxton, at the time the leader of the Independent Labour Party, to contribute a pamphlet that would outline the program that a Labour government should carry out. Eliot wrote to Maxton that "the notion of this series [is] to enable men and women in public life to put before the public their ideas on any subject with which they are especially engaged, in a cheap pamphlet which shall be at the same time more permanent, and more conspicuous, than periodical publication. [. . .] [I]t aims only at the rapid circulation of ideas in pamphlet form by persons of importance or of authority on their subjects and views" (Eliot, *Letters* 676). Indeed, a single author's pamphlet of approximately thirty pages that sold for one shilling was a distinctive format of modernist publication. A contribution in a pamphlet was different from that in a journal, in which the work of a writer such as Lawrence or Joyce would be juxtaposed with that of other writers. The latter form conveyed a risk for the authorial imprimatur; the "auratic" signature of Joyce or Lawrence could be overshadowed by that of other contributors. Designed and marketed by Faber and Faber, the pamphlet was undeniably an attractive cultural product.

Their appeal should have been further enhanced by their design and stylistic purposes, since the Criterion Miscellany pamphlets differed aesthetically from the series' parent journal, the *Criterion*. As Ann Ardis notes, the journal reproduced "the 'look' of a grand Victorian monthly review" characterized by "stately columns of black-and-white print unbroken by advertisements" (44n8). The pamphlets, on the other hand, had colorful covers, and some featured distinctive modernist designs and patterns. Lawrence's had mandarin orange wrappers, whereas Breton's *What Is Surrealism?* had turquoise-blue paper ones. As for Joyce's *Anna Livia Plurabelle,* the triangle on the cinnamon-colored cover of the pamphlet was designed by Joyce himself when he first prepared the text for publication in *transition* in 1927, and then again for Crosby Gaige in 1928.[4] The pattern of the triangle was further used for the cover of the Criterion Miscellany pamphlet. For all intents and purposes, the text of *Anna Livia Plurabelle* may have been the same as the one published in the American edition by Gaige; however, the format and its typographical innovations had the mark of Faber and Faber. They paid particular attention to the design of the books. Richard de la Mare, another Faber director who was later involved in the production of *Finnegans Wake*, contributed substantially to "their physical appearance [. . .] the kind of book for which the new firm became eminent. [. . .] [T]here developed a distinctive 'Faber' character" (Morley 65).

The medium of the pamphlet allowed the editors to foreground the style and voice of a singular author as it was captured in the specific historical moment. Such emphasis on the "here and now," even the ephemeral, may be intrinsically related to the historical role of the pamphlet. According to the *Oxford English Dictionary,* a pamphlet is "a short handwritten work or document of several pages fastened together; a handwritten poem, tract, or treatise." A pamphlet also refers to a text that handles political and social matters in a provocative manner, or, as the *OED* states, "a work of a polemical or political nature issued in this form." And Eliot was well aware of this incisive role of the pamphlet to stir public opinion, as his admiration for the Elizabethan pamphleteers testifies. In June 1929, prior to the launch of the Criterion Miscellany in July, Eliot gave a BBC radio talk entitled "The Elizabethan Grub Street" in which he explored the life and work of hack novelists and pamphleteers, including Robert Greene and Thomas Nashe. For Eliot, the significance of their writings lies in the fact that they can shed light on the public debates of sixteenth-century London because they wrote "controversial pamphlets to order, mostly (as was the custom of the time) highly vituperative; political or theological pamphlets— for Church affairs were as popular and as acrimonious then as they are now" (Eliot, "The Elizabethan Grub Street" 853). His fascination with Nashe's "art of vituperation"—a writer who was enmeshed in controversies "attacking or defending" throughout his life—can illuminate Eliot's strategies and qualities as an editor who in some cases acted also as an agent provocateur (Eliot, "The Elizabethan Grub Street" 854). Simultaneously, he was attracted by concurrent practices in the popularization of ideas. Such an influential outlet was C. K. Ogden's To-day and To-morrow series (1923–31). He had recruited scientists and women and men of letters to write on a variety of sociopolitical, scientific, and cultural topics. The promotion of the series as a whole is evident in the publisher's description placed in the final section of most booklets. As we read in Bolton Charles Waller's booklet on the future of Ireland (1928), they were "devoted to the future trend of Civilization, conceived as a whole; while others [dealt] with particular provinces" (Waller, final section 1). This successful project may have been a model for the Criterion Miscellany if we take into consideration that Eliot's endorsement was usually included in one of the final pages of the booklets, where extracts from reviews were listed: "*Nation*: 'We are able to peer into the future by means of that brilliant series [which] will constitute a precious document upon the present time.—*T. S. Eliot*" (Waller, final section 2). This point could well be read as Eliot's own objective for the Criterion Miscellany series. It highlights another facet of his editorial work: that of a key agent who not only impacted on the literary scene of the time but whose decisive choice of contributors established a forum for debate about urgent political and social issues—including censorship of literary works. Through this community of writers and readings, Eliot was actively engaged in what he had termed "a revolution of attitude" (Ayers, *1920s* 110).

Undoubtedly Joyce and Lawrence were already popular in Britain, and through various stratagems, the banned *Lady Chatterley's Lover* and *Ulysses* were widely read and circulated. *Ulysses* even travelled to London in the French Foreign Office bag for the night porter of the Euston Hotel (*Letters III* 206).[5] Harry T. Moore also offers accounts of elaborate systems of circulation of copies of *Lady Chatterley's Lover* in London and Britain; Lawrence's friends would receive copies from Florence and then ship them to those "who had sent paid orders" to [the publisher] Orioli. [. . .] Thus *Lady Chatterley* had a wide and effective distribution in England" (*Intelligent* 469). Despite the prevailing censorship, then, the work of Joyce and Lawrence had appeal and a devoted readership. Their new writings featured prominently in pamphlet format and with unique designs under the imprimatur of Eliot and Faber and Faber, a publishing house that by 1930 had become one of the most pioneering and culturally significant. The success was due to the *ethos* of the book committee, which consistently paid attention to "the intrinsic merits of a manuscript, or displayed more interest if it made any effective contribution to cultural conversation" (Morley 65–66). The distinctive presence of Faber and Faber in London's literary marketplace also attached cultural value to the work of Joyce and Lawrence—and contributed substantially to the furthering of their careers.

Despite such significant dissemination of their texts through this series, a critical discussion about the background of their collaboration with Eliot is limited. For instance, although David Ellis discusses some aspects of *Pornography and Obscenity* in his biography of Lawrence, in general Eliot's agency is underexplored. Possibly this is due to a further critical dichotomy that Leavis set up as he vigorously campaigned "*for* Lawrence's intellectual greatness" (Crick and DiSanto 145) and against Eliot's antipathy to Lawrence. As for Joyce studies, the issue of censorship has informed a long-standing predominant narrative according to which his work was received with uneasiness in England at the time, while the anthologizing and republication in various formats of Joyce's work after *Ulysses* has received little critical attention.

Eliot exploited the historical role of the pamphlet to criticize censorship and promote the work of Lawrence and Joyce, both of whom were seeking a new point of entry into London's publishing industry. Due to the general political climate, Eliot's journal the *Criterion* "frequently valued cultural commentary over literary criticism" (Ayers, "Cournos" 361). In a a series of editorials he wrote for the *Criterion* that appeared under the umbrella title "A Commentary," Eliot condemned policies that promoted censorship. In December 1928, he started his "Commentary" on censorship and Ireland by alerting readers about "rumours of fresh activity in the censorship of books. The Home Secretary has let fall a hint; there has been some correspondence in *The Times*: what is disquieting about this correspondence is that there appear to be persons prepared to defend the institution of the Censorship, which we should have thought patently indefensible" (Eliot 185).

His concerns were not restricted to English versions of censorship; he also referred to the Irish and American contexts. Eliot made reference to "an admirable essay on the proposed Irish censorship" (185–86) written by W. B. Yeats that was published in London's *Spectator* magazine (29 September 1928). Eliot shared his contemporary's concerns: "its enforcement would reduce Ireland to barbarism" (186). Eliot inevitably brought Joyce's case into the discussion, arguing that "censorship has made impossible a critical estimate of Joyce's *Ulysses* for at least a generation; by setting up a false relationship between art and morals it has obstructed the efforts of all those who recognize the true relationship between art and morals" (187–88).[6] Further, he referred to the established censorship in America as reported by another Irish writer, Sean O'Faolain, and drew attention to the emerging problem of censorship on both sides of the Atlantic.[7] In doing so, he acknowledged the contradictory nature of censorship and its effects in the publishing market.

As for the British market, this was affected by the structures that supported Home Secretary Joynson-Hicks, who was one of the most egregious figures of the period's dominant ideological trend toward "a peaceable kingdom" (J. Lawrence, "Forging" 557). He was notorious for his anti-Semitism and controversially reactionary politics, as well as his tactics of suppression during the British General Strike in 1926. By 1928, his activities involved being president of "the North Kensington Conservative and Unionist Association" (*Times* (London), 10 May 1928, 18). Joynson-Hicks had become directly or indirectly involved in a number of events that brought him and the institutions of censorship into confrontation with Lawrence. In January 1929, Lawrence posted from France two copies of the manuscript of *Pansies* "registering them as *papiers d'affaires*" to Curtis Brown in London, but these were confiscated "at the instigation of the Home Secretary" (Moore, *Intelligent* 484). The matter was raised in Parliament by the Labour Party when F. W. Pethick-Lawrence, on behalf of Ellen Wilkinson, MP and author of *Clash* (1929), asked

> whether the Home Secretary would tell who had acted, "before any question of publication arose," to seize Lawrence's manuscript in the post, and: "if he will give the names and official positions of the persons on whose advice he causes books and manuscripts to be seized and banned;

what are the qualifications of such persons for literary censorship; and whether, to assist authors and publishers, he will state what are the rules and regulations, the contravention of which causes a book to be seized and banned by his Department?" (Moore, *Intelligent* 485–86)

These developments had repercussions and affected Lawrence's other projects, specifically the exhibition of his paintings at the Warren Gallery in the summer of 1929. It was closed, despite the recent victory of the Labour Party in the 1929 general election, when the hope for new policies was still prevalent. As Ellis explains:

[O]n 7 June the new Labour cabinet under Ramsay MacDonald had taken control. [. . .] [The organizers of the exhibition of Lawrence's paintings] had no longer anything to fear from the zeal of Joynson-Hicks; but under the Obscene Publications Act of 1857 complaints from members of the public to the Commissioner of Police, as well as articles in the newspapers, would have been sufficient to explain the appearance of two detective inspectors at the Gallery on 5 July. (Ellis 490)

On that day, thirteen of the twenty-five paintings on display were confiscated, and the show ended abruptly. It was precisely this accumulation of political interventions in the cultural field that prompted Eliot to present Lawrence's reflections on art and literature in *Pornography and Obscenity*. It was published as pamphlet No. 5 in the Criterion Miscellany series in November 1929.

Lawrence the Pamphleteer

Lawrence had published an earlier version of the essay "Pornography and Obscenity" in a Parisian magazine, *This Quarter* (July–September 1929 issue) (*7L* 259n2). Yet after Faber's invitation, he revised it for inclusion in the Criterion Miscellany series. When he was first approached, Lawrence was surprised by the invitation. In September 1929, he wrote to Laurence Pollinger expressing his hesitation to write the pamphlet: "I don't know if I'll do the Faber article—what's the good! I'm sick to death of the British Public [*sic*], all publishers, and all magazines—and feel I never want to see a word of mine in public print again. But I'll read the 'Obscenity' article over, and if it interests me in itself I'll lengthen it" (*7L* 467–68). He was reluctant to publish it in England. He feared that its reception would be negative even if it came out by Faber and Faber. As he stated, "I should get about £10.— out of them and a batch more insults" (*7L* 468).

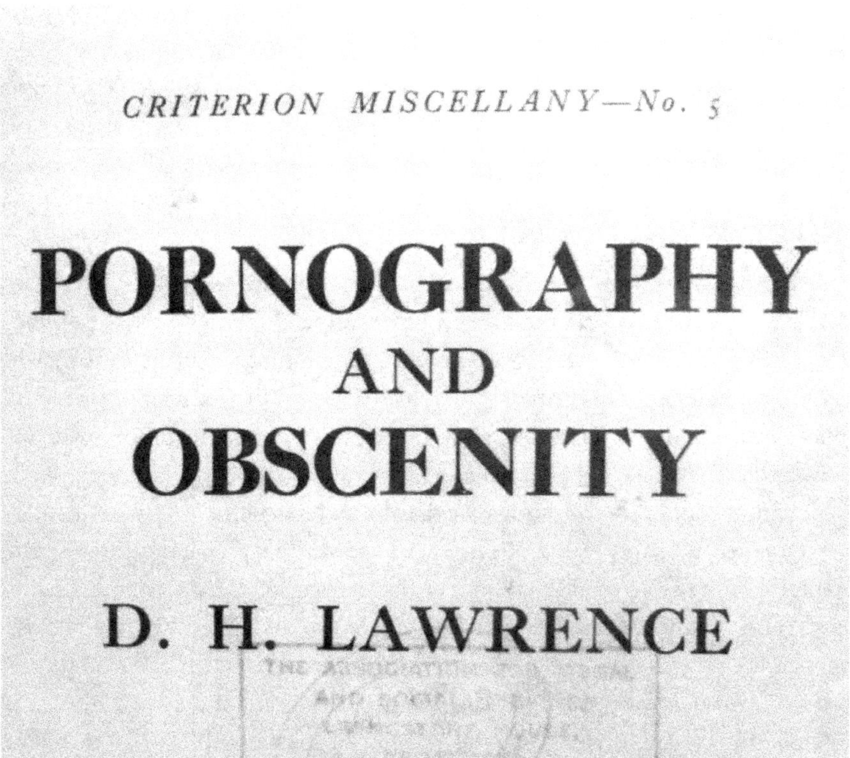

Figure 7.1. D. H. Lawrence's *Pornography and Obscenity*, Criterion Miscellany No. 5 (1929) (copy held at the Archives and Special Collections, LSE Library London). Image use courtesy of Faber and Faber Ltd.

Another reason for his reluctance was that he knew that Brentford (or Jix) also contributed. Lawrence expressed emphatically: "Of course I hate the thought of coming out in a series of Mr Jix" (7L 468). Similarly unpalatable was the realization that another contributor to the Criterion Miscellany series was H. G. Wells, whose pamphlet *Imperialism and the Open Conspiracy* was to be published in November 1929. As Lawrence wrote, "Why should I put pepper in their stale stew!" (7L 468). By comparing his writings to spice that could transform old-fashioned ideas and stylistic approaches to attractive publishing events, Lawrence was making an observation that might also be applied to Joyce's contribution: both writers were functioning as attractions for the potential readerships of the newly established Criterion Miscellany series. This may also explain why Faber had simultaneously commissioned Brentford and Lawrence. They had orchestrated an extraordinary debate in London's public sphere that could promote and advertise the series itself.

Intrigued by Faber's invitation, Lawrence started preparing the essay in September 1929. He wrote to Pollinger that he was "a bit surprised that Faber and Faber risk the obscenity article" (7L 503). By 8 September "he had extended the original article by a further 6,000 words" (Boulton, "Introduction" xxix). Lawrence was aware that he would have to adapt it to the historical specificities and knowledge of the readers of the pamphlets in the series. He starts with the observation that the terms "pornography" and "obscenity" cannot be easily defined: "What they are depends, as usual, entirely on the individual. What is pornography to one man is the laughter of genius to another" (Lawrence, *Pornography and Obscenity* 5). Throughout his polemic account, Lawrence offers examples of authors whose work was considered obscene in their time, focusing extensively on the Elizabethans and on Shakespeare.

Lawrence deals with the prevalent politics of censorship and refers to Brentford's much repeated argument that he only aimed at protecting the public interest. For him, obscenity was a crime committed against the public, as he had argued in his article in the issue of *Nineteenth Century* entitled "'Censorship' of Books." Under the signature "Brentford," it appeared in the August issue of the journal (207–11), and it is "a short preliminary version of his pamphlet *Do We Need a Censor?*" (Ellis 715n23). This article was his response to the April 1929 issue of the *Nineteenth Century*, in which various scientists and writers, including Havelock Ellis, E. M. Forster, and Virginia Woolf, protested against censorship after the ban on Radclyffe Hall's *The Well of Loneliness* (1928). These articles offered the impetus for the home secretary to defend his decision to ban the book. Lawrence had presumably read the article (Pollnitz 58) and responded in his pamphlet:

> Man is a changeable beast, and words change their meanings with him, and things are not what they seemed, and what's what becomes what isn't, and if we think we know where we are it's only because we are so rapidly being translated to somewhere else. We have to leave everything to the majority, everything to the majority, everything to the mob, the mob, the mob. They know what is obscene and what isn't, they do. [...] Mild little words that rhyme with spit or farce are the height of obscenity. [...] Vox populi, vox Dei. [...] At the same time, this vox Dei shouts with praise over moving-pictures and books and newspaper accounts that seem, to a sinful nature like mine, completely disgusting and obscene. Like a real prude and Puritan, I have to look the other way. (Lawrence, *Pornography and Obscenity* 6–7)

Lawrence's attack on the pictures and the daily press echoes Eliot's "Commentary" in the *Criterion* of October 1929. It deals mainly with the former home secretary's article in the *Nineteenth Century,* and it is written in a humorous and subtly sarcastic tone. Its subtitle is "Lord Brentford's Apology" (Eliot 1), and it begins:

> In the *Nineteenth Century* for August is published a very interesting article by the late Conservative Home Secretary over his new name. It confirms the opinion that we have always held; that the late Sir William Joynson-Hicks is a very honest, conscientious, public-spirited and bewildered man. The article is entitled "'Censorship' of Books." As the inverted commas suggest, Lord Brentford reminds us of what we already knew, that there is no "censorship" of books in Britain. (Eliot 1)

Eliot then proceeds to complain that despite his honesty and his well-intentioned policies, Brentford

> does not answer the criticisms, or respond to the proposals, made in THE CRITERION, of which we are sure he has never heard. It is for this reason that we venture to comment on his apology. Lord Brentford's defense of his action in the case of *The Well of Loneliness* is conducted against those opponents whom it is easiest to attack; those who believe that the book is a "work of art." [...] We have held, throughout, the view that the question of whether a work *is* [sic] a "work of art" is a red herring. [...] It is not a question of 'art' but of public liberties. (1–2)

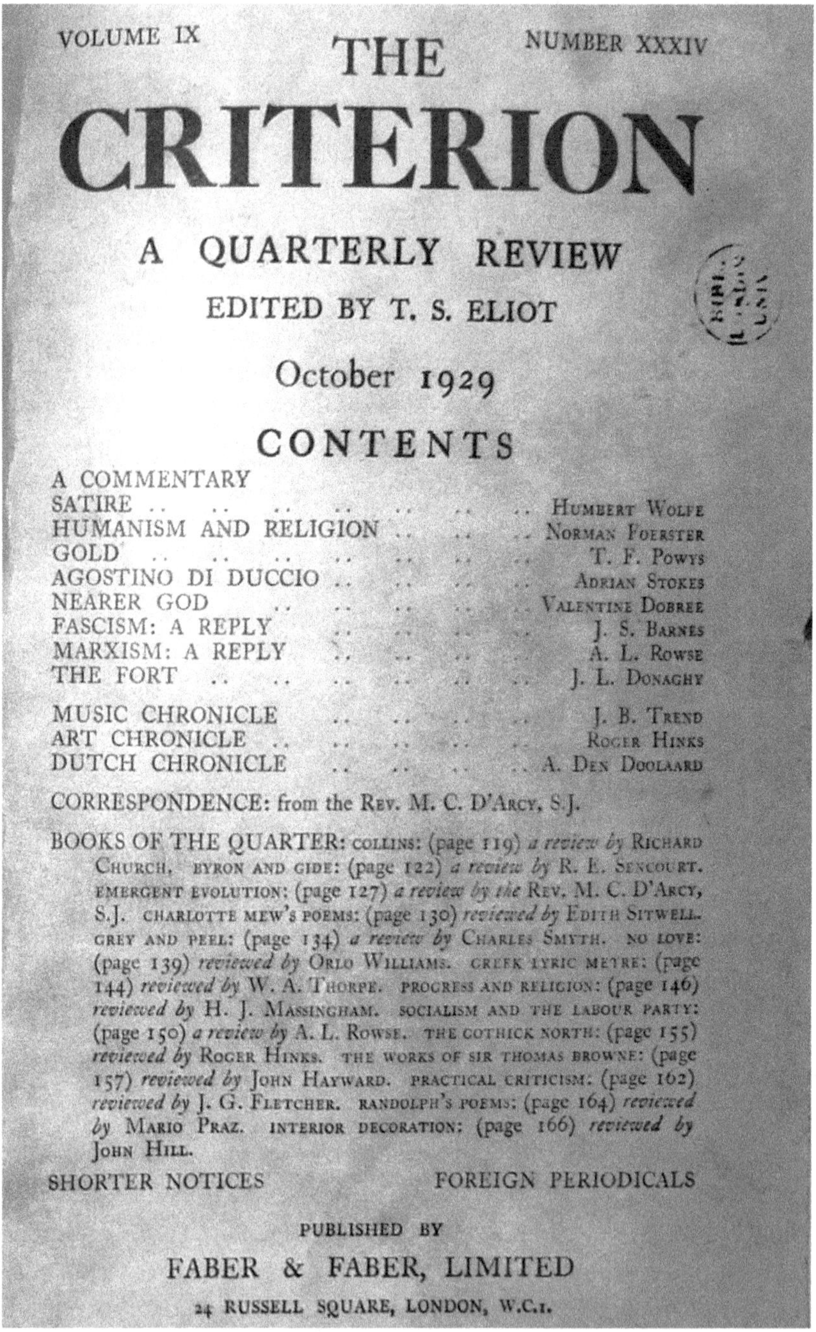

VOLUME IX   NUMBER XXXIV

THE
CRITERION

A QUARTERLY REVIEW

EDITED BY T. S. ELIOT

October 1929

CONTENTS

PUBLISHED BY

FABER & FABER, LIMITED

24 RUSSELL SQUARE, LONDON, W.C.1.

Figure 7.2. The *Criterion,* October 1929. The "Commentary" includes T. S. Eliot's response to Brentford's opinions about censorship. (Copy held at the Senate House Library, University of London.) Image use courtesy of Faber and Faber Ltd.

Here Eliot may press for public liberties, but Brentford had repeatedly argued that his policies protected public decency. Brentford claimed that obscenity was a crime that offended the law-abiding public. However, Eliot argued that this public—as well as politicians—were influenced to a large extent by the daily press. As he notes in the same "Commentary" of October 1929: "But what we should like to be able to gauge, is the extent to which public action is *hustled* [*sic*] by a certain section of the daily press. We have lately seen the daily press, which offers to its readers a small amount of news and an extensive space of bathing beauties, direct its readers to 'obscene' books and 'obscene' picture shows, and then exult in their condemnation. We also see the daily press providing 'policies' for political parties" (Eliot 5). In her discussion of Eliot's views on censorship as expressed in his editorials in the *Criterion*, Rachel Potter argues that Eliot disapproved of the prevalent "complex and wide-ranging structure of censorship" (85) and suggests that "in his references to the 'tyranny of morality' and the 'shouting of the mob,' he combines ideas about the bullying and censorious sensibility of public opinion in order to bring into the open the negative power of those 'public morals' which politicians and lawyers claim need protecting" (89). Although she notes that in 1929 Eliot protested against the confiscation of D. H. Lawrence's paintings and "as a consequence was instrumental in publishing Lawrence's pamphlet *Pornography and Obscenity* in the Criterion Miscellany series" (Potter 85), the concurrence of opinions in Eliot's editorial and Lawrence's pamphlet is underexplored. The political phenomenon of the popular press and the mob acting as literary critics and tastemakers was a key theme both in Lawrence's attack on Joynson-Hicks and in Eliot's "Commentary." In a way, this particular editorial of the *Criterion* could be read as an introduction to Lawrence's pamphlet. Eliot was in conversation with Lawrence's views, first developed in his article in *This Quarterly*, which Eliot had read, and it may be argued that indirectly he was promoting them. Eliot reminded the readers that "Mr. Lawrence is a British subject, one of half a dozen writers whose work commands respect in foreign countries" (4). As for the English soil, the *Criterion* had evidently endorsed Lawrence as the inclusion of his writings in its pages demonstrates: Lawrence's satirical short story "Mother and Daughter" was presented in the April 1929 issue. And throughout the 1920s other short stories and essays were welcomed there (Crick and DiSanto 132). By praising Lawrence in the "Commentary" of October 1929, Eliot was preparing the readership for the publication of Lawrence's pamphlet the following month. Thus it is worthwhile to consider Eliot's commentaries in the *Criterion* from a different perspective: as his response or even contribution to the public argument between Lawrence and Brentford within the context of the Criterion Miscellany series.

⌊Here we see how these pamphlets fulfill their historical role to provoke debate and instigate change of policies.⌋Eliot exploits this legacy and quality of the pamphlet by placing Lawrence and Brentford into oppositional terms. Earlier in February 1929, they were portrayed having a dispute in David Low's cartoon entitled *Jix, the Self-appointed Chucker-out*, which was published in London's *Evening Standard* newspaper. This cartoon featured a group of literary miscreants being thrown out of "The Literary Hyde Park" by Jix, who as home secretary had imposed restrictions on the use of the park so that this public space would not be morally degraded. Low lists the following ejected writers: "(Left to Right) A 'frank' woman novelist, Shakespere [*sic*], Shaw, Wells, Bennett, Aldous Huxley, D. H. Lawrence, James Joyce. Each is accompanied by his literary inspiration. (At back) Dickens and Jane Austen."[8] Lawrence was amused by the cartoon, but he wondered why Low didn't give him "an 'inspiration' along with the rest. Did he think my rage was my inspiring fount, so I didn't get a female?" (*7L* 198). Indeed, his rage against Jix proved to be his inspiration for one of the finest polemics against censorship. As this cartoon was much discussed in London's literary circles, it may have offered the impetus for Eliot to publicize the quarrel about artistic freedom. E. M. Forster later remarked that "it was a happy and indeed a witty thought of the publishers to induce the most remarkable of our novelists and our most notorious Home Secretary to write pamphlets on the subject of indecency" (*7L* 468n3). As Adam Parkes has stressed in his account of the relationship between modernist writers and censorship, "there was clearly a dialogue between censor and censored in the modernist period" (viii). ⌋

Such high-profile debate and even textual interaction between Lawrence and Brentford as contributors to pamphlets was achieved thanks to the editorial astuteness of Eliot. In the autumn of 1929, Lawrence's pamphlet *Pornography and Obscenity* was immediately followed by Brentford's political defense of censorship. Their publication in the Criterion Miscellany series may be viewed as Eliot's way of "rejuvenating the public sphere" (Morrisson 10). Such a debate could have ended a long-standing attack on public and private liberties by politicians who were dictated by the daily press. As Ayers observes, the modernist publishing constellations that emerged after the Great War embarked on a project of reconfiguring the position of writers in the public sphere. They created thus "platforms from which the arts could test their purpose and very possibility" at a time of wider democratization processes when it "seemed that the loudspeaker had replaced the process of dialogue" and by implication had "dealt a death blow to the idea of a 'public sphere'" (Ayers, *1920s* 107). In such a context of profound changes, the Criterion Miscellany series offered fertile ground for a formation of a new community of writers, texts, and readings.

Lawrence's pamphlet became much sought after in literary London. It was published on 14 November 1929 by Faber and Faber, who printed "five thousand copies" (Nourie 65). Within a month, it had sold six thousand copies, "more than any of the others" (*7L* 589), as he reported to Charles Lahr. Lawrence was happy with the sales and impact of *Pornography and Obscenity* in England, and on 9 December he wrote to Orioli that it "made quite a stir—sells 1200 copies a week!" (*7L* 588). These comments reflect Lawrence's enthusiasm about the reception of his pamphlet—a point that evidently contrasts with his earlier reservations and indignation against the British public and various culture's gatekeepers.

Do We Need a Censor?

When Eliot invited the Viscount Brentford to contribute his views on censorship (*7L* 468n3), he might have hoped that Brentford would study his commentaries in the *Criterion* and accordingly respond to them. The result was a pamphlet entitled *Do We Need a Censor?* Readers of Lawrence's dismantling of Brentford's views would have been either amused or upset by reading the opening section of the pamphlet, in which Brentford contended that any accusations about imposed and institutionalized censorship were unfounded.[9] Through the use of overgeneralizations and florid language, he disputes the existence of any such policies and proceeds to reassure the readers that "there is in England no censorship of books" (Brentford 9). He further elaborates that "no man has any more right to publish in this country matter which tends to the destruction of morals than he has to commit any other crime" (Brentford 11). The legal basis for such declarations is the Obscene Publications Act of 1857, which, as Brentford explains, "provides machinery" for handling indecent material (11). He substantiates this claim by contending that "the law in its application to frankly pornographic matter has well served its purpose, and so far as I am aware no complaint was made during my term of office of the steps taken by the departments concerned—The Home Office, Post Office, and Board of Customs—to suppress the traffic" (Brentford 11). This is not quite accurate because the confiscation of the manuscript of *Pansies* was "illegal" (Pollnitz 46), and there had also been complaints by Lawrence and a number of political activists.

Nonetheless, his tone changes when he refers to the conference organized in September 1929 by the World League for Sexual Reform. He notes specific actions and decisions taken at that conference at which Naomi Mitchison, a fervent supporter of Lawrence, contributed her views on contraception, subsequently published in a Criterion Miscellany pamphlet titled *Comments on Birth Control* (1930). Brentford opines: "and after an attack had been made on unenlightened magistrates, a resolution was passed holding that 'obscenity and impropriety are matters too subjective and indefinite to serve as a basis for laws. [. . .] On this ground we declare ourselves against all kinds of censorship on sex subjects on literature, scientific publications, pictures and other representations'" (17–18). The thesis of this organization echoes the view prominent in Lawrence's pamphlet about the difficulty in defining obscenity. To their protestations against the need for censorship, Brentford vehemently responds: "This is a position which I utterly and entirely repudiate" (18). Brentford even declares that his policies were endorsed by church officials of different religious groups and denominations (23). To validate his views, he concludes the pamphlet with a lengthy quotation of almost two pages that includes "some very remarkable words of the Cardinal Archbishop of Westminster, in the address which he gave at the Ninth National Catholic Congress at Westminster on the 13th September, 1929" (Brentford 22). The cardinal contended that "the writers of books, the painters of pictures [. . .] who render self-control more difficult for the average normal man or woman [. . .] are doing moral evil and are committing sin in the sight of God" (Brentford 23). Brentford explains that he identified with such views not because he was "a member of the Cardinal's Church. I am [. . .] a Protestant. But I am quite sure that these words will be concurred in by the heads of my own Church and by the heads of the great Nonconformist Churches" (23). To the proclamations made at the conference of the World League for Sexual Reform, Brentford offers the statements of a Church official (23). In doing so, he aimed to demonstrate the unanimous rejection of immoral literature by religious groups and their endorsement of his policies during the time he was home secretary.

Despite such support, Brentford's views proved unpopular. As Nourie informs us, "Lawrence was elated when his pamphlet sold better than Brentford's" (65). According to Nourie, Lawrence's was one of the most successful pamphlets of the forty-three published in the history of the series (64–65). Only Joyce's *Anna Livia Plurabelle* was more popular. Even though Joyce's texts were difficult, they attracted readers because there had not been an English edition of his work available to audiences since the censorship of *Ulysses*. The publication per se as well as the sales and the impact of their artistic stance had pleased both Joyce and Lawrence. They should have been even more satisfied with Eliot's provocative endorsement when he defended them in his assessment of the 1930 Lambeth Conference (the seventh decennial gathering of bishops of the Anglican Communion, who met in London to discuss doctrinal and other ethical positions).

Eliot's Criterion Miscellany pamphlet *Thoughts after Lambeth* (1931) is a telling example of his strategic campaign for the end of censorship against Joyce and Lawrence. In this pamphlet, which starts with the provocative line, "The Church of England washes its dirty linen in public" (*Lambeth* 5), Eliot begins by examining the *Report* of the conference and focuses on the section entitled "Youth and Its Vocation," which was covered extensively in the popular press. The bishops castigated the younger generation for being influenced by immoral publications, but they failed to name the authors of such material. He stressed that "the only two authors of 'recognised ability and position' officially disapproved in England, are Mr. James Joyce and D. H. Lawrence" (Eliot 8). Thus, Eliot argued, the bishops had "missed an opportunity of disassociating themselves from the condemnation of these two extremely serious and improving writers" (8–9). Eliot's stratagems for the valorization of the work of Lawrence and Joyce were not thus confined to the literary and political fields of London but carefully moved within religious circles as high as the Lambeth Conference. Although the Criterion Miscellany series had already featured an assessment of the conference (*The Lambeth Conference*, No. 24) by George Malcolm Thomson, the London-based Scottish writer and contributor to Ogden's To-day and To-morrow series with his *Caledonia, or the Future of the Scots* (1927), Eliot allowed time to reflect on the long-term implications of the resolutions and defend Lawrence and Joyce, whose major works, *Lady Chatterley's Lover* and *Ulysses*, were still banned.

Joyce the Pamphleteer

Even though there seems to be a distance in the order of their publication—Lawrence's was the fifth and Joyce's the fifteenth in the series—both Joyce and Lawrence were approached by Faber and Faber at around the same time. In fact, the arrangement for the publication of *Anna Livia Plurabelle* was made in July 1929 (*Letters I* 282) while Joyce was on holiday in England. The publication of Joyce's work in the form of the Criterion Miscellany pamphlets is of special interest for a new understanding of the strategic promotion of his work on two fronts: first, as part of his own long-standing ambitions to consolidate his position as a writer within the Anglophone publishing market; and second, in relation to the continuous efforts of Joyce and other key literary figures to overturn the ban on *Ulysses*. These aspirations are best articulated in Joyce's statement after the legal publication of *Ulysses* by Allen Lane in 1936: "I have been fighting for this for twenty years. [. . .] Now the war between England and me is over, and I am the conqueror" (*JJII* 693).

Publication in Eliot's Criterion Miscellany series played a pivotal role in Joyce's conquest of the English marketplace. The promotion of the *Anna Livia Plurabelle* and *Haveth Childers Everywhere* pamphlets by Faber and Faber and Eliot mark a crucial shift in Joyce's transition from author of the scandalous Paris-published *Ulysses* to a central figure within the London literary establishment and publishing market. Eliot's motivation to publish and promote Joyce's new work was in accordance with the interests of Faber and Faber. That Eliot believed in the cultural value of Joyce's work is beyond dispute, and his "championing of Joyce" had been consistently well-meant but conducted on his own terms (Nash 41). Eliot's direct support for publishing and promoting Joyce's earlier work has been much discussed. Criticism has paid particular attention to Eliot's essay "*Ulysses,* Order and Myth" in the *Dial* (1923), still considered one of the most well-known critical assessments of *Ulysses*. Similarly, he endorsed Joyce's experiments in *Work in Progress.* But in his influential position as one of the directors at Faber and Faber in the late 1920s, Eliot promoted more than just the cultural value of Joyce's work. He was also able to determine and promote the market value of *Work in Progress*. As has often been noted, in 1925 Eliot was offered employment at the then Faber and Gwyer because "he had good qualifications for a man of business [. . . and] he was in the firm as a man of business, as one of the inner council, making business decisions. And to the business he displayed a complete loyalty" (Morley 62–63).

Archival research, mainly into Eliot's correspondence with Joyce, in which sales numbers and contract details are mentioned, reveals evidence about the publication background of *Work in Progress*, many aspects of which have remained under-researched or relatively unknown.[10] *Anna Livia Plurabelle* entered the London market in June 1930 as part of Eliot's Criterion Miscellany pamphlets series.[11] Eliot's planning is evident here, especially in his attempt to position Joyce's work among new experiments in forms and styles of writing as well as among interventions in current political and moral issues. Joyce's new work after *Ulysses* was thus published in a series that acquired a reputation among conservative and Puritan supporters through its publication of views on censorship by the former home secretary. What better publicity for Joyce than to be included in such a series and with such a potential readership? Readers of the time who browsed Joyce's *Anna Livia Plurabelle* pamphlet (June 1930, No. 15) would have noticed that in the list of the series, Brentford was included as a contributor of one of the previous pamphlets. Considering that *Ulysses* was still censored and that in 1932 Joyce defined himself as a "banned writer" (Joyce, "From a Banned Writer" 260–61), the mere fact that Joyce's name featured alongside Joynson-Hicks is indicative of the promotional techniques that underpinned Eliot's series. His shift to a more central position within London's publishing market appears prominent after these pamphlets are published following the dialogue between Lawrence and Brentford, and Eliot's commentaries in the *Criterion* and his blurb writing for the Criterion Miscellany (Morley 68).

Upon opening the *Anna Livia Plurabelle* pamphlet, the reader is immediately reminded of the ban on *Ulysses*. The blurb on the inside flap of the front cover (possibly written by Eliot) reads: "Despite the extent of discussion about Mr. Joyce's writings, this is the first time for over twenty years that an English publisher has separately set up a new specimen. Here is an episode, complete in itself, which forms the conclusion of the first section of *Work in Progress.*" Eliot's promotion of Joyce's work in the Criterion Miscellany pamphlets is a manifestation of his consistent interventions into shaping the cultural formations of interwar Britain. Just as he endorsed Lawrence in the "Commentary" of the *Criterion* of October 1929, here Eliot repositioned Joyce in the center of publishing developments in literary London. The championing of Joyce's work by Faber and Faber placed his work within contemporary debates about cultural value that the sociopolitical institutions of censorship contested but indirectly promoted.

The pamphlet, which presents the story of the riverine figure Anna Livia as told by two washerwomen while washing dirty clothes on the banks of the Liffey, proved a successful publication, going to a third impression within a month.[12] Joyce was so motivated to promote the work further that he wrote jingles to advertise *Anna Livia Plurabelle*:

Buy a book in brown paper
From Faber & Faber
To see Annie Liffey trip, tumble and caper.
Sevensinns in her singthings,
Plurabelle on her prose,
Seashell ebb music wayriver she flows. (*JJII* 616–17fn)

CRITERION MISCELLANY—No. 15

ANNA LIVIA PLURABELLE

JAMES JOYCE

ONE SHILLING NET

FABER & FABER

Figure 7.3. The cover of the first edition of James Joyce's *Anna Livia Plurabelle*, 1930 (copy held at the Special Collections, University of Kent, Canterbury). Image use courtesy of Faber and Faber Ltd.

As for the pamphlet *Haveth Childers Everywhere*, which depicts the achievements of HCE, husband of Anna Livia, as a builder of cities and conqueror of her love, Joyce sent to the publicity department of Faber and Faber the following jingle:

> Humptydump Dublin squeaks through his norse,
> Humptydump Dublin hath a horrible vorse
> And with all his kinks english
> Plus his irismanx brogues
> Humptydump Dublin's grandada of all rogues. (*JJII* 617fn)

While Anna Livia is presented as a highly immoral figure, "sevensinns in her singthings," that is, seven sins in her sin things, HCE is depicted as the Irish version of the Humpty Dumpty character of the nursery rhyme but with a twist: he is an arch-rogue. To represent such an amalgamation, the pamphlet *Haveth Childers Everywhere* relies on two linguistic strands: it draws on the "kinks English"—or grammatically precise English language as presented in the book *The King's English* (1906) by the linguists and translators Henry Watson Fowler and Francis George Fowler—and on "irismanx brogues," that is, Irish and other Gaelic-Norse ("norse") traditions including the Manx language and culture of the Isle of Man. By characterizing HCE as "Humptydump Dublin's grandada of all rogues," the jingle foregrounds issues of cultural inheritance and value and stresses Joyce's efforts to renew English language and literature in these Criterion Miscellany pamphlets and subsequently in *Finnegans Wake*. By presenting HCE and Anna Livia, the main figures in the two pamphlets, in such way, Joyce questions assumptions around moral and linguistic indecency. He transforms the title of the book *The King's English* to "kinks English," and he invites the reader to make connections between the idiosyncratic elements that characterize his elaborate syntactically sentences, marked by portmanteau words and by a lack of "linguistic morality" (Gibson 235) that the Fowlers, and by extension Brentford as the exemplification of Puritan England, prescribed. In this way he contributes to the dialogue about censorship and cultural production inaugurated by Eliot and Lawrence.

According to Richard Ellmann, the publicity department of Faber and Faber used the jingles only "on a mimeographed publicity release," and presented them as explanatory notes for the pamphlets. Joyce was displeased because he was adamant that the verses would contribute to an increase in the sales of the pamphlets (*JJII* 617). He possibly hoped that the jingles would bring considerable income wherever the pamphlets circulated, as the last line of his verse for

Anna Livia Plurabelle indicates: "Seashell ebb music wayriver she flows." The structure of this line might evoke Stephen Dedalus' perception of the seascape in the "Proteus" episode of *Ulysses*. It is represented through metaphors, compound words, and onomatopoeia: "seaspawn and seawrack, the nearing tide [. . .] his boots crush crackling wrack and shells [. . .] Crush, crack, crick, crick. Wild sea money. Dominie Deasy kens them a'" (*U* 3.2–20.). As Stephen hears the crushing sound of the shells—"wild sea money" (Gifford 46)—he recalls the advice regarding economising that Mr Deasy had given him earlier in the "Nestor" episode (*U* 2.237–39). While Deasy prided himself in knowing what money is, Stephen was reflecting on the symbolic power and beauty value of some "whelks and money cowries and leopard shells" (*U* 2.213–14). Indeed, shells and especially money cowries were often used as currency in the past (Washington-Weik 117). And Joyce's portmanteau words in the final line of his jingle for *Anna Livia Plurabelle* might express his aspirations that the sales of his Criterion Miscellany pamphlets in London's marketplace would result in money flowing into Faber and Faber and eventually into his bank account.

In his letters to Joyce, Eliot frequently mentioned how satisfied Faber and Faber was with the sales of the pamphlet. In one of these letters, Eliot enthusiastically expressed the view that the *Anna Livia Plurabelle* pamphlet would be selling well indefinitely and would serve as an invaluable advertisement for *Finnegans Wake*.[13] In another letter, Eliot also noted that the publication of the *Haveth Childers Everywhere* pamphlet, initially planned for December 1930, was well subscribed in advance by booksellers, an indication that the general reading public was interested in Joyce's London-published work.[14] Eliot's endorsement of Joyce's work was always backed up by sales and demand. By 16 December 1931, Faber and Faber had sold 6,100 copies of *Anna Livia Plurabelle* and 3,532 copies of *Haveth Childers Everywhere*, while by mid-February 1932, Eliot reported that the sales of the two pamphlets had reached 6,546 and 3,655 copies, respectively.[15]

"Creeping into Immortality"

Although *Finnegans Wake* is still considered Joyce's most difficult and impenetrable text, the success of the *Anna Livia Plurabelle* and *Haveth Childers Everywhere* pamphlets, published in Eliot's series, dispels retrospective assumptions that Joyce was rejected or ignored in Britain due to the censorship of *Ulysses* and that Joyce was not interested in pursuing contacts with the British literary establishment (and vice versa). In July 1931, Eliot wrote to Joyce outlining the highly advantageous terms of the contract for *Finnegans Wake*, which Faber and Faber was eager to publish.[16] The contract, and Faber's involvement in a campaign to lift the ban on *Ulysses,* led to the book's legal publication in England in 1936 by Allen Lane. When *Finnegans Wake* was being prepared for publication, the designers of Faber and Faber worked further on the shape of the beginning of the most famous and beloved section of *Anna Livia Plurabelle.* Although the first version of the delta on a smaller scale, only using the first two lines, appeared in the 1928 American publication, the impressive typographic opening of *Anna Livia Plurabelle,* employed also subsequently in the relevant section of *Finnegans Wake,* the "triangular block of text," was finalized by Faber and Faber (McCarthy 174).

O

tell me all about

Anna Livia! I want to hear all

about Anna Livia. Well, you know Anna Livia? Yes,

of course, we all know Anna Livia. Tell me all. Tell

me now. You'll die when you hear. Well, you know,

(Joyce, *Anna Livia Plurabelle*, fourth impression 5)

As for Lawrence, the impact of his involvement with Eliot's publishing venture the Criterion Miscellany was also remarkable. According to Harry T. Moore, "it was perhaps the popular success of this pamphlet [*Pornography and Obscenity*] that encouraged Lawrence to expand his 'Jolly Roger' introduction to the Paris *Lady Chatterley* by five times its original length. The result, *À Propos of Lady Chatterley's Lover,* which the Mandrake Press published in June 1930, was the finest of all his pronouncements on the subject of sex, literature, and censorship" (Moore, *Intelligent* 511). The Criterion Miscellany series also published *Nettles: Satirical Poems by D. H. Lawrence.* The poems were prepared in November 1929 in the aftermath of the confiscation of the manuscript of *Pansies* and the suppression of the exhibition of his paintings at the Warren Gallery. This collection of ruthlessly comic and sometimes even bitter poems covered political and social matters, such as press censorship, elections, change of government, and the new political rhetoric of the 1920s that emerged in the House of Commons through the presence of the Clydesiders, a group "of the Labour Party and Independent Labour Party [including James Maxton] which was associated with Glasgow and the neighbouring industrial area" (*OED*). In his poem "Clydesider" (11–12), Lawrence offers an allegorical snapshot of the political debates of the time. In the poems that open the volume, authority figures and exponents of divergent political views (from the conservatives to the communists) are represented as aunties and are criticized: "each comes in for her fair share of censure" (Jones, "Nettling"). And this spirit evokes again Eliot's scathing attacks on the varied manifestations of censorship and on the ways politicians handled them. According to Nourie, *Nettles* "was published in an edition of three thousand copies" (65), indicating the publisher's belief in the impact that Lawrence's poems would have. The success of Lawrence's contributions led Faber and Faber to produce a new edition of his writings in one volume in 1936. That volume featured the essay on pornography and *Nettles*, but also included Lawrence's essay "Introduction to Painting," which in some parts alludes to the closing of his exhibition at the Warren Gallery in 1929.[17]

Despite the prevalent censorship and conservatism, the work of Lawrence and Joyce was culturally validated and disseminated thanks to the agency of Eliot at Faber and Faber. They featured prominently as members of a group of pamphleteers whose work and views constituted significant contributions to public debates about literature and artistic freedom. Contrary to the forceful role of censorship in England to restrict their presence in the literary marketplace, their work was successful in London and beyond and sold well. The Criterion Miscellany pamphlets created a much-needed forum for the two "banned" authors by putting them into textual conversations both with each other and with other influential figures. In this process, the Criterion Miscellany series played the role of springboard for both of them to "creep to immortality" together.

Notes

1. See F. R. Leavis, *The Great Tradition* 37–39.

2. From "About the Modernist Studies Association" at its website, http://msa.press.jhu.edu/about/index.html.

3. As Nourie further elaborates, "Eliot knew that the success of Lawrence's and Joyce's publications when compared with the other titles in the series was not due to any pamphleteering strengths but to the literary reputations of their authors and the fact that they were first editions of previously unpublished works" (65).

4. See VI.J.8 (see also VI.B.9): "Work in Progress"/*Finnegans Wake* Miscellaneous Manuscripts: "Anna Livia Plurabelle" Design (probably 1928); information listed at the website of the The Poetry Collection, University at Buffalo, http://library.buffalo.edu/pl/collections/jamesjoyce/catalog/vij8.htm, accessed 14 February 2013.

5. It is worth recalling that the confiscation at Croydon Aerodrome of a copy of

the Egoist Press edition of *Ulysses* sent by air from Paris in December 1922 effected the ban of the book from London. Then all ports were on alert, and "when the Egoist consignment sailed into Folkestone, it sailed into the arms of the law" (Lidderdale and Nicholson 216). Selling *Ulysses* was forbidden and so, too, was using the postal system to send such a book. After the ban, British readers had to order their copies of *Ulysses* from Paris. By May 1931, the safest way to evade surveillance was through air mail order. As Joyce wrote from London, "there is less surveillance by air" (Banta and Silverman 170).

6. The structures of censorship that prevented *Ulysses* from being widely circulated through London's publishing industry, the largest in the world, should be examined in relation to the conservative politics of the period, which led to the censorship of numerous other contemporary authors. In 1920s Britain, the prevailing conservative cultural politics were aiming to counteract emerging contemporary currents of post-war resentment, sociopolitical upheaval, and reactive hedonism.

7. Drawing on Sean O'Faolain's accounts of censorship in Boston, Eliot observed how profitable censorship can be for the publishing industry: "the censoring of a book by Boston stimulates its sales in other parts of the country. And this is one of the most pernicious effects of a censorship. It lowers taste in literature. A good book, a conscientious work of art may become popular for the wrong reason" (*Letters* 187).

8. The cartoon can be viewed at the website of the British Cartoon Archive Centre at the University of Kent, www.cartoons.ac.uk/browse/cartoon_item/anytext=chucker-out?page=2.

9. To get a sense of the prevalent tone, a few lines from the beginning are worth quoting:

[T]he institution, towards the end of my term of office as Home Secretary, of legal proceedings in respect of two books provoked a storm of comment—both well and ill informed—on the supposed literary censorship in this country, and I was attacked, at times in far from moderate language, for trying to "establish a dictatorship in the realm of literature and morals" and for imposing a "ban" on works in which authors and others of distinction in the world of letters had found considerable literary merit. (Brentford 5)

10. The details mentioned in this essay are the results of archival research that was made possible thanks to the 2007 Christine Bolt Scholarship, University of Kent.

11. This is the first publication of the "ALP" extract in Britain. It was first published in the Parisian magazine *Le Navire d'Argent* in 1925. In November 1927, it was republished in *transition* 8. Crosby Gaige published a deluxe edition of the section in New York in 1928.

12. Eliot to Ogden, 30 June 1930, partly quoted in number 316 of *Christie's Catalogue of Sales*, 204.

13. Eliot to Joyce, 29 October 1930, The Poetry Collection, University at Buffalo Library.

14. Eliot to Joyce, 11 December 1930, The Poetry Collection, University at Buffalo Library.

15. Eliot to Joyce, 16 December 1931, The Poetry Collection, University at Buffalo Library; Eliot to Joyce, 17 February 1932, The Poetry Collection, University at Buffalo Library. By 11 June 1948, the *ALP* pamphlet had sold 10,166 copies and the *HCE*, 5,590 (Slocum and Cahoon 46, 54).

16. Eliot to Joyce, 6 July 1931, The Poetry Collection, University at Buffalo Library.

17. See D. H. Lawrence, *Pornography and So On*, the Faber Library No. 34, containing "Pornography and Obscenity," "Introduction to Painting," and *Nettles*.

Works Cited

Ardis, Ann. "Magazine Dialogism." *Transatlantic Print Culture, 1880–1940: Emerging Media, Emerging Modernisms*. Ed. Ann L. Ardis and Patrick Collier. New York: Palgrave Macmillan, 2008. 30–47.

Ayers, David. *English Literature of the 1920s*. Edinburgh: Edinburgh UP, 1999.

———. "John Cournos and the Politics of Russian Literature in *The Criterion*." *Modernism/modernity* 18.2 (April 2011): 355–69.

Banta, Melissa, and Oscar A. Silverman, eds. *James Joyce's Letters to Sylvia Beach, 1921–1940*. Bloomington: Indiana UP, 1987.

Boulton, James T. "Introduction. Lawrence: Journalist and Essayist." *D. H. Lawrence: Late Essays and Articles*. Ed. James T. Boulton. Cambridge: Cambridge UP, 2004. xix–xxxvii.

Brentford, Viscount (Sir William Joynson-Hicks). "'Censorship' of Books." *The Nineteenth Century and After* 106 (August 1979): 207–11.

———. *Do We Need a Censor?* Criterion Miscellany No. 6. London: Faber and Faber, 1929.

British Library. "In a Bloomsbury Square: T. S. Eliot the Publisher." Accessed 4 February 2013. http://pressandpolicy.bl.uk/Press-Releases/-In-a-Bloomsbury-Square-T-S-Eliot-the-Publisher-2de.aspx.

Christie's Catalogue of Sales. Printed Books and Manuscripts including Modern Literature and Science. New York: Christie, Manson, and Woods, 20 May 1988.

Crick, Brian, and Michael DiSanto. "D. H. Lawrence, 'An Opportunity and a Test': The Leavis–Eliot Controversy Revisited." *Cambridge Quarterly* 38.2 (2009): 130–46.

Eliot, T. S. "A Commentary." *Criterion: A Quarterly Review* 8.31 (December 1928): 185–90.

———. "A Commentary." *Criterion: A Quarterly Review* 9.34 (October 1929): 1–6.

———. "The Elizabethan Grub Street." *Listener* 1.23 (19 June 1929): 853–54.

———. *The Letters of T. S. Eliot: 1928–1929*. Ed. Valerie Eliot and John Haffenden. London: Faber and Faber, 2013.

———. *Thoughts after Lambeth*. Criterion Miscellany No. 30. London: Faber and Faber, 1931.

Ellis, David. *D. H. Lawrence: Dying Game 1922–1930.* Vol. 3 of *The Cambridge Biography of D. H. Lawrence.* Cambridge: Cambridge UP, 1998.

Gibson, Andrew. "Joyce through the Fowlers: 'Eumaeus,' *The King's English* and *Modern English Usage.*" *Joycean Unions: Post-Millennial Essays from East to West.* Ed. R. Brandon Kershner and Tekla Mecsnóber. Rodopi: Amsterdam; New York, 2013. 225–244.

Gifford, Don, with Robert J. Seidman. *Ulysses Annotated. Notes for James Joyce's Ulysses.* 2nd ed., revised and enlarged by Don Gifford. Berkeley: University of California Press, 1989.

Harding, Jason. *The* Criterion: *Cultural Politics and Periodical Networks in Inter-War Britain.* Oxford: Oxford UP, 2002.

Jaffe, Aaron. *Modernism and the Culture of Celebrity.* Cambridge: Cambridge UP, 2005.

Jones, Bethan. "Nettling Authority: Lawrence's Reaction to Censorship in His Late Poetry." *Études Lawrenciennes* 41 (2010): 9–26. http://lawrence.revues.org/139. Accessed 18 May 2014.

Joyce, James. *Anna Livia Plurabelle: Fragment of* Work in Progress. Criterion Miscellany No. 15. London: Faber and Faber, 1930. Fourth impression, 1932.

———. "From a Banned Writer to a Banned Singer." *New Statesman and Nation* (London) 3.53 (27 February 1932): 260–61.

———. *Haveth Childers Everywhere.* Criterion Miscellany No. 26. London: Faber and Faber 1931.

Latham, Sean. *"Am I a Snob?" Modernism and the Novel.* Ithaca, NY: Cornell UP, 2003.

Lawrence, D. H. "Mother and Daughter." *Criterion* 8.32 (1929): 394–419.

———. *Pornography and Obscenity.* Criterion Miscellany No. 5. London: Faber and Faber, 1929.

———. *Pornography and So On.* Faber Library No. 34. London: Faber and Faber, 1936.

Lawrence, Jon. "Forging a Peaceable Kingdom: War, Violence, and Fear of Brutalization in Post–First World War Britain." *Journal of Modern History* 75.3 (September 2003): 557–89.

Leavis, F. R. *The Great Tradition: George Eliot, Henry James, Joseph Conrad.* Harmondsworth, UK: Penguin, 1972.

Lidderdale, Jane, and Mary Nicholson. *Dear Miss Weaver: Harriet Shaw Weaver 1876–1961.* London: Faber and Faber, 1970.

Low, David. "Jix, The Self-appointed Chucker-out." British Cartoon Archive Centre, University of Kent. Accessed 13 February 2013. www.cartoons.ac.uk/browse/cartoon_item/anytext=chucker-out?page=2.

McCarthy, Patrick. "Making Herself Tidal: Chapter I.8." *How Joyce Wrote Finnegans Wake: A Chapter-by-Chapter Genetic Guide.* Ed. Luca Crispi and Sam Slote. Madison: U of Wisconsin P, 2007. 163–80.

Moore, Harry T. *The Intelligent Heart: The Story of D. H. Lawrence.* Harmondsworth, UK: Penguin, 1960.

Morley, F. V. "T. S. Eliot as a Publisher." *T. S. Eliot: A Symposium*. Ed. Richard March and Tambimuttu. London: Editions Poetry London, 1948. 60–70.

Morrisson, Mark. *The Public Face of Modernism: Little Magazines, Audiences, and Reception, 1905–1920*. Madison: U of Wisconsin P, 2001.

Nash, John. "Genre, Place and Value: Joyce's Reception, 1904–1941." *James Joyce in Context*. Ed. John McCourt. Cambridge: Cambridge UP, 2009. 41–51.

Nourie, Alan R. "The *Criterion Miscellany*: A Lost Series." *Serials Librarian* 12.3/4 (1987): 61–68.

O'Faolain, Sean. "Censorship in America." *Irish Statesman* 6 October 1928.

Parkes, Adam. *Modernism and the Theater of Censorship*. Oxford: Oxford UP, 1996.

Pollnitz, Christopher. "The Censorship and Transmission of D. H. Lawrence's *Pansies*: The Home Office and the 'Foul-Mouthed Fellow.'" *Journal of Modern Literature* 28.3 (Spring 2005): 44–71.

Potter, Rachel. "Censorship." *T. S. Eliot in Context*. Ed. Jason Harding. Cambridge: Cambridge UP, 2011. 83–92.

Saunders, Max, and Brian Hurwitz. "The To-day and To-morrow Series and the Popularization of Science: An Introduction." *Interdisciplinary Science Reviews* 34.1 (March 2009): 3–8.

Slocum, John J., and Herbert Cahoon. *A Bibliography of James Joyce, 1882–1941*. London: Rupert Hart-Davis, 1953.

Spiers, John. "Introduction: Wondering about 'the Causes of Causes': The Publisher's Series, Its Cultural Work and Meanings." *The Culture of the Publisher's Series: Publishers and the Shaping of Taste*. Ed. John Spiers. London: Palgrave Macmillan, 2011. 1–61.

Waller, Bolton Charles. *Hibernia: Or, The Future of Ireland*. London: Kegan Paul, 1928.

Washington-Weik, Natalie. "Cowry Shells (Cowries)." *Encyclopedia of the Middle Passage*. Ed. Toyin Falola and Amanda Warnock. Westport, Conn.: Greenwood, 2007. 117–18.

Yeats, W. B. "The Irish Censorship." *The Spectator* (29 September 1928).

The Real can be experienced only as traumatic gaps in the symbolic order

8

An Encounter with the Real

A Lacanian Motif in Joyce's "The Dead" and Lawrence's "The Shadow in the Rose Garden"

HIDENAGA ARAI

In *After Strange Gods*, T. S. Eliot compares "The Shadow in the Rose Garden" (1914) and "The Dead" (1914), considering Lawrence, who wrote the former, to be "an almost perfect example of the heretic" while appreciating Joyce, who wrote the latter, as "the most ethically orthodox" of the eminent writers of his time (38).[1] In spite of Eliot's polarizing view of the two modernist writers, and the various differences that actually do exist between "The Dead" and "The Shadow in the Rose Garden," there seems to be a fundamental affinity between the works.[2] Eliot construes the common theme of the two short stories to be "disillusion": "a husband is disillusioned about his relations with his wife" (35). It is ironic that Eliot refers to this similarity, for this "disillusion" could refer, in both stories, to the husband's awakening from a fantasy not only to discover the hidden past of his wife but also, more radically, to recognize the actuality of an uncanny world that lies beneath the surface. By uncanny world, I refer to what Jacques Lacan terms "the Real." From the Lacanian viewpoint, what we usually see as reality is no more than a fantasy that can undergo a fundamental transformation when we encounter the Real.[3] The purpose of the present essay is to identify common ground between the two allegedly contrasting writers, James Joyce and D. H. Lawrence, by investigating "The Dead" and "The Shadow in the Rose Garden" in terms of concepts introduced by Lacan and Slavoj Žižek, particularly the idea of the Real. I intend this comparative discussion to contribute not only to the study of Joyce and Lawrence but also to modernism in general.

IT WOULD BE ADVISABLE to begin by examining Eliot's contention in greater detail. He states that "cruelty" characterizes scenes in "The Shadow in the Rose Garden," such as when the wife sees her former lover again by chance and then reveals the reunion to her husband: "The disclosure is made with something nearly approaching conscious cruelty. There is cruelty, too, in the circumstances in which she had met her former lover: 'And I saw him to-day,' she said. 'He is not dead, he's mad.' Her husband looked at her, startled. 'Mad!' he said involuntarily. 'A lunatic,' she said" (Eliot 36). What Eliot calls cruelty in Lawrence's short story is generalizable to his fiction at large and related to his characters' lack of morality or sociality: "What I wish chiefly to notice at this point, is what strikes me in all of the relations of Lawrence's men and women: the absence of any moral or social sense. [. . .] [T]he characters themselves, who are supposed to be recognizably human beings, betray no respect for, or even awareness of, moral obligations, and seem to be unfurnished with even the most commonplace kind of conscience" (36–37).

On the other hand, Eliot quotes a passage from the ending of "The Dead" that describes Gabriel's reaction after he learns that his wife, Gretta, had a lover in Galway who died young, saying he highly values Joyce's "orthodoxy of sensibility" and "sense of tradition" (38):

> the husband realises that what this boy had given her was something finer than anything he had to give. And as the wife falls asleep at last:
> Generous tears filled Gabriel's eyes. He had never felt like that himself towards any woman, but he knew that such a feeling must be love. The tears gathered more thickly in his eyes and in the partial darkness he imagined he saw the form of a young man standing under a dripping tree. Other forms were near. His soul had approached that region where dwell the vast hosts of the dead. (Eliot 37)

IT IS TRUE THAT, on the surface, the ending of Joyce's story contrasts sharply with that of Lawrence's; while quietude is dominant in "The Dead," as the wife and then the husband fall asleep, the last conversation of the couple in "The Shadow in the Rose Garden" seems filled with irritation and anger, or what Eliot terms cruelty. Moreover, "The Dead" ends slowly, as Gabriel becomes unconscious, while "The Shadow in the Rose Garden" ends abruptly when Frank leaves his wife and goes out. All this may testify to the incommensurable difference between the two modernist works.

However, the nature of Gabriel's unfamiliar "feeling" described in the quotation above should be scrutinized because it has some affinity with Frank's and his wife's feelings at the end of Lawrence's story. Their feelings relate to the disillusion Eliot mentions; however, the analogy goes wider and deeper than one may initially assume. It is noteworthy that, even if Gabriel thinks that "such a feeling must be love," this love can be seen as an outgrowth of disillusion. This is further affirmed if we read the preceding paragraph, in which Gabriel thinks about himself and his wife, who has fallen fast asleep after disclosing the existence of her past boyfriend: "So she had had that romance in her life: a man had died for her sake. It hardly pained him now to think how poor a part he, her husband, had played in her life. He watched her while she slept as though he and she had never lived together as man and wife. [. . .] [A]s he thought of what she must have been then, in that time of her first girlish beauty, a strange friendly pity for her entered his soul" (D 222). The phrase "as though he and she had never lived together as man and wife" is particularly significant because it suggests the possibility that he is no longer constrained by the marital bond. In fact, "a strange friendly pity" is a rather peculiar feeling for a husband to have toward his wife. Since this "friendly pity" is described as "strange," it is most probable that he has never felt like this before. In other words, this pity closely relates or is extremely similar to the "love" Gabriel feels for the first time; although he romanticizes pity as love, it may well be the kind of feeling that not a husband but a friend or literal stranger would have. An hour earlier, Gabriel had experienced a "riot of emotions" (D 222) toward Gretta, but there is now some distance or a breach between the two. In fact, Gabriel's "love," which cannot be ordinary conjugal love, appears tantamount to the feeling that Frank and his wife experience in Lawrence's story.

In order to confirm this equivalence, it is necessary to inspect the concluding passage of "The Shadow in the Rose Garden," including the following portion quoted by Eliot:

> He stood with expressionless, almost childlike set face, revolving many thoughts, whilst his heart was mad with anguish.
> Suddenly she added:
> "And I saw him to-day," she said. "He is not dead, he's mad."
> Her husband looked at her, startled.
> "Mad!" he said involuntarily.
> "A lunatic," she said. It almost cost her her reason to utter the word.
> There was a pause.
> "Did he know you?" asked the husband, in a small voice.
> "No," she said.

He stood and looked at her. At last he had learned the width of the breach between them. She still squatted on the bed. He could not go near her. It would be violation to each of them to be brought into contact with the other. The thing must work itself out. They were both shocked so much, they were impersonal, and no longer hated each other. After some minutes he left her and went out. (*PO* 132)

Frank, like Gabriel, suffers from envy, anger, and hatred at first, but eventually, having "learned the width of the breach between them," he reaches a state of impersonality that is devoid of human feelings such as hatred: "They were both shocked so much, they were impersonal, and no longer hated each other." To be sure, Frank does not shed any generous tears. Yet it seems certain that, for Frank, as for Gabriel, his wife has suddenly become, as it were, a stranger to him. And, in spite of Eliot's argument, the disappearance of feelings like hatred in Frank and his wife strongly resembles the concomitant disappearance of "cruelty" from "The Shadow in the Rose Garden."

Moreover, Frank and his wife become impersonal in a way that corresponds to Gabriel's loss of identity, which Joyce depicts immediately after describing the generous tears that Eliot cites: "His soul had approached that region where dwell the vast hosts of the dead. He was conscious of, but could not apprehend, their wayward and flickering existence. His own identity was fading out into a grey impalpable world: the solid world itself which these dead had one time reared and lived in was dissolving and dwindling" (*D* 223). Not only the "fading out" of Gabriel's identity but also the "dissolving and dwindling" of "the solid world" are narrated here. In Lawrence's story, after the couple has become "impersonal," they must face some radical transformation of the familiar world as well. It is safe to presume that the change in the subject's personality or identity in each story is accompanied by a change in the world or objects therein.

Whether intentional or not, Eliot's differentiation between Joyce and Lawrence disregards the moment of transfiguration that occurs at the end of each story. If we examine the passages ignored or neglected by Eliot, congruence rather than dissonance between "The Dead" and "The Shadow in the Rose Garden" becomes evident, thereby destabilizing Eliot's claim regarding the heretic or the orthodox.

WHAT BRINGS ABOUT the compelling change, not only of the subject but also of the object, in the first place? Is it the impersonalization or the disintegration of identity? This phenomenon is too profound to be understood as disillusion. In order to navigate this problem, some concepts proposed by Jacques Lacan and Slavoj Žižek will provide a useful perspective that can help us grasp the changes or transformations experienced by the male protagonists of both "The Dead" and "The Shadow in the Rose Garden."

To begin with, Lacan's analysis of Freud's dream of Irma's injection is examined because a parallel exists between Freud and Gabriel and Frank. Lacan distinguishes two parts of Freud's dream. In the first part, Freud sees into the mouth of Irma, his patient, and finds there "the primitive object," or "the image of death in which everything comes to its end." Irma's mouth reveals nothing but "that which is least penetrable in the real, of the real lacking any possible mediation, of the ultimate real, of the essential object which isn't an object any longer, but this something faced with which all words cease and all categories fail, the object of anxiety *par excellence*" (Lacan, *Seminar* 164).

In the second part, Freud becomes frightened and escapes, calling upon "the congress of all those who know." Then, after the cause of Irma's disorder turns out to be an injection given to her by his friend Otto, the formula for trimethylamine appears to Freud. According to Lacan, in the transition from the first part to the second part of the dream, Freud "becomes something totally different, there's no Freud any longer, there is no longer anyone who can say *I*" (Lacan, *Seminar* 159, 164).

This transformation of the subject caused by the encounter with the Real can be said to have happened to both Gabriel and Frank. It is when they become upset after discovering their wives' past romances that they glimpse the Real. Gabriel finds out that "distant music" or the song "The Lass of Aughrim" has preoccupied his wife since she first heard it immediately after the end of Misses Morkan's annual dance and that the song is linked to her memories of a deceased boy named Michael Furey, who used to sing it. Pretending to be indifferent, Gabriel ironically asks her about the boy and then feels drawn to the world of death: "Gabriel felt humiliated by the failure of his irony and by the evocation of this figure from the dead, a boy in the gasworks" (*D* 219). Still, "this figure from the dead" cannot be equated with what Lacan calls "the object of anxiety *par excellence*" because Gabriel feels "humiliated" rather than anxious.

It is when Gabriel asks about the cause of Michael's death that he irrevocably confronts the Real:

—And what did he die of so young, Gretta? Consumption, was it?
—I think he died for me, she answered.

A vague terror seized Gabriel at this answer as if, at that hour when he had hoped to triumph, some impalpable and vindictive being was coming against him, gathering forces against him in its vague world. (*D* 220)

The description "some impalpable and vindictive being" in "its vague world" corresponds to the Real. Enduring this terror "with an effort of reason," Gabriel listens to how Michael died. Then, after his wife goes to sleep, he lies down beside her and thinks about how death is inevitable for each one of us. This might suggest that Gabriel has accepted "the image of death in which everything comes to its end" (Lacan, *Seminar* 164).

Soon afterwards, the feeling of terror begins to release its hold over Gabriel, who is going to shed "[g]enerous tears":

One by one they were all becoming shades. Better pass boldly into that other world, in the full glory of some passion, than fade and wither dismally with age. He thought of how she who lay beside him had locked in her heart for so many years that image of her lover's eyes when he had told her that he did not wish to live.

Generous tears filled Gabriel's eyes. He had never felt like that himself towards any woman but he knew that such a feeling must be love. (*D* 223)

This description shows that, after his encounter with the Real, Gabriel "becomes something totally different." (Lacan, *Seminar* 164). Actually, as indicated above, the paragraph that begins with "[g]enerous tears" concludes with the following sentence: "His own identity was fading out into a grey impalpable world: the solid world itself which these dead had one time reared and lived in was dissolving and dwindling" (*D* 223). Therefore, it is possible to consider that in this scene there is no longer any Gabriel: "there is no longer anyone who can say I" (Lacan, *Seminar* 164).

It could be said that Frank experiences the same transformation in "The Shadow in the Rose Garden." For Frank, the Real emerges through the figure of Archie, who intervenes as a third person in the husband-wife dyad that has turned into an overtly hostile relationship. Although Archie is not dead while Michael is, the two are alike in that they exist between life and death. Michael Furey is still alive in Gretta's memories, affecting not only her life but that of her husband as well. On the other hand, Archie, who was found to be alive, does not belong in everyday life as he did before and is unable to recognize his old lover, Frank's wife. In either case, existing on the line dividing life from death, both Michael and Archie exert great influence over each couple. Undoubtedly Archie, just like Michael, triggers the transformation or impersonalization of the male protagonist. At the end of the story, there is no longer any Frank: "there is no longer anyone who can say *I*" (Lacan, *Seminar* 164).

FROM ANOTHER LACANIAN VIEWPOINT, the transformation of the hus-bands' subjects could be considered "the *act* in the Lacanian sense": "*symbolic suicide*: an act of 'losing all,' of withdrawing from symbolic reality" which Žižek refers to in his discussion of Roberto Rossellini's film *Stromboli* (*Enjoy* 43). Finding the same withdrawal or conversion at work in Freud's dream of Irma, Žižek suggests that the opening of Irma's throat corresponds to the crater of the volcano that the heroine of the film, Karin (Ingrid Bergman), faces after run-ning away from the oppressive village (*Enjoy* 63–64n21).[5] According to Žižek, despairing in the face of the powerful volcano's smoke, Karin encounters "the *Real*," but "[a]fter we pass through the 'zero point' of the symbolic suicide, what a moment ago appeared as the whirlpool of rage sweeping away all determinate existence changes miraculously into supreme bliss—*as soon as we renounce all symbolic ties*" (43).

The passage in which this "supreme bliss" is represented in "The Dead" is undoubtedly the description of Gabriel's generous tears. Combining the first and second parts, already quoted above, I will cite the entire paragraph in order to confirm the homology between Freud's dream of Irma or Karin in *Stromboli* and Gabriel in "The Dead":

> Generous tears filled Gabriel's eyes. He had never felt like that himself to-wards any woman but he knew that such a feeling must be love. The tears gathered more thickly in his eyes and in the partial darkness he imagined he saw the form of a young man standing under a dripping tree. Other forms were near. His soul had approached that region where dwell the vast hosts of the dead. He was conscious of, but could not apprehend, their wayward and flickering existence. His own identity was fading out into a grey impalpable world: the solid world itself which these dead had one time reared and lived in was dissolving and dwindling. (*D* 223)

Gabriel's eyes are filled with generous tears, and he feels love that he has never felt toward any woman for a reason that is apparently comprehensible. It is because, as Gabriel's identity is "fading out" and "the solid world itself" is "dis-solving and dwindling," he is experiencing some miraculous and "supreme bliss" and is being freed from "*all symbolic ties*" and from his "narcissistic per-spective" (Žižek, *Enjoy* 43, 64).

On the other hand, it may be difficult to say that Frank is also in "supreme bliss" at the end of "The Shadow in the Rose Garden." However, it seems undeniable that the conversion that occurs in Frank resembles that which occurs in Gabriel and Karin: "At last he had learned the width of the breach between them. [. . .] They were both shocked so much, they were impersonal, and no longer hated each other. After some minutes he left her and went out" (*PO* 132). As Frank learns of the unbridgeable "breach," becomes "impersonal," and leaves his wife's side, his withdrawal appears to be nothing but "the *act* in the Lacanian sense," or "*symbolic suicide*: an act of 'losing all,' of withdrawing from symbolic reality." In fact, as will be discussed later, the ending of "The Shadow in the Rose Garden" resembles that of *Stromboli*.

THE ENDING OF "THE DEAD" IS, of course, different from that of "The Shadow in the Rose Garden" in that, unlike Frank, whose next action or destination is unforeseeable, Gabriel has a semblance of a plan: "The time had come for him to set out on his journey westward" (*D* 223). What is the function or implication of this "journey westward" and its relation to Michael Furey ("some impalpable and vindictive being") or "distant music" ("The Lass of Aughrim")? For that matter, how can we interpret the ending of "The Dead" from the perspective of Lacan or Žižek? The story ends in the following manner:

> A few light taps upon the pane made him turn to the window. It had begun to snow again. He watched sleepily the flakes, silver and dark, falling obliquely against the lamplight. The time had come for him to set out on his journey westward. Yes, the newspapers were right: snow was general all over Ireland. It was falling on every part of the dark central plain, on the treeless hills, falling softly upon the Bog of Allen and, farther westward, softly falling into the dark mutinous Shannon waves. It was falling, too, upon every part of the lonely churchyard on the hill where Michael Furey lay buried. It lay thickly drifted on the crooked crosses and headstones, on the spears of the little gate, on the barren thorns. His soul swooned slowly as he heard the snow falling faintly through the universe and faintly falling, like the descent of their last end, upon all the living and the dead. (*D* 223–24)

In *The Sublime Object of Ideology*, Žižek turns to Lacan's teaching that "we have to distinguish at least three types of object" (182). The difference among Gabriel's objects can be clarified by adopting the Lacanian concepts of the Imaginary, the Symbolic, and the Real. In the schema of Lacan/Žižek, Gabriel's three objects appear in the process of the symbolization of the Imaginary ("distant music": "The Lass of Aughrim"), the realization of the Symbolic (Michael Furey: "some impalpable and vindictive being"), and the imaginarization of the Real (Ireland or the west of Ireland) (Žižek, *Sublime Object* 182–85).

"Distant music," or "The Lass of Aughrim," is "a leftover, remnants which cannot be reduced to a network of formal relations proper to the symbolic structure"; however, it is "paradoxically, at the same time, the positive condition for the effectuation of the formal structure," or "an object of exchange circulating among subjects, serving as a kind of guarantee, pawn, on their symbolic relationship" (*Sublime Object* 182). Distant music, which Gretta and Gabriel come across unexpectedly, is precisely "a leftover, remnants." It can neither be formally included in Misses Morkan's party nor in Gretta and Gabriel's relationship as wife and husband. Still, it is "an object of exchange circulating" between the couple, as Gretta becomes so fascinated with the song that she cannot help inquiring about the name, while Gabriel feels attracted to his wife as if he has been infected by her unusual form of fever:

> Gabriel watched his wife who did not join in the conversation. [. . .]
> At last she turned towards them and Gabriel saw that there was colour on her cheeks and that her eyes were shining. A sudden tide of joy went leaping out of his heart.
> —Mr D'Arcy, she said, what is the name of that song you were singing?
> —It's called *The Lass of Aughrim*, said Mr D'Arcy, but I couldn't remember it properly. Why? Do you know it?
> —*The Lass of Aughrim*, she repeated. I couldn't think of the name. (*D* 211–12)

It could be said that since the name of "distant music" turns out to be "The Lass of Aughrim," this information allows the Imaginary to be symbolized for Gabriel as well as Gretta.

However, after they arrive at the hotel, their conversation about the song leads Gretta to disclose the story of her young lover, Michael Furey, thereby causing Gabriel to come in contact with the Real. As a result, "The Lass of Aughrim" is no longer his object as it is replaced by Michael Furey, who used to sing the song. For Gabriel, Michael Furey is another type of object, one that appears in the transition from the Symbolic to the Real: "the *objet petit a*, the lack, the leftover of the Real setting in motion the symbolic movement of interpretation, a void in the centre of the symbolic order, a pure semblance of the 'mystery' to be explained, interpreted" (Žižek, *Sublime Object* 185). The existence of Michael Furey is nothing less than a "'mystery' to be explained, interpreted" for Gabriel, who asks Gretta about the boy, feigning indifference. This query eventually causes the appearance of the Real through "some impalpable and vindictive being" (D 220). This uncanny being, "Michael Furey," is a denotation of "the leftover of the Real" or "a pure semblance of the 'mystery.'"

The encounter with the Real causes an unfamiliar breach in the mundane reality or fantasy, that is, it causes a "void in the centre of the symbolic order." Unless the breach is closed or the void filled with fantasy once again, we will be unable to stand the horror and will fall into madness. In this sense, even the image of "some impalpable and vindictive being" is a kind of fantasy invoked to fill the void in Gabriel's symbolic order. According to Žižek, the object related to the Real is the sublime object, which is "a mere secondary positivization of the 'nothing,' the void," and "holds the place of, stands in for, what has to be excluded, foreclosed, if 'reality' is to retain its consistency" (*Tarrying with the Negative* 38). The representation of "some impalpable and vindictive being" is what "holds the place of, stands in for" the nothingness or the void in Gabriel's reality.

A third type of object, which has "a massive, oppressive material presence," is "a mute embodiment of an impossible *jouissance*" and "the impassive, imaginary objectification of the Real" (Žižek, *Sublime Object* 184–85). Žižek takes examples from a series of Hitchcock's films: he references the birds in *The Birds* and "the body of the giant ship at the end of the street in which Marnie's mother lives" in *Marnie* (184). It seems that "snow" in the last paragraph of "The Dead" corresponds with this third type of object. Like birds, snow flies in the sky and can be "a massive, oppressive material presence" as snow is "general all over Ireland," falling upon "all the living and the dead" (D 223–24). In addition, the announcement that "[t]he time had come for [Gabriel] to set out on his journey westward" seems to indicate that Ireland, or the west of Ireland, can be equated with "a mute embodiment of an impossible *jouissance*" (Žižek, *Sublime Object* 184). In other words, (the west of) Ireland, covered with snow, is the object that emerges in the process of the imaginarization of the Real.[6]

WITH REGARD TO THE THREE types of objects, almost the same holds true for "The Shadow in the Rose Garden." In the case of Lawrence's story, the seaside place that Frank and his wife visit on holiday is the first object, acting as "a leftover, remnants which cannot be reduced to a network of formal relations proper to the symbolic structure" (Žižek, *Sublime Object* 182). This seaside place is what enables the couple to escape from everyday life and everyday feelings. The place may not be "an object of exchange circulating among subjects," but it is the object about which the couple argues, exchanging their thoughts and feelings. It could be said, then, that the place brings about the symbolization of the Imaginary for Frank. However, as in Joyce's story, the disclosure of his wife's relationship with her former lover, Archie, forces Frank into contact with the Real. As a result, the seaside place is replaced by Archie, who becomes Frank's second object.

Like Michael Furey is for Gabriel, Archie is "the 'mystery' to be explained, interpreted" for Frank (Žižek, *Sublime Object* 185). In order to solve the mystery, Frank demands to know more about Archie and his wife's romantic relationship. His queries conclusively force the Real to reveal itself as madness,[7] which in turn shows Archie to be a denotation that is no more than "the leftover of the Real" or "a pure semblance of the 'mystery'" (Žižek, *Sublime Object* 185).

In the meantime, it should be noted that, for Frank in "The Shadow in the Rose Garden," whereas the seaside place is the object of the symbolization of the Imaginary and Archie as a "lunatic" is that of the realization of the Symbolic, the third object of the imaginarization of the Real—which is (the west of) Ireland for Gabriel—seems to be absent. This absence, which closely relates to the rather abrupt ending or open-endedness of this work, may leave the reader unsatisfied or frustrated, particularly when compared to the ending of "The Dead."

However, on the basis of Žižek's discussion, such open-endedness appears to take on positive significance. Žižek states that whether Karin in *Stromboli* is leaving or returning to the village at the end is indeterminate: "By this very irresolution of its ending, *Stromboli* marks the proper dimension of the act: it ends at the precise point at which the *act* is already accomplished, although no *action* is yet performed" (*Enjoy* 43). As mentioned previously, Karin commits an act of "*symbolic suicide*: an act of 'losing all,' of withdrawing from symbolic reality," and it is this act, not her action (leaving or returning to the village), that "enables us to begin anew from the 'zero point,' from that point of absolute freedom" (*Enjoy* 43). Therefore, it is not far-fetched to also understand "The Shadow in the Rose Garden" as ending at the precise point at which the Lacanian act is already accomplished by Frank, although it is ultimately indeterminate whether he is leaving his wife once and for all or only momentarily.[8] In any event, the absolute freedom attained by Frank is significant for the story as well; because of the irresolution or suspension of its ending, Lawrence's story has an effect similar to that of Rossellini's films. According to Žižek, "the 'symbolic' suicide cancels the very presupposition of the 'big Other'—in a way, it is the negative, the reversal, the 'undoing' of the founding ideological gesture of (presup)posing the Other," and "insofar as Rossellini's films endeavor to enact this suspension, they are unideological, they enable us to break out of the ideological closure" (*Enjoy* 59).

T. S. ELIOT'S INTERPRETATION of "The Shadow in the Rose Garden" by D. H. Lawrence can be regarded as an attempt at "ideological closure." By labeling the story cruel and insisting that Lawrence's characters do not have any sense of "moral obligations" or "conscience," he attempts to confine Lawrence to the stigma of "the heretic" (37). However, as this essay has discussed, Lawrence's story indicates a ground that Lacan calls the Real; it goes without saying that this ground has nothing to do with "moral obligations" or "conscience." The Real is nothing other than that which dismantles everyday reality, including "moral obligations" or "conscience." As shown by the paragraph on Frank's impersonality, which immediately follows the passage cited by Eliot, it is evident that Lawrence is interested in the characters that lie below the surfaces of everyday personalities. It is not clear whether Eliot omits the reference to impersonality deliberately, but it is undeniably symptomatic because he does exactly the same thing when citing the passage on Gabriel's generous tears from "The Dead"; the subsequent passage, in which Gabriel's identity fades out, is omitted just like its counterpart in "The Shadow in the Rose Garden." In both stories, the important moment in which identity or personality disappears is notably eliminated. In this regard, Eliot's interpretation of "The Dead" by Joyce can be seen as another attempt at "ideological closure." Apart from the paradoxical revelation of the affinity of these two modernist stories, which occurs somewhat as a result of Eliot's symptomatic method of partial quotation, an inquiry into the congruence between the stories in terms of an encounter with the Real as a Lacanian motif can, as I have shown, bring into sharp relief a common theme. Namely, it can highlight the transformation of the subject and the object, thereby indicating the possibility of further investigations into the congruencies between two ostensibly divergent writers, James Joyce and D. H. Lawrence.

Notes

1. For a quick refutation of Eliot, see Spender 167–75. Spender maintains that "[t] o call Joyce a traditionalist means a lot, but to call Lawrence a heretic means nothing. For if the tradition is all that matters, it finally disposes of Lawrence as a serious writer. On the other hand, if Lawrence does matter, then we have got to revise our use of the word tradition, and the machine that Eliot has constructed falls to pieces" (172–73).

2. Martin F. Kearney introduces Brenda Maddox's suggestion that "The Dead" may have influenced "The Shadow in the Rose Garden" (47).

3. According to Lacan, "[t]he real is beyond the *automaton*, the return, the coming-back, the insistence of the signs, by which we see ourselves governed by the pleasure principle" and "[t]he function of the *tuché*, of the real as encounter—the encounter in so far as it may be missed, in so far as it is essentially the missed encounter—first presented itself in the history of psycho-analysis in a form that was in itself already enough to arouse our attention, that of the trauma" (*Four Fundamental Concepts* 53–55).

4. Garry M. Leonard argues that the price of Gabriel's glimpse into the Real is that "the falsity of his subjective consciousness, and all its myriad deceptions, attacks him at once and divorces him from his own reflection" (307).

5. According to Žižek, "[t]he dual, imaginary dialogue with Irma, dominated by Freud's narcissistic interests, culminates in a look into her open mouth; suddenly, this horror (where the throat's opening clearly corresponds to the crater in *Stromboli*) changes miraculously into a sort of ataraxia, the subject floats freely in symbolic bliss—as soon as the dreamer (Freud) renounces his narcissistic perspective" (*Enjoy* 63–64n21).

6. For a thematic connection between the song "The Lass of Aughrim" and the west of Ireland, and the implications of "his journey westward" being Gabriel's epiphany, see Owens. Referring to Owens' equation of "the West" with "the collective unconscious of the nation" (Owens 85), Earl G. Ingersoll maintains: "It is a journey toward the feminine, evident in the 'strange friendly pity' he feels for the 'no longer beautiful' Gretta and '[p]oor Aunt Julia [. . .] soon to be a shade.' [. . .] Having discovered his lack in a Lacanian sense, Gabriel paradoxically may set out at last on the journey toward empowerment" (154). Shelly Brivic indicates that "Joyce, Lacan, and Žižek all see the world as made up of language and they all focus relentlessly on departure, transition, and discovery" (xii).

7. For the relation of the Lacanian Real to modernism and Foucauldian madness, see Restuccia 28–68. Restuccia suggests that modernism is "fascinated with the Real" (29), and that Foucault's *Madness and Civilization* "serves as a springboard into the topic of modernism's relation—or failed, desiring relation—to Lacan's register of the Real" (33).

8. For a better understanding of the division of critical opinion on the prospects of Frank and his wife, see Thornton 95–96n58. Thornton himself believes that the ending of the story "contains some bases for hope": "Their terrible confrontation may well have

breached the barriers that have so long separated them, and may provide the basis for deeper and more honest engagement" (42).

Works Cited

Brivic, Shelly. *Joyce through Lacan and Žižek: Explorations.* New York: Palgrave Macmillan, 2008.

Eliot, Thomas S. *After Strange Gods: A Primer of Modern Heresy.* London: Faber and Faber, 1934.

Ingersoll, Earl G. *Engendered Trope in Joyce's* Dubliners. Carbondale: Southern Illinois UP, 1996.

Kearney, Martin F. *Major Short Stories of D. H. Lawrence: A Handbook.* New York: Garland, 1998.

Lacan, Jacques. *The Four Fundamental Concepts of Psycho-Analysis.* Ed. Jacques-Alain Miller. Trans. Alan Sheridan. New York: Norton, 1981.

———. *The Seminar of Jacques Lacan: Book II: The Ego in Freud's Theory and in the Technique of Psychoanalysis 1954–1955.* 1978. Ed. Jacques-Alain Miller. Trans. Sylvana Tomaselli. New York: Norton, 1991.

Leonard, Garry M. *Reading* Dubliners *Again: A Lacanian Perspective.* Syracuse, NY: Syracuse UP, 1993.

Maddox, Brenda. "Lawrence's 'Shadow in the Rose Garden' and Joyce's 'The Dead.'" Paper presented at the Sixth International D. H. Lawrence Conference, University of Nottingham, UK, 13 July 1996.

Owens, Cóilín. "The Mystique of the West in Joyce's 'The Dead.'" *Irish University Review* 22.1 (1992): 80–91.

Restuccia, Frances L. *Amorous Acts: Lacanian Ethics in Modernism, Film, and Queer Theory.* Stanford, CA: Stanford UP, 2006.

Spender, Stephen. *The Destructive Element: A Study of Modern Writers and Beliefs.* London: Jonathan Cape, 1935.

Thornton, Weldon. *D. H. Lawrence: A Study of the Short Fiction.* New York: Twayne, 1993.

Žižek, Slavoj. *Enjoy Your Symptom! Jacques Lacan in Hollywood and Out.* New York: Routledge, 1992.

———. *The Sublime Object of Ideology.* London: Verso, 1989.

———. *Tarrying with the Negative: Kant, Hegel, and the Critique of Ideology.* Durham, NC: Duke UP, 1993.

9

Masochism and Marriage in *The Rainbow* and *Ulysses*

JOHANNES HENDRIKUS BURGERS AND JENNIFER MITCHELL

In 1916, while staying with Frieda and D. H. Lawrence in Cornwall, Katherine Mansfield was privy to one of their frequent and horrifying domestic disputes. The spark of the argument was a comment Frieda made about Shelley, which sent Lawrence into an uncontrollable and protracted rage. According to Mansfield, "He beat her—he beat her to death—her head and face and breast and pulled out her hair [. . .]" (Maddox 226). In 1918, Frank Budgen had to comfort a distraught Nora Barnacle because James Joyce had asked her to "go with other men so that he would have something to write about" (Budgen 188). Undoubtedly, both Lawrence and Joyce were masters of their craft, but from an outsider's perspective, they were challenging partners. Yet their relationships were far more complex than these biographical slivers reveal. Nora and James enjoyed reading the works of the erotic writer Leopold von Sacher-Masoch together and indulging in bondage fantasies. Brenda Maddox argues that there was a theatricality about the Lawrences' public fights, which bordered on histrionics and were usually followed by a saccharine reconciliation (225). Frieda was not always the victim and on one occasion broke a plate on Lawrence's head (Maddox 158). Clearly, both couples lived their relationships with a passionate intensity that defied legacies of Victorian propriety.

Lawrence perhaps best expounds such a version of love in his aptly titled 1918 essay "Love," which resonates not only in his own work but also in Joyce's: "love is a travelling, a motion, a speed of coming together. Love is the force of creation. But all force, spiritual or physical, has its polarity, its positive and its negative" (*1P* 151). Lawrence approaches love as embracing and demanding a set of extreme emotional binaries. Love cannot be roses and smiles without being thorns and tears. A similar polarity is visible when a despondent Jim asks Nora in a letter, "Are you too, then, like me, one moment high as the stars, the next lower than the lowest wretches?" (*Letters II* 243). This turmoil in their own lives is often visible in their fictional characters. True, turbulent and troubled relationships are common in modernist texts, but Lawrence and Joyce are all the more shocking because their characters relish recalcitrance and find pleasure in pain. Yet, rather than signifying a divergence from a healthy relationship, the intense conflicts between characters are normalized and treated as central to any relational power dynamic. As a result, we contend that Lawrence's and Joyce's work was responding to contemporaneous discussions about masochism by sexologists. Particularly, they are critically responding to a very narrow definition of masochism current among sexologists who treated it as a perversion. Instead, they see the submissive and performative nature of masochism as constitutive of everyday interactions between successful couples. This representation of what we identify as "everyday masochism" in a happy marriage is particularly well developed in *The Rainbow* and *Ulysses*.

This argument extends and amplifies a longer genealogy of scholarship about sexuality in Lawrence and Joyce. Within this tradition, the proclivity for pleasure through pain in modernist writing has generally been explored through the lens of "sadomasochism." To this end, "sadomasochism" has often been used as an all-inclusive term to describe what we contend are two distinct behavioral and relational mechanisms: sadism and masochism. The concept "sadomasochism" elides the specific and complex power dynamics at play in any given relationship and therefore sacrifices heuristic precision for categorical breadth. Lawrentian and Joycean scholarship is not an exception to this tendency, especially with respect to *The Rainbow* and *Ulysses*.[1] Here, the concepts of sadism and masochism tend to be placed, as complements, under the umbrella of sadomasochism. Yet, such broad categorization erases the complexities of masochism as its own dynamic.

As a means of reappraising the tradition of sexuality scholarship on Joyce and Lawrence, we consider masochism a category distinct from sadomasochism. Both authors were deeply interested in the way that masochistic relationships pervaded everyday relationships. In particular, the protagonists of both *The Rainbow* and *Ulysses* define the success of their relationships through their mutual submission. This interpretation opens up a new critical space for dialogue about representations of sexuality in Lawrence and Joyce, particularly because it demonstrates that these texts were in conversation with one another, despite the mutual disdain of the authors.

This argument is presented in three distinct sections. The first section refines the analytical term "masochism" by disarticulating it from "sadomasochism." The second section on Lawrence examines the second generation of

Brangwen marriages in *The Rainbow* to locate Lawrence's doctrine of ordinary masochisms. Finally, we show how the masochistic Leopold Bloom creates the means of his own torture by inciting Molly to cheat on him. Ultimately, this essay suggests that the duality inherent in Lawrence's and Joyce's own relationships is tied to the perhaps surprising theoretical overlap in their works.

Theories of Masochism

When sexology was an emerging field in the middle of the nineteenth century, it found much of its inspiration in literature. It is therefore no surprise that the term "sadomasochism" was inspired by the notorious works of the Marquis de Sade and Leopold von Sacher-Masoch. Despite the distinctly literary projects of these authors, early sexologists like Richard von Krafft-Ebing grouped sadism and masochism together, suggesting that they ostensibly stem from similar sensations—some combination of humiliation, debasement, pain, and pleasure. Thus for Krafft-Ebing, "sadism is the experience of sexual, pleasurable sensations (including orgasm) produced by acts of cruelty, bodily punishment [. . .] an innate desire to humiliate, hurt, wound or even destroy others," while masochism is "the association of passively endured cruelty and violence with lust" (152, 159). The two are therefore the inverse of one another. Other sexual theorists like Wilhelm Stekel, Havelock Ellis, and Sigmund Freud made relatively similar arguments (Ellis 199; Stekel 14; Freud 24). That is not to say that there were not important nuances among the theories but rather that they all saw these behaviors as part of an overarching sadomasochistic complex. Primarily, sadistic impulses in men were excused as an exaggeration of traditional, sexualized masculinity, while masochistic impulses in women were treated as an intrinsic part of their biological and social makeup (Ellis 88; Bonaparte 170–71).

In *Coldness and Cruelty*, Gilles Deleuze significantly departs from this sexological tradition by explicitly bifurcating sadomasochism into its constituent terms. He does so by recovering their spiritual grandfathers, Sacher-Masoch and Sade. Deleuze argues that both men exemplify two distinct sexual impulses governed by different sets of foundational principles that never meet on the same terms: "a genuine sadist could never tolerate a masochistic victim. [. . .] Neither would the masochist tolerate a truly sadistic torturer" (40–41). For the sadist, the sexual pleasure inherent in sadistic behavior lies in the complete absence of pleasure for the victim, just as the torturer who satisfies the masochist must be molded, educated, and coerced into such a position of authority. Despite the impulse to believe that sadism is active and masochism passive, both the sadist and the masochist are active participants in their own distinct fantasies. Accordingly, the masochistic complex and the sadistic complex are complete unto themselves.

Even after their forty-year tenure, Deleuze's theories are still powerfully resonant, and there are many Deleuzian echoes in contemporary theory. For example, in *Homos*, Leo Bersani relies on the broad term "S/M," which breaks down the boundary between sadism and masochism. Yet he still accedes to "primacy of masochism" and the "appeal of powerlessness" within said "S/M" relationship, revealing the Deleuzian roots of his argument (95). Also using the theoretical groundwork laid by Deleuze, Slavoj Žižek further emphasizes the primary distinctions between sadism and masochism: it is the masochist who "stages his own servitude" (92). The apparent reluctance to move beyond Deleuze's compelling framework speaks to its critical acuity. By embracing this approach to masochism, we consider the way in which Lawrence's and Joyce's masochists create the situations in which their masochistic fantasies are fulfilled. Moving beyond Deleuze, we contend that masochism does not exclusively find its full expression in explicitly sexual power dynamics; rather, the masochism inherent in ordinary relationships and everyday life is not only of equal intensity and satisfaction but can also be a vital element within a successful marriage.

Marriage as Masochism: Anna and Will Brangwen

Surveying the body of gender- and sexuality-focused criticism about D. H. Lawrence's *The Rainbow* (1915), Marianna Torgovnick argues that there is a "time warp" in which critics make little or no reference to the development and influence of potentially relevant theories including structuralism, psychoanalysis, and feminism (33). Remarkably, she finds that the overabundance of explicit sex and sexual philosophizing that appears in the novel has led to few sexually focused readings. Torgovnick, in an effort to reposition Lawrence within this discourse on sexuality, recuperates the contextual discourses about sexuality in circulation while he was writing *The Rainbow*. By citing the groundbreaking work of Richard von Krafft-Ebing, Havelock Ellis, and Sigmund Freud as "possible model[s]" for Lawrence (45), Torgovnick usefully establishes connections between Lawrence's work and contemporaneous theories about sex that undoubtedly inform his writing.

More interested in the intersections between Lawrence and Ellis, Torgovnick does not fully unpack the full potential of her mention of Sacher-Masoch's *Venus in Furs* (1870) in relation to Lawrence. This is, in fact, something that had earlier been fleshed out by Emile Delavenay, who admits that while Lawrence never directly references Sacher-Masoch, there are deep "psychological similarities between the two authors," suggesting that it might be possible to trace a "direct line of literary descent" from Masoch to Lawrence (121, 143). Indeed, the boudoir novel salaciously and meticulously documents Severin constructing his own punishment through the erstwhile innocent Wanda. The active role of the masochist echoes throughout Lawrence and especially the *Rainbow*. In many cases, the masochistic elements that Lawrence appropriates—the tendencies on behalf of his characters to gain pleasure from the pain they experience—become the cornerstones of the relationships that comprise the narrative. Importantly, these masochistic elements exist in the everyday lives and interactions of Lawrence's characters. They have, accordingly, been difficult for critics to negotiate, even though they are ripe for inventive analysis. To this end, we follow the path laid by Deleuze in his return to masochism's literary origins and use Sacher-Masoch's text as a lens through which to explore *The Rainbow* and its pioneering, reactionary model of masochism.

The novel focuses primarily on the differences in courtship, flirtation, marriage, and love over the course of three generations of Brangwens. Initially, Tom Brangwen marries a mysterious foreigner, Lydia. As the novel progresses, Lydia's daughter from a previous marriage, Anna, marries her cousin Will. Finally, Will and Anna's daughter Ursula experiments romantically but refrains from settling down. The frank and tumultuous sexual haven that Anna and Will Brangwen experience within the confines of their marriage appears to pose an interpretive problem for critics determined to see Lawrence as conservative, as misogynist, as queer, as homophobic, and as fascist.[2] As a couple, Anna and Will are rarely mentioned in *Rainbow* scholarship if at all. James Twitchell, focusing predominantly on the vampiric characteristics often ascribed to Lawrentian women, groups Anna and Will in a bevy of other couples: Gudrun and Gerald, Ursula and Anton, Tom and Lydia. Twitchell views Tom and Lydia's marriage as the only relationship that comes to some semblance of long-lasting fruition, citing their inaction and stability as distinct from the other ultimately destructive pairings. This reading of *The Rainbow* does Anna and Will a disservice by prioritizing the least exciting relationship in the text. Yet Twitchell is following a longer tradition in his reading of the novel. In his early 1931 review, John Middleton Murry argues that in the first generation

(Tom and Lydia), "man is really man," while in the next generation (Will and Anna) "woman begins to establish the mastery" (74).

Despite Murry's reservations, Anna and Will are arguably evenly matched partners. They experience the same sets of problematic emotions and impulses, thereby complicating the gendered prioritization that critics often ascribe to Lawrence. In fact, the creation of this perpetually shifting balance is a substantial part of Lawrence's experimentation with Sacher-Masoch. By applying his innovative and often shocking fantasies to women as well as men, Lawrence creates a heterosexual masochistic complex in which both participants play a variety of roles to satiate themselves and their partners. For Lawrence, love and marriage are inextricably tied to masochism, which he sees as part of the consistent foundation upon which all human relationships are built. In "Love," he asks the pivotal question facing his characters: "What worse bondage can we conceive than the bond of love?" (1P 151–52). Viewing love in terms of bondage—perhaps taking his cue from Ellis' conception of courtship—enables Lawrence to establish equivalence between the two; that equivalence reveals masochism and love as mutually inflected, mutually dependent, and mutually influential in the world of romance. In his theoretical approach to love, Lawrence's discourse speaks directly to the language of masochism as, of course, distinct from sadism.

Lawrence moves beyond the whip-possessing, fur-clad dominatrix of Sacher-Masoch's *Venus in Furs* to less obvious and more ordinary, even inescapable, forms of masochism. By using variations of the surprisingly flexible masochistic contract, a literal set of "laws that regulate the partnership" (Smirnoff 65), Lawrence identifies the pervasive presence of masochism in marriage. These rules establish a set of guidelines and conditions that, by virtue of the weight given to them by those entering into the contract, create a specific role each participant must play. In Sacher-Masoch's own contract with Wanda, his wife, she is set up to demand the following of her servant: "My Slave [. . .] You shall renounce your identity completely. You shall submit totally to my will. [. . .] You shall be neither a son nor a brother nor a friend; you shall be no more than my slave groveling in the dust. [. . .] You have nothing save me; for you I am everything, your life, your future, your happiness, your unhappiness, your torment and your joy" (278–79). Masochism, for Sacher-Masoch, necessitates a power hierarchy in which one partner appears to be wholly in control and the other wholly subjected. Severin, the theoretical victim of *Venus in Furs*, constantly places himself at the mercy of a woman he coerces into a position of physical and emotional tortures.[3] Not only is Severin subject to the whims and fancies of the cruel women he creates, but he stops being called "Severin" so that his own identity can be broken down, reshaped, and reconstructed within the confines of the contract. Both participants in the contract undergo a revision of their respective identities. In similar fashion, Will and Anna experience a redefinition of their identity from complete individual to lover, spouse, and dependent as they become husband and wife. Marriage for the duo reveals secrets, emotions, concerns, and confusion. Early in their marriage, Will discovers a new woman in Anna, one who is "reckless," "independent," and "indifferent" (*R* 177, 126, 96), while Anna finds Will "hard," "evil," and "cruel" (*R* 118, 141, 164). Both see the revelation of these frightening new characteristics as directly related to their newly attained marital status—an indication of the immediacy of identity shifts within marriage. These sudden realizations spawn Will's moment of clarity about the condition of marriage: "When he was a child, he had thought a woman was a woman merely by virtue of her skirts and petticoats. And now, lo, the whole world could be divested of its garment, the garment could lie there shed away intact, and one could stand in a new world, a new earth, naked in a new, naked universe. It was too astounding and miraculous. This then was marriage!" (*R* 139–40). Here, Will faces the shedding of the external signifiers that both he and Anna possessed before their marriage. Will, much like Severin, comes to the realization that external signifiers, like the garment, are symptomatic of the complicated relationship between the two spouses. Although identity for Severin is tied to adornments, for Will those adornments are simply masks that dissolve within marriage. Interested more in what this dissolution yields, the removed-garment metaphor is a recurring one that enables Lawrence to genuinely locate his concerns in commonplace trivialities.

While not nearly as explicit, formal, or rigid as Sacher-Masoch's contracts, Lawrence sees the marriage contract as something that just as necessarily gives birth to new individuals who are bound and subject to each other. Furthermore, the rebirth of Anna and Will within their relationship is a direct result of the institution of marriage and the contract that it entails. Consequently, the marriage contract is the primary form of the masochistic contract as it can be found in ordinary lives. As Tom Brangwen so hesitantly states in his toast to the couple, the definition of man and woman, of husband and wife, exists in and of marriage: "for a man to be a man, it takes a woman—. [. . .] And for a woman to be a woman it takes a *man*—. [. . .] Therefore we have marriage" (*R* 128).[4] The exchange of vows, for Lawrence, implies an exchange of identities, in which the real self will be revealed within the marriage contract, just as the masochistic contract claims to reveal the inner selves of its participants. These respectively undiscovered selves need the formality of marriage and of the masochistic contract in order to shed their guises and come into themselves. Within the contract (marital and masochistic) Lawrence locates the often painful and shocking transformation of individuality that productive relationships tend to demand. In his attitudes toward marriage, Lawrence is deliberately engaged with issues of bondage and love, masochism and coupling, all in order to rework some of the underlying principles that govern Sacher-Masoch's masochism into the less rigid, more fluid, and much more ordinary masochisms that exist in everyday institutions.

Focusing more heavily on what he sees as the emotional victimization and torture experienced by *both* partners in any love-based relationship, Lawrence is overtly engaged with the overlaps between pleasure and pain. Most obviously, that emotional torture appears in *The Rainbow* vis-à-vis the experience of a frustrating combination of opposing and consuming emotions, described as bliss, joy, misery, and repulsion; it is within that realm of binaries that Lawrence situates all important romantic relationships. Lawrence's philosophy on love emphasizes union through an embracing of polarity: "There must be two in one, always two in one—the sweet love of communion and the fierce, proud love of sensual fulfillment, both together in one love" (1P 154–55). This "one love" manifests itself, for Lawrence's characters, in conflicting and competing emotions and impulses, and what seem like their catastrophic consequences. The "gladness" that Will feels upon his possession of Anna is perpetually countered by his "hatred" of her. Will cannot manage his role in their relationship until he accepts this problematic duality and its accompanying feelings of isolation, victimization, anger, and hurt as unavoidable, even natural. Much more importantly, however, Will's experience is not an exclusively male one because Anna, too, faces the mix of fear, sadness, bitterness, magnetism, and love. Here Lawrence innovatively suggests that the masochistic complex exists in precisely the same form in women as in men—a drastic deviation from the misogynistic diagnoses of sexology and psychoanalysis.

Much like Severin, who is perpetually "condemned" (238) by competing feelings of terror, shame, fear, love, attraction, and hatred, both Will and Anna find themselves constantly torn between their feelings of extreme adulation and severe loathing. At the mercy of the mistress that he himself creates, Severin craves the complex impossibility of such emotions coexisting. Initially overwhelmed by that impossibility, both Will and Anna fear for their future, individually and as a couple. Yet, just as Severin finds himself overstimulated and sexually satisfied, and deliberately dissatisfied, so, too, Will and Anna grow into their rocky feelings. They constantly torment one another and themselves by reading into gestures, expressions, and circumstances. Lawrence uses bodily and religious language and imagery to capture the enormity of their coexisting animosity and adoration. Seeing Anna cry, Will's "eyes glittered [. . .] as if with malignant desire," upon which he was "possessed by the evil spirit [. . .] [which] tortured him and wracked him, and fought in him" (*R* 143). The coexistence and interrelatedness of Will's glittering eyes and the cruelty that Anna sees in him in conjunction with the desire that Anna feels as a result of this insight are part and parcel of the masochistic complex as it exists for Lawrence in everyday life. In case the reader misses Lawrence's deliberate highlighting of the ordinariness of that complex, he uses simple imagery that captures the cyclical give-and-take of day and night to represent precisely the same cycle that Anna and Will perpetuate: "So they remained as separate in the light, and in the thick darkness, married. He supported her daytime authority, kept it inviolable at last. And she, in all the darkness, belonged to him, to his close, insinuating, hypnotic familiarity" (*R* 201). For Lawrence, the ups and downs of Will and Anna's marriage are as natural, and as inevitable, as the transition from day into night and back into day again. The constantly shifting power balance that allows Anna and Will to exist, and more importantly, to thrive, enables them to channel the inner turmoil that they experience on a daily basis into the fuel for their lustful relationship, thereby virtually destroying the boundary that separates pleasure and pain. Will and Anna, then, become representatives of Lawrence's doctrine on marriage and masochism; in their embracing of the paradoxically painful and pleasurable polarities within marriage, Will and Anna prove their equality. Notably, it is not an equality based on romantic notions of two equal and complementary forces. Rather, it is an equality achieved when two oppositional forces meet on unequal terms and are able to harmonize through mutual submission, an equality part and parcel to the everyday tug and pull of the masochism inherent in the marriage contract.

Bondage on the Island of Calypso

There can be little doubt that James Joyce was also influenced by the works of Sacher-Masoch. Not only did the Austrian stimulate the Irishman on an intellectual level, but Joyce also used *Venus in Furs* as a personal sex guide. In one letter to Nora, Jim pleads, "I would like to be flogged by you" (*Letters II* 243). In another missive, he has it in mind to dress her up as his own Venus in

Furs, buying for her "a splendid set of sable furs, cap, stole, and muff" (*Letters II* 254). Due to this overt predilection for masochism on Joyce's part, and the whipping and fisting Bella/Bello metes out on the obliging Bloom in "Circe," it is no surprise that there is an extensive body of research on Joyce and sexuality generally, and masochism in particular. Indeed, as early as 1954, Richard Ellmann fleshed out the parallels between *Venus in Furs* and the "Circe" episode in *Ulysses* (*JJII* 371–73).

Since that moment, and in contrast to Lawrentian scholarship, there has been a rich tradition of fruitful readings of *Ulysses* through the lens of sexuality. Two distinct, although not necessarily mutually exclusive, genealogies of research have emerged: one follows heavily in the footsteps of the textual, biographical, and historical tradition of Joyce studies, while the other tends to approach the text through a theoretical, largely psychoanalytic, lens. The former school is best exemplified by Richard Brown's comprehensive study *Joyce and Sexuality* (1985).[6] These works put *Ulysses* in conversation with contemporaneous sexological literature and controversies. Alternatively, the theoretical school understands masochism through a host of different psychoanalytic models.[7] The theoretical school has provided useful insight into the intersections of textuality, sexuality, and aesthetics, especially in showing that sexuality is integral to the form of the novel.

Curiously, despite the sometimes vast differences in approach, the use of masochism as a point of entry into *Ulysses* has focused almost exclusively on two episodes: Bloom's masturbation in "Nausicaa" and his domination by Bella/Bello in "Circe." Of these two episodes, the latter receives the overwhelming amount of attention. There are three reasons for this uneven distribution. First, "Circe" deals extensively with masochism and sadism. Second, as Leo Bersani has pointed out, the scene lends itself well to psychoanalysis while at the same time, interestingly, resisting such a reading (166). Third, "Circe" is one of the most experimental episodes in *Ulysses* and, therefore, interesting for its aesthetic treatment of perversion.

This is not to say that critics have unilaterally focused their attention on "Circe" without contextualizing it within the rest of the work. Nevertheless, there is room for more exploration in other chapters. Doing so reveals that masochism in *Ulysses* does not exclusively hinge on explicit sexual acts. Our reading, therefore, takes as a starting point other scholars who argue that Joyce conceived of sexuality as a broad spectrum of power dynamics between men and women. Indeed, he believed a wide variety of sexual tastes are intrinsic to human psychology (Brown 83). Bloom's masochistic desire, which is expressed through textual experimentation in "Circe," is not separate from but is complementary to the more pervasive and sustained masochistic drive that structures his interactions throughout the day.

The finest examples of this everyday masochism permeate the "Calypso" episode, in which Bloom and Molly are first introduced. Perhaps the most easily readable episode in *Ulysses*, it is often overlooked because so little seems to happen in terms of both style and plot development. Yet it is the only episode in which there is direct dialogue between husband and wife.[8] The scene, then, becomes a productive site for investigating the way Bloom's masochism articulates itself through ordinary relational power dynamics. The episode opens with the couple's morning routine: Molly lies in bed while Bloom makes her breakfast, steps out to the butcher, serves her breakfast, catches up with her, eats his own breakfast, and finally defecates. Complementing Bloom's ironic Odysseus, Molly functions as an ironic Penelope. Consequently, she appears more like Calypso, the nymph who keeps Odysseus on her island, in this chapter than Penelope. Molly's demands also hold Bloom in bondage. Yet it is a willing bondage, and he serves her with subservient satisfaction (Boone 70–71).

As Bloom prepares her food, he anticipates her desires in detail: "Another slice of bread and butter: three, four: right. She didn't like her plate full. Right" (*U* 4.11–12). The repetition of "right" indicates not only that he is actively thinking about her but that he is checking himself in his thoughts about her, as though arriving with a full plate would incur punishment. A similar type of obsequiousness is visible when he goes up to ask her if she wants anything for breakfast. Rather than entering the room, he "paused by the bedroom door," hearing his own voice "softly" in the "bare hall" (*U* 4.49–52). The extreme awareness of his actions—pausing, speaking softly, monitoring the volume of the sound, and standing in the empty hallway outside the bedroom—all speak to a level of consideration beyond mere uxoriousness and much closer to more formal submission. Bloom is thereby casting himself as a potential victim of Molly's wrath, even though the sleeping Molly is most likely unaware of this.

Molly's obliviousness to Bloom's fantasy adheres to the essentially active and surreptitious nature of masochism. As Deleuze points out, the masochist has to educate and persuade the woman dominating him "in accordance with his secret project" (41). Molly becomes dominant in the relationship despite herself because Bloom endows her with an exaggerated power and vindictiveness. On the surface, though, Molly has a very limited set of punishments to dole out. She cannot withhold sex from him because it is he who refrains from sex with her. She has no desire to beat him because, as her reading habits reveal, she is not into books about bondage but only books about sex. Even her last act of punishing Bloom, sleeping with Blazes Boylan, is a fulfillment of Bloom's desire. The elaborate rituals he goes through on her behalf are of no consequence to her, which emphasizes Bloom's control of the situation. Bloom thus imagines Molly hurting him though she has no intention of doing so. In a slightly different theoretical context, Tonya Krouse explains that "Bloom's masochistic pleasure depends upon the women performing the dominant role in the sado-masochistic scene as if they will, in fact, cause Bloom real harm" (127). For the most part the satisfaction in masochism for Bloom is based on an imaginary wrong that will be perpetrated against him.

Admittedly, one could offer that the most hurtful wrong meted out to Bloom, his cuckolding by Boylan, is very much real. While the physical act is certainly real, the importance of the act is entirely dependent on how Bloom frames this wrong within marital and social convention. He posits it as a grave misdeed exactly because this enhances his pleasure. Even his cuckolding by Boylan is an imaginary wrong because it is not inherently wrong, only wrong with regard to traditional marital conventions.

This initially jarring captive behavior early on in the episode is explained later through the insinuation of masochism in Dlugacz's pork butcher shop. Here Bloom runs into the servant girl from next door with "vigorous hips" and a "[s]trong pair of arms," who he fondly recalls "[w]hacking a carpet on the clothesline" (*U* 4.148–50). The image of a robust woman flogging foreshadows the masochistic phantasmagoria he experiences later in the day. He is afraid that she might take the last kidney but is happy that she only wants "Denny's sausages" (*U* 4.147). Bloom intends to follow her furtively out of the store but is thwarted by the butcher who is too slow when helping him. The missed chance to walk behind her "moving hams" (*U* 4.172) instead turns into masochistic pleasure: "The sting of disregard glowed to weak pleasure within his breast" (*U* 4.176–77). To add to the sensation of rejection, he postulates that she will go and sleep with someone else, "a constable off duty cuddling her in Eccles lane. They like them sizeable. Prime sausage. O please, Mr Policeman, I'm lost in the wood" (*U* 4.177–79). Bloom gets sexual pleasure through her imagined infidelity (Brivic, *Freud and Jung* 154). His complete humiliation and emasculation through being cuckolded by a stronger, more commanding male authority is one of the central themes of his day. In no uncertain terms it is, for Bloom, the mental foreplay to the actual infidelity later in the day.

A similar power dynamic is visible when he returns to Molly. Upon arriving home, he finds two letters, one from Milly, the other from Boylan, which he recognizes by the homophonic "Bold hand" addressed to "Mrs. Marion Bloom" (*U* 4.244). The bold hand highlights both Blazes' masculinity and the confidence with which he approaches Molly.[9] A "conquering hero" (*U* 11.340), Boylan is the most stereotypical representation of male virility in the novel (Boone 69). He stands in direct contrast to Bloom, who writes secretly to Martha Clifford as Henry Flower in "Sirens" and masks his handwriting by using "Greek ees" (*U* 11.860). Accordingly, he treats Boylan's letter as a cherished symbol of his emasculation. What he does with the letter, therefore, is particularly important. Rather than leave it for Molly to find in his absence, and thereby avoid confronting the imminent cuckoldry, he brings the letter and its humiliating consequences to her.

Bringing her the plans for her infidelity betrays Bloom's actual position as submissive. When Bloom enters the room, the narrative establishes Molly's spatial dominance. She sits propped up in the bed while Bloom shuffles about her. He opens the blinds at her request and tidies up the room. When he goes down to grab her breakfast after she tells him to "[h]urry up with that tea" (*U* 4.263), he comes back with his arms laden with her food and drink and is forced to "[n]udg[e] the door open with his knee" (*U* 4.300). In so many ways, Bloom is manacled in and by his service to Molly. Her "bulk" (*U* 4.304), "large soft bubs" (*U* 4.304–5), and her fragrance that inundates the "air" (*U* 4.306) are all indicative of her dominance. In short, Molly is ubiquitous, and Bloom willingly swims within and about her.

This dynamic consistently demonstrates Bloom's submissiveness to Molly. Importantly, he himself desires and creates this submission. As Krouse aptly points out, "Bloom in fact has the power, and those who dominate him submit to that power" (127). Even though he sees Molly hide the letter from Blazes under her pillow, clearly wanting to disguise her tryst, he prods her about it, asking, "Who was the letter from?" and thinking immediately, "Bold hand. Marion" (*U* 4.310–11). He knows the answers to his own questions, yet he persists. Upon his inquiries, she reveals that she will sing "Là ci darem la mano" from Mozart's *Don Giovanni* with Boylan for the music recital. The song—in which Don Giovanni tries to seduce the innocent peasant girl Zerlina away from her fiancé—will be particularly important for Bloom throughout the day. In the song, Zerlina's first lines are "vorrei e non vorrei," meaning "I would like to and I would not like to." However, Bloom misremembers the line as stating "voglio e non vorrei," which means "I want to and would not like to." Traditionally, this has been read as foreshadowing of Molly's behavior because the indicative "want" is stronger than the modality of the conditional "would not like to" (Hall 80). That is, she wants to have sex with Boylan even though she would not like to. Bloom thinks about this phrase at key moments throughout the day: when he is about to read the letter from Martha Clifford (*U* 5.224), as he is ostracized during the funeral cortege (*U* 6.238), at his work (*U* 7.152), when he's confronted by the imaginary Molly and Mrs. Breen in Bella Cohen's brothel (*U* 15.355, 473), and when he tries to start a friendship with Stephen (*U* 16.342). He constantly wonders if he is pronouncing it correctly, but in doing so he is actually replicating the paradoxical dynamic of his masochistic complex. After all, the definite feeling of "want" is caused by the hypothetical notion of "I would not like to." Bloom wants Molly to cheat on him in actuality precisely because he would not like it theoretically. That is, he wants real punishments because he imagines them to be wrong.

This linguistic tension replicates what Žižek identifies as the theatricality within masochism: "masochism [. . .] is inherently theatrical: violence is for the most part feigned, and even when it is 'real,' it functions as a component of a scene, as part of a theatrical performance" (92). In relation to Bloom and Molly, it is clear that his masochistic fantasies rely on an imagined ideal of her. In his mind this idea is performing a certain role even though Molly herself is not aware of it. It is not simply actualized physical or emotional abuse that Bloom finds pleasurable, but the drama of the assumed abuse—of which he is the author, director, and actor.

This mutually reinforcing circuit and Molly's unwitting participation in it is underscored when Bloom picks up one of the pulp novels he gave Molly, *Ruby: The Pride of the Ring*. The image on the flipped-open page depicts Ruby lying on the floor and a "Fierce Italian with a carriagewhip" (*U* 4.346–47). The picture awakens Bloom's masochistic desire but fails to thrill Molly because she does not find "anything smutty in it" (*U* 4.355). She would rather have a book by Paul de Kock because she likes his name. The books do not serve the purpose of educating Molly as Bloom hopes.

In fact, Molly is apprehensive about Bloom's masochistic overtures; like Severin's Wanda she needs to be coaxed and coerced into fulfilling the role of a dominatrix. This is visible in her adultery with Boylan. While Molly does achieve multiple orgasms during their encounter, it does not lead to a happy memory for her. For one, he is too stereotypically masculine for her. Her description of intercourse with him is hardly enticing; he is like, "a Stallion driving it up into you because thats all they want out of you with that determined vicious look in his eye" (*U* 18.152–53). She even confesses that, "I had to half shut my eyes" (*U* 18.153–54), a reaction that is closer to agony than ecstasy.

She ultimately does not want him to be part of her and says she "made him pull out and do it on me" (*U* 18.154–55). In not allowing Boylan to perform *eiaculatio seminis inter vas naturale mulieris* (*U* 10.168), she does not officially commit adultery fully according to Catholic doctrine.[10] Interestingly, she does reveal that she let Boylan ejaculate inside of her on a previous occasion. This increased distancing from him speaks to a rejection of the sexual fantasy as it becomes a reality. Once she realizes what she is doing, she feels regretful. It is hardly the sordid sexual tryst Bloom imagines himself watching through a keyhole and masturbating to in "Circe." Indeed, it is Bloom's imagined fantasy of infidelity that is far more damning than the actual engagement suggests.

At the end of the day, it is Bloom she prefers, even if she has a hard time enjoying his penchant for analingus and coprophilia. The desire for analingus has been read as masochistic (Kleinberg 177).[11] The humiliation involved in tasting excrement is exciting to Bloom. When he "kissed the plum mellow yellow smellow melons of her rump" (*U* 17.2241), it evokes in him a "silent contemplation: a tentative velation: a gradual abasement: a solicitious aversion: a proximate erection" (*U* 17.2245–46). The process of licking her anus is so humiliating and degrading that it unlocks Bloom's deepest masochistic satisfactions. Molly, conversely, does not enjoy it. In a fit of irritation she fantasizes that "he can stick his tongue 7 miles up my hole as hes there my brown part then Ill tell him I want £1" (*U* 18.1521–23). For her the only possible pleasure she might receive from analingus is remuneration. Yet in the end she accepts his submission: "I know every turn in him Ill tighten my bottom well and let out a few smutty words smellrump or lick my shit. [. . .] Ill be quite gay and friendly over it" (*U* 18.1530–33). She resigns herself to sex acts that give her absolutely no physical pleasure because they are pleasurable to Bloom. She is not, as it might appear on the surface, dominating him; rather, he is pulling the strings of her apparent domination. It is at this moment that Molly actually most closely resembles Severin's Wanda and Deleuze's understanding of the coerced dominatrix. Molly, like Wanda, gives into desires that do not arouse her in any way and becomes Bloom's ideal. She loses physical interest in Bloom, as Wanda loses interest in Severin.

Ultimately, a mutually accepted masochism is the basis of their complicated if happy relationship. Despite the infidelity he foisted upon her and the infidelity she committed, Molly submits to Bloom and Bloom submits to Molly. It is significant that their marriage is reaffirmed in the last lines of the novel, as Molly imagines the moment Bloom asked her to marry him. She recounts: "I asked him with my eyes to ask again yes and then he asked me would I yes to say yes my mountain flower and first I put my arms around him yes and drew him down to me so he could feel my breasts all perfume yes and his heart was going like mad and yes I said yes I will Yes" (*U* 18.1605–9). The initial rejection on the part of Molly—"I asked him with my eyes to ask again"—shows perhaps an understanding that Bloom needs to be rejected in order to feel accepted. When he is accepted, she draws him down, physically dominating him. This power of hers over Bloom, his willingness to submit, forms the basis of her trust in him. Yet, Molly's submission to Bloom's submissiveness also allows him to trust her. By returning to the moment of their engagement, Joyce demonstrates that the power dynamic has not essentially changed over the course of the day (Siegel 67). Bloom, as a masochist, begins the day in control and ends the day in control; the illusion that Molly is in charge is symptomatic of her adherence to Bloom's masochistic ideal.

This common trust and submission enables us to reconcile infidelity with constancy, coprophilia with loving embrace, and degradation with ecstasy. It is a contradiction that Joyce himself lived. In one letter, he tells Nora, "Every coarse word in speech offends me now for I feel that it would offend you," while later he writes, "I am delighted to see you do like being fucked arseways" (*SL* 165, 184). This game of dominance and submission becomes central to Joyce's conception and representation of marriage. Indeed, Leopold and Molly also continuously perform this very same tug and pull of mutual submission. What is more, even though we are privy to their marriage for only one long day, arguably their masochism is experienced as everyday.

D. H. Lawrence and James Joyce are strikingly different authors—with different styles, aesthetics, and priorities. They were, in fact, so different that their mutual animosity is well known and chronicled. Yet, sometime during the early part of the twentieth century, both novelists started to cultivate their own responses to the sexological and psychoanalytical debate about masochism. Those responses, for both men, include an attempt to remove masochism from the realm of clinical aberration and reinvent it as a far more ordinary experiential model. Such an impulse, though, is still constrained by the contemporaneous dialogue about masochism to which both men are contributing. As Lawrence writes *The Rainbow*, masochism is a peripheral subject of interest for a public first being introduced to sexology. When Joyce is finishing *Ulysses*, however, masochism is a term with far greater scope. Indeed, the public's reception to and involvement in the discourses about masochism may become the delineating factor in the authors' approach to the subject.

Both Joyce and Lawrence are deliberately engaged in broadening cultural

approaches to masochism. Will and Anna's masochistic complex suggests that
Lawrence is reacting directly to the gender distinctions laid out by sexologists.
Both Krafft-Ebing and Ellis locate the masochistic perversion primarily in men
as a direct result of woman's seemingly innate masochistic position. Ellis explains that "in women a certain degree of sexual subjection, the primary stage
of masochism, may fairly be regarded as almost normal" (207). By presenting
readers with representations of masochism that both men and women experience, Lawrence denounces the gender specificity of sexological classifications
of masochism, instead celebrating the potential for gender equality that masochism could and should represent to its participants.

Although Joyce incorporates more explicit sexualized representations of
masochism, he still uses marriage as the site through which the most ordinary
masochisms are experienced and expressed. Indeed, it is Joyce's experimentation with the power dynamics explicit and implicit in marriage that allows
readers to understand the remarkable dynamic between Molly and Bloom.

Anita Phillips argues that masochism "has signally failed to defend itself
as a human tendency" (7). The writings of Lawrence and Joyce directly contradict such sweeping generalizations. To be sure, it is vital for our understanding of the history of masochism to recognize the ways in which modernists, including Joyce and Lawrence, were actively defending masochism
by relocating it within the confines of ordinary marriage. They were thereby
not only speaking back to the scientific language that diagnosed masochism
but at the same time attempting to reveal its existence in daily trivialities. It
is perhaps one of the few moments where Lawrence and Joyce were having
the same conversation.

Notes

1. The critical reliance upon "sadomasochism" as a theoretical lens for approaching the works of D. H. Lawrence is varied in its scope. See, for example, Schapiro,
D. H. Lawrence and the Paradoxes of Psychic Life, and Frost's *Sex Drives*, both of which
approach D. H. Lawrence in light of contemporary theoretical approaches to sadomasochism.

2. Critics who investigate the relationships that appear in Lawrence's fiction tend
to want to create a unified portrait of Lawrence that can be read into his characters
and their interactions with one another. Interestingly, descriptions of Ursula's lesbian
teacher and her arguably gay uncle are used to reveal Lawrence's homophobia, while
the gladiatorial scene in *Women in Love* is used to support readings of Lawrence's appreciation for homoerotic, even homosexual love. Those readings are always exclusive

and totalizing, and as a result, ineffective; they require their respective critics to ignore, overlook, or dismiss textual evidence that complicates their readings.

3. Severin as "victim" is difficult to distance from Sacher-Masoch as masochist. In an essay entitled "The Masochistic Contract," Victor N. Smirnoff writes about the conflation between fact and fiction that appears in *Venus in Furs*; perhaps, more precisely, he means that the boundary between Sacher-Masoch's biographical history and Severin's experiences is often a blurry one, if it exists at all. Moreover, the appendices that appear as a part of *Venus in Furs* are about Sacher-Masoch's childhood, love affairs, marriages, and memories. It is virtually impossible, then, to conceive of either partner as "passive;" rather, they are wholly active participants in their mutually fulfilling roles.

4. Although this quote seems controversially traditional in its definition of marriage, Lawrence's approach to defining marriage and gender roles therein is quite groundbreaking for its time. Lawrence constructs a masochistic complex that removes a traditional gender hierarchy while using a seemingly heteronormative paradigm.

5. Will's "adultery" is the perfect example of the necessity of this acceptance. It is only after he realizes the lack of fulfillment generated by the relationships he could have with other women—sexual, emotional, superficial, or otherwise—that Will wholeheartedly embraces the shifting power dynamic within his relationship with Anna.

6. To that list can also be added Mullin's *James Joyce, Sexuality and Social Purity*, Plock's *Joyce, Medicine, and Modernity*, Frost's "With This Ring I Thee Own," and Watt's "Nothing for a Woman in That." Another school of thought that also makes use of the historicist vein in Joyce studies investigates the common association between masochism and Jewishness. Two major explorations in this field, Reizbaum's *James Joyce's Judaic Other* and Davison's *James Joyce, Ulysses, and the Construction of Jewish Identity*, explore this to some extent. Byrnes investigates the idea most fully in "Bloom's Sexual Tropes."

7. Even though Joyce largely disavowed Freud, many of the psychoanalytical readings have their roots in Freudian psychology. The most central of these accounts is by Schecner, *Joyce in Nighttown*. Brivic builds on this Freudian account of Joyce by also incorporating Jung in *Joyce between Freud and Jung*. He later explores a Lacanian reading in *Joyce through Lacan and Žižek*. There are also some readings that incorporate Michel Foucault at length; these readings tend to read Bloom's sexuality into larger political power dynamics: Krouse, *The Opposite of Desire*, and Streit, *Joyce/Foucault*. Although somewhat more historical, Froula uses Amy Kaplan in *Modernism's Body*. There are also some inroads into more Anglo-American psychological models, specifically Daniel Ferrer's use of Klein in "Circe, Regret and Regression." Balázs uses relational psychoanalytic theory generally and Jessica Benjamin specifically in "Recognizing Masochism." Still, the overwhelming amount of criticism relies on Deleuze with or without Guattari: Cotter, *James Joyce and the Perverse Ideal*; Henke, *James Joyce and the Politics of Desire*; Lamos, *Deviant Modernism*; Restuccia, "Molly in Furs"; and Siegel, *Male Masochism*.

8. True, Bloom and Molly speak at the end of "Nausicaa," but this is largely filtered through the voice of the catechistic narrator.

9. By addressing the letter to "Mrs. Marion Bloom," Boylan actively disregards the early-twentieth-century convention of using the husband's name when writing to the wife (Gifford 76).

10. Ejaculation of semen into the natural female vessel.

11. It should be noted that Kleinberg speaks of rimming in an exclusively homosexual context and as an exclusively homosexual act. However, his argument also fits perfectly well for Leopold Bloom.

Works Cited

Balázs, Thomas P. "Recognizing Masochism: Psychoanalysis and the Politics of Sexual Submission in Ulysses." *Joyce Studies Annual* 13 (2002): 160–91.

Bersani, Leo. *The Culture of Redemption*. Cambridge: Harvard UP, 1990.

———. *Homos*. Cambridge: Harvard UP, 1996.

Bonaparte, Marie. *Female Sexuality*. Trans. John Rodker. New York: International UP, 1953.

Boone, Joseph Allen. "A New Approach to Bloom as 'Womanly Man': The Mixed Middling's Progress in *Ulysses*." *James Joyce Quarterly* 20.1 (1982): 67–85.

Brivic, Sheldon. *Joyce between Freud and Jung*. Literary Criticism Series. Port Washington, NY: Kennikat, 1980.

———. *Joyce through Lacan and Žižek: Explorations*. New Directions in Irish and Irish American Literature. New York: Palgrave Macmillan, 2008.

Brown, Richard. *James Joyce and Sexuality*. New York: Cambridge UP, 1985.

Budgen, Frank. *Myselves When Young*. New York: Oxford UP, 1970.

Byrnes, Robert. "Bloom's Sexual Tropes: Stigmata of the 'Degenerate' Jew." *James Joyce Quarterly* 27.2 (1990): 303–23.

Cotter, David. *James Joyce and the Perverse Ideal*. Studies in Major Literary Authors. New York: Routledge, 2003.

Davison, Neil R. *James Joyce,* Ulysses, *and the Construction of Jewish Identity: Culture, Biography, and "The Jew" in Modernist Europe*. New York: Cambridge UP, 1996.

Delavenay, Emile. "D. H. Lawrence and Sacher-Masoch." *D. H. Lawrence Review* 6.2 (1973): 119–48.

Deleuze, Gilles. *Coldness and Cruelty*. 1967. *Masochism*. New York: Zone, 1992.

Ellis, Havelock. *Psychology of Sex: A Manual for Students*. New York: Emerson, 1938.

Ellmann, Richard. "The Backgrounds of Ulysses." *Kenyon Review* 16.3 (1954): 337–86.

Ferrer, Daniel. "Circe, Regret and Regression." *Post-Structuralist Joyce: Essays from the French*. Ed. Derek Attridge and Daniel Ferrer. New York: Cambridge UP, 1984. 127–44.

Freud, Sigmund. "The Sexual Abberations." *Three Essays on the Theory of Sexuality*. 1962. Trans. James Strachey. New York: Basic, 2000. 1–38.

Frost, Laura. *Sex Drives: Fantasies of Fascism in Literary Modernism*. Ithaca, NY: Cornell UP, 2001.

————. "'With This Ring I Thee Own': Masochism and Social Reform in *Ulysses*." *Sex Positives? The Cultural Politics of Dissident Sexualities*. Ed. Thomas C. Foster, Carol Siegel, and Ellen E. Berry. New York: New York UP, 1997.

Froula, Christine. *Modernism's Body: Sex, Culture, and Joyce*. New York: Columbia UP, 1996.

Gifford, Don, and Robert J. Seidman. *Ulysses Annotated: Notes for James Joyce's* Ulysses. Berkeley: U of California P, 1988.

Hall, Vernon, Jr. "Joyce's Use of Da Ponte and Mozart's *Don Giovanni*." *PMLA* 66.2 (1951): 78–84.

Henke, Suzette A. *James Joyce and the Politics of Desire*. New York: Routledge, 1990.

Kleinberg, Seymour. *Alienated Affections: Being Gay in America*. New York: St. Martin's, 1980.

Krafft-Ebing, Richard von. *Psychopathia Sexualis*. 1912. New York: G. P. Putnam's Sons, 1965.

Krouse, Tonya. *The Opposite of Desire: Sex and Pleasure in the Modernist Novel*. Lanham, MD: Lexington, 2009.

Lamos, Colleen. *Deviant Modernism: Sexual and Textual Errancy in T. S. Eliot, James Joyce, and Marcel Proust*. New York: Cambridge UP, 1998.

Langbaum, Robert. "Lords of Life, Kings in Exile: Identity and Sexuality in D. H. Lawrence." *American Scholar* (1976): 807–15.

Lawrence, Frieda. *The Memoirs and Correspondence*. Ed. E. W. Tedlock. London: Heinemann, 1961.

Maddox, Brenda. *D. H. Lawrence: The Story of a Marriage*. New York: Simon and Schuster, 1994.

Mullin, Katherine. *James Joyce, Sexuality and Social Purity*. New York: Cambridge UP, 2003.

Murry, John Middleton. "The Rainbow" (1931). *D. H. Lawrence:* The Rainbow *and* Women in Love: *A Casebook*. Ed. Colin Clarke. London: MacMillan, 1969. 73–76.

Phillips, Anita. *A Defense of Masochism*. New York: St. Martin's, 1998.

Plock, Vike Martina. *Joyce, Medicine, and Modernity*. Florida James Joyce Series. Gainesville: UP of Florida, 2010.

Reizbaum, Marilyn. *James Joyce's Judaic Other*. Stanford, CA: Stanford UP, 1999.

Restuccia, Frances L. "Molly in Furs: Deleuzean/Masochian Masochism in the Writing of James Joyce." *NOVEL: A Forum on Fiction* 18.2 (1985): 101–16.

Sacher-Masoch, Leopold von. *Venus in Furs*. 1870. *Masochism*. New York: Zone, 1992.

Schapiro, Barbara Ann. *D. H. Lawrence and the Paradoxes of Psychic Life*. Albany: State U of New York P, 1999.

Shechner, Mark. *Joyce in Nighttown: A Psychoanalytic Inquiry into* Ulysses. Berkeley: U of California P, 1974.

Siegel, Carol. *Male Masochism: Modern Revisions of the Story of Love*. Bloomington: Indiana UP, 1995.

Smirnoff, Victor N. "The Masochistic Contract." *Essential Papers on Masochism.* Ed. Margaret Ann Fitzpatrick Hanly. New York: New York UP, 1995. 62–73.

Stekel, Wilhelm. 1939. *Sadism and Masochism: The Psychology of Hatred and Cruelty.* New York: Washington Square Press, 1968.

Streit, Wolfgang. *Joyce/Foucault: Sexual Confessions.* Ann Arbor: U of Michigan P, 2004.

Torgovnick, Marianna. "Narrating Sexuality: *The Rainbow.*" *The Cambridge Companion to D. H. Lawrence.* Ed. Anne Fernihough. Cambridge: Cambridge UP, 2001. 33–48.

Twitchell, James. "Lawrence's Lamias: Predatory Women in *The Rainbow* and *Women in Love.*" *The Critical Response to D. H. Lawrence.* Ed. Jan Pilditch. Westport, CT: Greenwood, 2001. 82–100.

Watt, Stephen. "'Nothing for a Woman in That': James Lovebirch and Masochistic Fantasy in *Ulysses.*" *Joyce and Popular Culture.* Ed. R. B. Kershner. Gainesville: UP of Florida, 1996. 74–88.

Žižek, Slavoj. "Courtly Love, or, Woman as Thing." *The Metastases of Enjoyment: On Women and Causality.* London: Verso, 2005.

10

That Long Kiss

Comparing Joyce and Lawrence

ENDA DUFFY

> *after that long kiss I near lost my breath*
> *yes he said I was a flower of the mountain.*
>
> James Joyce, *Ulysses*

While the kiss—of friendship, greeting, religious ceremony, sexual desire, or betrayal—has known many historical iterations, the kiss as a public declaration of sexual desire might be thought of as a modernist invention. Cinema is the new modernist art form; the signal human gesture it brought to mass public attention may be the kiss. One of the key technical innovations of cinema, the close-up, helped make the kiss *the* lingered-over scene of modernist-era mass entertainment. Yet the passionate kiss as public spectacle was more than a revolt against propriety by new mass media; two of the most famous European protomodernist artworks are of couples kissing: Rodin's sculpture *The Kiss* of 1882 and Klimt's *Der Kuss* of 1907–8. One of Thomas Edison's very first movies was *The Mary Irwin Kiss*—almost certainly the first kiss shown on moving film (Gray 60).[1] As the *Los Angeles Times* reported on the kiss of Mary Irwin and John Rice, "Their smiles and glances and expressive gestures, and the final joyous, overpowering luscious osculation was repeated again and again, while the audience fairly shrieked and howled approval" (qtd. in Musser 83). At the moment of modernism, kissing scenes in high and popular art forms mark a determination to put on public view what had previously been considered the realm of "private life." Openly showing scenes of sexual desire, artists needed to formulate discourses and imageries of previously unspoken experiences. This incremental countercensorship was one avatar of the more radical shocks that the avant-garde modernisms would inflict on public sensibilities—shocks often premised on breaking taboos regarding sexual display. Since judgments of Joyce and Lawrence have focused first on how each developed discourses of sexuality, it is worth considering how each handled the literary kiss.

The reputations of Joyce and Lawrence, regarding their respective representations of sexuality and much else, have diverged in the last thirty years. Joyce's reputation, already high (he even appeared on the cover of *Time* in 1939) has continued to rise; he is an instantly recognizable global icon of modernist culture, akin to Einstein, Picasso, and Proust. The sense of him as the greatest twentieth-century novelist and literary innovator seems unassailable; his fame as a writer who dealt fearlessly with sexuality is almost equal to that of Freud. He is now often cited also as the original postcolonial writer, an inspiration for South American magic realism and other movements. As such he may be the first modern global author, and he has finally been accepted and celebrated as such in his own country, Ireland. Even Joyce's face, known to the world from relatively few photographs, has become one of the recognizable icons of twentieth-century pre–World War II high culture.

Is Joyce's pervasive fame simply an accident of global celebrity culture or evidence of cultural value that will in some sense endure? The case of Lawrence, at any rate, provides grounds for caution. Lawrence's reputation, which until the 1970s was at least equal to that of Joyce, has since suffered a decline. Lawrence has not only become less familiar to students of English literature, but his novels themselves appear to have grown less readable. As his reputation dims, Lawrence's novels, especially such later ambitious and esoteric ones as *Aaron's Rod* (set in Florence), *Kangaroo* (set in Australia), and *The Plumed Serpent* (set in Mexico) can seem like relics of a time and of concerns not now quite ours. Just as we can look at the best modernist architecture, such as the villas of Le Corbusier, and find it timeless and modern, Joyce's language can still strike the reader as contemporary; Lawrence's prose and his ideas, on the other hand, can seem passé. Likewise, Joyce's approach to human relations, sexual and otherwise, can still seem to matter urgently, while Lawrence's interventions, notoriously so in the realm of politics, sometimes seem spoken in a voice whose pastness we must overcome to enjoy the prose.

Yet we must question the ways in which these two reputations developed. A series of factors have served Joyce's reputation well in the new global republic of literature. Paramount is the issue of Joyce's Americanness—the senses in which the "Joyce" we know was invented by American criticism. His own management of his global reputation set the scene. As Hugh Kenner describes it in *The Pound Era*, for example, Joyce gets to play the discovered literary star, plucked from Ireland, to Pound's tirelessly inventive and enterprising literary agent-manager. Joyce's early publication in the *Little Review*, the interest taken in his work by the Irish American John Quinn, and the publication of *Ulysses* by the American avant-garde bookseller Sylvia Beach (in Paris) all cemented a sense of literary ownership of Joyce among the tastemakers of the nation that was, after World War II, the center of global influence. Kenner and Ellmann, as postwar American critics, invented the version of Joyce we still revere. For both, Joyce's rejection of Irishness suggested a break achievable by the modern individual from provincialism to cosmopolitanism—the desirable trajectory for the new American citizen of the world. Joyce is a star author created by the American imperial imagination at its most liberal but also its most globally ambitious. This version of Joyce grew in favor as the U.S. university system expanded in the 1960s; at that moment, too, his bawdiness could be read as a prophecy of the new sexual freedoms. Despite disruptive postcolonial readings, this is the version of Joyce that still undergirds his global prestige.

Conversely, it may be precisely Lawrence's Englishness—despite his own vehement desire to escape from all England stood for—that has pulled his reputation, especially as a global modernist, downward. The somewhat begrudging respect for Lawrence's work by the formidable and, in British and Commonwealth universities, highly influential F. R. Leavis, author of the canon-making *The Great Tradition,* was both an honor and his downfall. Leavis published *The Great Tradition*, in which Austen, George Eliot, Joseph Conrad, and Henry James were praised, in 1948; it marks the central British postwar bid to demarcate the English canon. In 1958, he added Lawrence to the select company with *D. H. Lawrence, Novelist.* He explicitly compared Lawrence to Joyce, finding the Irish writer deficient in moral purpose:

> It is this spirit, by virtue of which he [Lawrence] can truly say that what he writes must be written from the depth of his religious experience, that makes him, in my opinion, so much more significant in relation to the past and future, so much more truly creative as a technical inventor, an innovator, a master of language, than James Joyce. [In Joyce] there is no organic principle determining, informing and controlling into a vital whole, the elaborate analogical structure, the extraordinary variety of technical devices, the attempts at an exhaustive rendering of consciousness, for which *Ulysses* is remarkable, and which got it accepted by a cosmopolitan literary world as a new start. It is rather, I think, a dead end, or at least a pointer to disintegration. (Leavis 25–26)

Leavis' endorsement marked Lawrence's acceptance at the grandest levels of postwar British academic criticism, so that he became a much-taught writer in the expanding British and postcolonial university systems. Yet it also cast him as a national writer whose reception even at home never quite ceased to be contentious. Lawrence's own version of the modernist war against sexual repression was what most appealed to his American critics; his 1954 biography by Harry T. Moore, originally entitled *The Intelligent Heart*, was reissued in 1974 as *The Priest of Love* (and made into a film in 1981). As interest in the politics of modernism grew, however, Lawrence's quasi-fascist impulses stood out as an embarrassment. His version of a popularized Nietzscheism, channeled through Whitman, Hardy, and artists such as Frank Brangwyn, had led him to an ardent primitivism and a fascination with powerful (male) leaders. His horror of the mass existence of modern urbanism led not to socialism (as in the case of Sean O'Casey) but to a muddled politics that valued charisma. Given all this, the taste for Lawrence's writing ebbed.

In these critical eddies what is forgotten is Lawrence's revolutionary breakthrough: the fact that he may have been the very first truly working-class writer to have entered the English canon. It might be claimed that it was the tremendous psychic, affective, and cultural energies expended in the effort to achieve this breakthrough that found its outcome in his increasingly shrill social attitudes in *The Plumed Serpent* and *Kangaroo*. His embodiment of the idea that in the twentieth century one could leave the working class was partly what made his work popular among students in post–World War II British universities. As class has grown less visible, for whatever reasons, as an issue in literary studies, it is the misogyny, the quasi-fascist tendencies, and the primitivism that may have been born of attempts to deal with his class ambivalence that have now doomed him in the eyes of readers.[2]

Nevertheless, Lawrence's biography draws us back to the class question. The issue of Joyce's class origins is usually subsumed in the tale of his father's alcoholism; however, his family came from a small but select group of well-established upper-middle-class Catholics in Ireland. Joyce attended Ireland's most elite Jesuit schools; even when the family were more or less impoverished, his friends (with Nora Barnacle the single exception) were almost wholly from the privileged class into which he had been born, and he was welcomed to musical evenings in the drawing room of David Sheehy, Member of Parliament.[3] He inherited a confidence born of his family's initial class position, along with an assumption, despite his professed reserve, that he could always tap into networks of others from his class—a talent he used to advantage. The absence of developed working-class characters from his fiction also indicates his assumption that the only class that mattered—for Dublin, for Ireland, for urban civic life, and for modernity—was his own. In this, he again turned out to be on the side of history, for his was precisely the class that in the early twentieth century was coming into its own. In Ireland, members of the Catholic bourgeoisie came to power with independence from Britain in 1921, and this rise, in turn, must be considered as part of the general emergence in the West in the twentieth century of a huge new middle class.

Despite the well-chronicled sinking of the Joyce family into poverty, therefore, Lawrence's class trajectory was in fact altogether more fraught and precarious. As the son of a coal miner and a woman who had married somewhat "beneath her," his initial climb into middle-class respectability was accomplished by the conventional route, for the time, of teacher training college and a post as a teacher. His relatively swift acceptance, once he became a writer, by the bohemian and even aristocratic world that included the Woolfs and Lady Ottoline Morel was influenced by the Fabianism of the day and by a culture that, in the moment of the rise of the Labor Party and of the General Strike, was hungry for working-class voices. If Joyce displayed his bourgeois class confidence to a fault by ostentatiously disporting himself, once he became famous, as the model upper-bourgeois living in spacious Arrondissement 7 apartments and allowing himself to be photographed in his own drawing room in a velvet dressing gown, Lawrence, *au-contraire*, once he had gained entrée to upper class circles, adopted a hand-to-mouth bohemianism.

Joyce, encountering Nora, had the class confidence to elope with a chambermaid, a rebellious act at the time: his confidence, one might claim, allowed him to stage his own intimate life as the enactment of a primitivist impulse to encounter the western, rural-Irish world for which he harbored a fearful fascination. Lawrence, on the other hand, married a German aristocrat; in his case, the scene of desire enacted the subaltern's relations to those in power. Joyce, despite his "exile" and his numerous addresses, lived a version of a conventional high-bourgeois life. Lawrence brilliantly and restlessly traveled the world, from Cornwall to Mexico to Taos to Sri Lanka to Australia to Italy and France. It seems ironic that the duller of these choices has worn best: Joyce's settled milieu of parlor, piano, and writing room produced *Finnegans Wake*, while Lawrence's keyed-up restlessness in the same years generated his contentious late Nietzschean visionary politics.

Yet despite their different authorial self-presentations, the two have much in common. Born in the early 1880s, both came from provincial backwaters that each made famous in his writing. Both, as scholarship boys, benefited from the new, free, and widespread availability of high culture and literature in particular at the end of the nineteenth century: Joyce was sending his brother to find *Jude the Obscure* in the Capel St. Library (Stanislaus, misreading, asked for *Jude the Obscene*) (S. Joyce 101). Lawrence, even better read, wrote his *Study of Thomas Hardy* in 1914. Their family circumstances, despite the differences already outlined, also had similarities: the alcoholic father, ineffectual yet a striking presence, whom the son resented but eventually acknowledged as profoundly influential; the tragic and much-loved mother; the struggle to study and "get on" amid a crowded home life and the degradations of poverty. This precipitated in each author a furious sense of his own distinctiveness and made each intensely skeptical of middle-class pieties. It meant that their bildungsroman narratives share a compelling contrast between accounts of the particularities of everyday life bedeviled by poverty, and flashes of profound yearning for forms of aesthetic experience.

The famous Joycean epiphanies, along with the intense reconnoitering of the natural world and of Lawrence's own sexuality recorded in *The White Peacock*, show us extraordinarily sensitive young authors receptive to a fin de siècle mixture of Nietzscheism, symbolist intensity, and both high Victorian culture and emerging popular culture variants, from music hall songs to sensation fiction. For each, the sense of the poverty and relative narrowness of his background, sharpened by access to high culture, led to the construction of synthetic but signature modes of literary expression. From relatively unlikely sources, the Irish youth whom the Trinity College Provost John Pentland Mahaffy would characterize as akin to "[a] corner-bo[y] who spit into the Liffey" (*JJII* 58) and Lawrence, the coal miner's son from Yorkshire, each synthesized a range of utterly new language forms, vehicles for feelings and ideas unseen in Anglophone literature before. To compare the literary value of Joyce and Lawrence, it is the specific form of these languages that we must explore.

We must also resolve to see beyond the occasional snide comments that at times each made about the other. These almost always appear to be the carpings bred of petty jealousy.[4] Lawrence, according to the unreliable Compton Mackenzie in his memoir *My Life and Times*, is said to have called *Ulysses* "more disgusting than Casanova," and he did describe *Finnegans Wake*, an extract of which he read in *transition*, as "just stewed up fragments of quotation in a would-be dirty mind" (167). Like Yeats, he admitted not to be able to read more than bits of *Ulysses*, claiming "Ulysses wearied me" (*4L* 345). Joyce repaid this attitude by telling Harriet Weaver that *Lady Chatterley's Lover* was "propaganda in favor of something, which, outside D. H. L.'s country at any rate, makes all the propaganda for itself" (*SL* 359). If "D. H. L.'s country" refers here to England, then it is suggestive of how their national—Irish versus British— difference influenced their opinions of each other. Rather than hypothesizing a literary feud on the evidence of scattered comments, however, we should take Lawrence's own advice: "Never trust the artist. Trust the tale. The proper function of a critic is to save the tale from the artist who created it" (*SCAL* 2). At this distance, the antipathy these two writers felt for each other's work (and for each other, for Joyce in 1929, Harry Crosby reported, declined to meet Lawrence) appears a small thing when confronted with the sheer technical and expressive innovation in the writings of each.

To compare these literary innovation projects, let us return to their texts— and, as one example, to how each represents the kiss. In each of the following passages, we read of a kiss offered in the context of heterosexual desire. The first is the kiss of Stephen Dedalus, Belvedere college student, and the "young woman dressed in a long pink gown" (*P1* 100), the prostitute he encounters in the Dublin red-light district, in chapter 2 of *A Portrait*:

> —Give me a kiss, she said.
>
> His lips would not bend to kiss her. He wanted to be held firmly in her arms, to be caressed slowly, slowly, slowly. In her arms he felt that he had suddenly become strong and fearless and sure of himself. But his lips would not bend to kiss her.
>
> With a sudden movement she bowed his head and joined her lips to his and he read the meaning of her movements in her frank uplifted eyes. It was too much for him. He closed his eyes, surrendered himself to her, body and mind, conscious of nothing in the world but the soft pressure of her softly parting lips. They pressed upon his brain as upon his lips as though they were the vehicle of a vague speech; and between them he felt an unknown and timid pressure, darker than the swoon of sin, softer than sound or odor. (*P1* 101)

In *The Rainbow*, the kiss of Ursula and Skrebensky, not quite as illicit, takes place over two days. On the first, "they played at kisses" (*R* 272); on the next, they enter a church:

> Here she would open her female flower like a flame, in this dimness that was more passionate than light.
>
> They hung apart a moment, then willfully turned to each other for the desired contact. She put her arms round him, she cleaved her body

to his, and with her hands pressed upon his shoulders, on his back, she seemed to feel right through him, to know his young, tense body right through. And it was so fine, so hard, yet so exquisitely subject and under his control. She reached him her mouth and drank his full kiss, drank it fuller and fuller.

And it was good, it was very, very good. She seemed to be filled with his kiss, filled as if she had drunk strong, glowing sunshine. She glowed all inside, the sunshine seemed to beat upon her heart underneath, she had drunk so beautifully. [. . .] And radiant as an angel she went with him out of the church, as if her feet were beams of light that walked on flowers for footsteps.

He went beside her, his soul clenched, his body unsatisfied. (*R* 274)

There are other celebrated kisses in the work of each: consider Molly's "after that long kiss I near lost my breath" of *Ulysses* (*U* 18.1575–76). Paul and Clara kiss passionately by the river in chapter 12 of *Sons and Lovers*. If Joyce and Lawrence are two writers of the first, heroic stage of Anglophone modernism that brought sex into public discourse, then these kiss scenes may be read as limit texts, where human intimacies hitherto left mostly unspoken are finally publicized. Note first, therefore, the touching awkwardness in the writing of each of these passages. Both are the literary counterparts of the close-up screen kiss. What does the literary text achieve in writing this intimacy that is lost in the cinema close-up?

Joyce's and Lawrence's kiss descriptions have each an awkward edge. Our embarrassed laughter resembles our reaction to the kinetoscope *Mary Irwin Kiss*: all three are novelties, first depictions. At this distance, it is easy to underestimate this novelty; the writers were delineating a gesture whose forms and variations had hardly ever, in such detail, been described before in high literature in English. Their accounts stage the cobbling together, in modernist experiment, of discourses that in aggregate aim to express the complex of feelings, desires, sensations, and thoughts of the experience described. Thus both authors offer versions of intensified naturalism. They attempt to describe, with a novel exactitude, experiences up to now publicly unspoken. For both, this revolutionary project marks the most brilliant moments of the prose of each. In Joyce, it propels his directness about human physicality, as when in *Ulysses* Molly clambers out of bed as she feels her period coming. More pervasively, it leads to the page-by-page annotation in that novel of a cascading account of tics, itches, sensations, and fidgets, as well as the half thoughts that each of these arouses. It is through them that *Ulysses*, scrupulously, achieves its accounting not of great arcs of human emotion or motivation but, instead, of the exact sensations through which we experience, literally, being alive.

In Lawrence, meanwhile, the novel's power comes from an analogous drive differently expressed. Lawrence, too, wants to "get at" the actual physical sensations and only secondarily the consciousness work involved in being fully alive. (Mostly, he was hostile to a surfeit of consciousness in modern subjects). The discourse he marshals, and then fuses, follows a very different formula to that of Joyce. The fascination of his writing, too, however, stems from the same impulse, emerging in his work as a textual reaching for intensities of language and feeling that seem to us as readers now perhaps less fully modernist than Joyce's (that is, less a montage of clashing heteroglossic styles) but that also strive to annotate the exact experience of a range of raw physical sensations. How each of these writers achieved this becomes clear as we close-read the limit-accounts of the close-up kiss.

For the writer who wishes to come in close to the kissing couple, the relentless stare of the mechanical camera eye filming the close-up is not available. Rather, employing language, he musters a potentially vast array of already existing discourses, from the medical to the poetic, developed to describe all manner of human actions, reactions, and desires, to annotate the gestural and affective fluctuations. Consider, then, how similar the discursive resources mobilized by each are. Both feature tropes of surrender: for Joyce, "He closed his eyes, surrendering himself to her, body and mind" (*P1* 101); for Lawrence, "She cleaved her body to his" (*R* 274). (Joyce's is a lovemaking cliché; Lawrence introduces the biblical "cleaved.")

Next, each switches between accounts of thought and of sensation, from mindfulness to the sensing physical body. Joyce opens with "He wanted to be held firmly in her arms," superseded by "It was too much for him. [. . .] the dark pressure of her softly parting lips" (*P1* 101). The switch from mindful volition to physical sensation is accomplished by a sentence in which the body part becomes volitional: "But his lips would not bend to kiss her" (*P1* 101). In Lawrence, the trajectory from quasi-conscious volition to sensation is less clear-cut but still visible: "Here she would assert her indomitable, gorgeous female self" gives way to "she seemed to be filled with his kiss" (*R* 274). The difference in each passage springs from variations in the point of view. In Joyce, the viewpoint is unabashedly Stephen's, the focus his mixture of sexual desire and embarrassed guilt. In Lawrence, the viewpoint is largely, but not wholly, that of Ursula; it as if the authorial camera moves forward and back, at moments offering us a view of both lovers and suggesting at those moments a narrator who is offering us a judgment on Ursula's fluctuating desires, feelings, sensations, and thoughts rather than giving us access to her unmediated viewpoint. When we hear that "Her eyes lit up with daring," she is being viewed from without (R 274); in the next sentence, "Here, here she would assert her indomitable, gorgeous female self, here" (R 274), we sense that we are having her intention at that moment signaled through her consciousness directly to us, or alternately, or even simultaneously, we sense that here is a narrator's judgment of what will occur, using a language of primitivist gender "archetypes."

All this, in each writer, is interspersed with dashes of discourses from a myriad of sources: in Lawrence, a lurid, Pateresque pastoralism ("she would open her flower like a flame" [R 274]), a language of romantic contact culled from Victorian sensation fiction ("She seemed [. . .] to know his young, tense body right through" [R 274]), from the poems of the pre-Raphaelites, of drinking, weather, angel's wings, and heartbeats ("filled as if she had drunk strong, glowing sunshine [which . . .] seemed to beat upon her heart" [R 274]). Joyce, more Jesuitical than pre-Raphaelite, still succumbs ostentatiously to symbolist flourishes ("darker than the swoon of sin, softer than sound or odor" [P1 107]), a language of devotional gestures transferred to the profane ("she bowed his head and joined her lips to his" [P1 107]), and a languid, decadent textuality of exaggerated repetitions ("to be caressed slowly, slowly, slowly" [P1 107]). Arrestingly, he limns the move from thinking to sensing in the kiss as the reading of signs in a mode worthy of Wilde or Derrida: "he read the meaning of her movements [. . .] as though they were the vehicle of a vague speech" (P1 101).

This polyphony of dissociated, paradoxical discourses marshaled by each to describe the kiss comes across as an authorial rummaging among the moth-eaten Victorian draperies in which love and desire could be dressed. Their almost embarrassing proliferation suggests a textual impulse to annotate, by any means necessary, the *physical* reality of what was actually felt: "between [his lips] he felt an unknown and timid pressure, [. . .] softer" (P1 101), and "She reached him her mouth and drank his full kiss, drank it fuller and fuller. And it was good" (R 274). In each, these moments that focus on sensation tease us with hints of the undescribed: Joyce speaks of an "unknown pressure"; Lawrence merely repeats twice the exasperatingly nondescriptive "good." This generality reflects each character's sense that he or she can barely assimilate this experience. But it also suggests each author signaling that he has not yet plumbed the depths of this experience, that his efforts are a work in progress, and that each text, even if more explicit than formerly, still plays at discretion. In both, the kiss is a synecdoche for sex, itself undescribed.

Both writers annotate a human gesture hitherto seldom described in English literature; they do so in terms of the physical sensations it arouses. Yet each marshals different discursive apparatuses to represent these sensations, thus achieving remarkably different effects. In part, this results from how the different religious discourses learned in each writer's childhood, although for each repudiated early, still impinge on their accounts. In Stephen's case, the symbolist decadence of the chapter's ending is the counterpoint to the deliciously surmounted guilt of the Catholic youth. For Ursula, the sense of the kiss as a more intense communion with her natural or pastoral selfhood suggests the residual rhetoric of Lawrence's Nonconformist, "chapel" upbringing in encounter with a Nietzschean ideology of personal force and a Bergsonian belief in the *élan vital*.

Both authors are invested, if in different ways, in the notion of a radically independent, self-constituted, and powerful human subject; for the characters each describes, the kiss is as much a struggle with another person as it is any kind of communion or communication. For both, too, the discourses marshaled effectively disallow the chance for any single ideological perspective—regarding modern selfhood, gender roles, or the place of humans in the order of things, for example—to dominate. Thus both also seem radically uncertain about what meaning they might grant the kiss after they have revealed it. With modernist obscurity, these are, in their different ways, radically uncertain kisses, moments of stoppage or uneasy truce in intersubjective power struggles in which the excitement, which Lawrence called the "electricity" (*Women in Love* 93), has as much to do with an interpersonal competitiveness as with sexual attraction, and in which the excessiveness of the language, which in each reaches a near-mawkish intensity at the kiss, implies a nervy sense of the incompleteness of the project to annotate either the full sensuality or the social implications of each encounter.

In "Notes on Gesture" of 1992, Giorgio Agamben declared that "[b]y the end of the nineteenth century, the Western bourgeoisie had definitely lost its gestures" (48). He cites the research of Georges de la Tourette and other fin de siècle scientists on the fidgeting body, and the photographic studies of gesture by Muybridge and Marey, and goes on to claim that "[i]n the cinema, a society that has lost its gestures tries at once to reclaim what it has lost and to record its loss" (52). The jerky movements of Stravinsky's *Rite of Spring*, the spasmodic rhythms of some avant-garde music, and the endless interest in the gait of the pedestrian in Joyce, Musil, Woolf, and Eliot all support Agamben's declaration. Modernist literature's emphasis is geared to specific physical gestures, to the sensations they induce and the desires they satisfy. Of this Joyce's and Lawrence's depictions of the kiss, precisely because of their discursive be-fuddlement, are outstanding examples. Both writers are engaged in a project to annotate human gestures with an exactitude previously unseen in literature. Each brings to bear on the previously occluded gesture a mix of discourses, which map it with a postnaturalist specificity, and each refuses any single inter-pretation of its significance. It is left to us as readers to ask: why should human gesture come in for such intense scrutiny at this moment?

Was gesture a near-obsession because for some reason, as Agamben sug-gests, a massive overhaul of the bourgeoisie's gestural repertoire was at that moment taking place? Was a new range of gestures being invented? For ex-ample, could the passionate, mouth-to-mouth kiss have been less common before the modernist era? If the kiss as we know it is a modernist invention—a gesture with a cultural history that appeared, and was then described and celebrated—will it eventually, at least in its current form, fade? If Agamben is correct, we must ask why the old gestures did not suffice any longer. If gestures are expressions of human sensations and emotions, a means to give such feel-ings human form through the movements of the body, then does a gestural breakdown also imply a breakdown of accepted human feelings and sensations themselves? How are the old gestures replaced by new ones? Finally, could this replacement be a definition of the cultural activity of modernism itself? It is not hard to imagine a history of gesture—for example, bowing in court is now largely passé—but to imagine a concomitant history of feeling itself—to think, for instance, that the very nature of sexual desire or love has changed over time—is a more controversial idea. It is against this background of the history of modern gesture and an implied related history of feeling that we must read Joyce's and Lawrence's kiss accounts. They are signal moments in the history of modern feeling and modern gesture, when we witness the old protocols fall while new ones, with immense implications for what the texts tells us about structures of feeling, are inaugurated.

How can we assign significance to such possibly revolutionary accounts of gesture, sensation, and feeling in modernist writing? Darwin, Victorian nar-rator of a modern "natural history," that is, of the story of nature as one of his-torical change, grappled with the question of a natural history of the emotions in *The Expression of Emotions in Man and Animals*. Our task in reading Joyce and Lawrence is to relate this possible *natural* history to more local histories, of communities, nations, group formations, and the sensate, emotional sub-jects who inhabit them. Joyce and Lawrence, very like scientists after Darwin from Charcot to Angelo Mosso,[5] recorded with an incredible exactitude the alterations in gesture that correlated to sensations and emotional responses. The scientists professed a therapeutic logic, determined to chart normative gestures and cure deviations, or to harness the expressions of human energy for maximal efficiency. Art had no such justification for attending to gesture so that literature, dance, and painting became sites where wild new gestures could be entertained and the sensations they engendered understood.

The kiss is hardly a wild new gesture. By giving it its literary close-up, nevertheless, both Lawrence and Joyce show a commitment to the evidence of the sensing body, and a determination to imagine that body and its subject-owner's potential for moving, sensing, feeling, and acting outside the bounds imposed by preexisting ideologies. Both Lawrence and Joyce improvised not only new polyphonal discourses of embodiment but also discourses adequate to new gestures of human relationality, generators of potentially new sensations, even new drives. Their language experiments strive to attend more attentively than ever before to the realities of actual sensate experience. Their work does not, in the passages read here, at once reframe that experience within new paradigms of sociopolitical efficacy; that is the task of their readers. Describing the kiss through a host of discourses, they each annotate a familiar gesture, opening another delicate move of the human ballet to our delighted gaze.

Notes

1. For more on the prevalence of the "Kiss film" in early silent film, see Gray, "The Kiss in the Tunnel."

2. Martin Amis called Lawrence "perhaps the most foul-tempered writer of all time (beater of women and animals, racist, anti-Semite, etc.)" (qtd. in Kunkel). For an academic affirmation of this attitude (by an admirer of Lawrence), see Eagleton, *The English Novel* 258–60. For feminist aversion to Lawrence, see Millet's landmark *Sexual Politics*, esp. chap. 5. For a counterargument, see Balbert, *D. H. Lawrence and the Phallic Imagination*. For an excellent feminist treatment of Lawrence that acknowledges his "misogynist poetics," see Sword, *Engendering Inspiration* 75–118.

3. See the excellent guide by Igoe, *James Joyce's Dublin Houses* 44–56.

4. On their enmity, see Delany's "A Would-Be-Dirty Mind" 76–82.

5. On the work of Mosso, Marey, and others, see Rabinbach, *The Human Motor*.

Works Cited

Agamben, Giorgio. "Notes on Gesture." *Means without End: Notes on Politics.* Trans. Vincenzo Binetti and Cesare Casarino. Minneapolis: U of Minnesota P, 1992. 49–62.

Balbert, Peter. *D. H. Lawrence and the Phallic Imagination: Essays on Sexual Identity and Feminist Misreading.* New York: St. Martin's, 1989.

Darwin, Charles. *The Expression of Emotions in Man and Animals.* 1872. Chicago: U of Chicago P, 1965.

Delany, Paul. "'A Would-Be-Dirty Mind': D. H. Lawrence as an Enemy of Joyce." *Joyce in the Hibernian Metropolis.* Ed. Morris Beja and David Norris. Columbus: Ohio State UP, 1996.

Eagleton, Terry. *The English Novel: An Introduction.* Oxford: Wiley-Blackwell, 2004.

Faulkner, William. *Women in Love.* Ed. David Farmer, Lindeth Vasey, and John Worthen. Cambridge, Cambridge UP, 1987.

Gray, Frank. "*The Kiss in the Tunnel* 1896: G. A. Smith and the Emergence of the Edited Film in England." *The Silent Cinema Reader.* Ed. Lee Grieveson and Peter Krämer. New York: Routledge, 2003. 51–62.

Igoe, Vivien. *James Joyce's Dublin Houses and Nora Barnacle's Galway.* London: Mandarin, 1990.

Joyce, Stanislaus. *My Brother's Keeper: James Joyce's Early Years.* New York: Viking, 1958.

Kenner, Hugh. *The Pound Era.* Berkeley: U of California P, 1973.

Kunkel, Benjamin. "The Deep End: A New Life of D. H. Lawrence." *New Yorker* 19 December 2005: 35.

Leavis, F. R. *D. H. Lawrence, Novelist.* London: Chatto and Windus, 1955.

———. *The Great Tradition.* New York: George Stewart, 1950.

Mackenzie, Compton. *My Life and Times: Octave Five, 1915–1923.* London: Chatto and Windus, 1966.

Millet, Kate. *Sexual Politics.* 1970. Champaign: U of Illinois P, 2000.

Moore, Harry T. *The Priest of Love: A Life of D. H. Lawrence.* Carbondale: Southern Illinois UP, 1977.

Musser, Charles. *Before the Nickelodeon: Edwin S. Porter and the Edison Manufacturing Company.* Berkeley: U of California P, 1991.

Rabinbach, Anson. *The Human Motor: Energy, Fatigue and the Origins of Modernity.* Berkeley: U of California P, 1992.

Sword, Helen. *Engendering Inspiration: Visionary Strategies in Rilke, Lawrence and H. D.* Ann Arbor: U of Michigan P, 1995.

11

"Result of the Rockinghorse Races"

The Ironic Culture of Racing in Joyce's *Ulysses*
and Lawrence's "The Rocking-Horse Winner"

CARL F. MILLER

> *Horseness is the whatness of allhorse*
>
> James Joyce, *Ulysses*

While the critical comparisons between James Joyce and D. H. Lawrence have at times centered on issues of exile, colonialism, and gender and relationships, all of these considerations intersect in their writing within the unlikely subject of horse racing. The sport offers a crucial theme in both Joyce's masterpiece *Ulysses* (1922) and Lawrence's classic short story "The Rocking-Horse Winner" (1926), as both works are set in a time when horse racing was perhaps the most culturally ubiquitous sport in Europe, a reality driven by a host of complex socioeconomic factors. While analyses of horse racing in *Ulysses* have been offered by a number of prominent Joyce scholars from Stanley Sultan to Vincent Cheng, the sport remains a largely marginalized and self-contained concern within the book as a whole. In truth, horse racing and its accordant concerns offer insight into the characters and culture of *Ulysses* in ways that few other narrative or symbolic factors in the book do, with the sport presenting an effective barometer of everything from class standing to colonial subjugation to gender affiliation.

While racing's culture of materialism and addiction is only peripherally evident in *Ulysses*, "The Rocking-Horse Winner" showcases it as the text's central subject. The mantra in Lawrence's story—"There must be more money!"—emphasizes a sense of economic desperation that can never be quenched and that instead only deepens over time, even as Paul turns ten shillings into eighty thousand pounds. Paul's rocking horse becomes the vehicle for his obsessive drive to select winning racehorses, a compulsion as notable for its unbelievable success as for its tragicomic ending. This study will emphasize the way that both Joyce and Lawrence utilize horse racing as a hallmark of their respective cultures, the perverse economic and social system such cultures produce, and the dramatic significance of racing and gambling in each of these memorable works.

"A Bloody Dark Horse"

While horses feature repetitively in *Ulysses*, it can be easy to dismiss such mention as a result of the book's sheer volume; Rafael García León says most readers would conclude that "there are so many horses because one can find in *Ulysses* a great deal of almost everything" (3). However, such immensity does not account for why the horse is the most common animal in the book, or why the Ascot Gold Cup is such a repeatedly referenced event, and these questions strike at the core of Joyce's cultural and symbolic intent.

To begin with, Joyce had an evident familiarity with and affinity for horse racing. He was an occasional visitor to races in Ireland, which he would attend with like-minded friends, and he often listened to radio programs from Athlone, whose eclectic material included everything from traditional Irish songs to racing information and results (Atherton 53). This was an interest that Joyce shared with the majority of the men in Dublin, as horse racing was perhaps the most culturally inclusive sport in Ireland in the early twentieth century. Richard Holt explains that while "racing had the aura of aristocracy about it [as] 'the sport of kings,'" it nevertheless "appealed both to the smart and fashionable and to the ordinary man, the punter with a few pence to put on" (211). While there are numerous references within *Ulysses* to other sports (including tennis, rugby, and boxing), none are as universally linked to Dublin's popular culture. For example, the Gordon-Bennett Cup—the preeminent European automobile race of the time and an event that had been held in Ireland in 1903—bears scant mention in *Ulysses*, despite having been contested the following day. The auto race represents a technological fascination with a relatively unfamiliar medium, as most spectators had never owned a motorcar or even ridden in one. Horse racing, on the other hand, offers a more mainstream consideration, as horses were still the dominant mode of transportation in 1904 Dublin, and racing them was a dominant sport within the culture at large.

With this degree of familiarity comes a high level of comfort in discussing horses for most of the characters in the novel. While most have a rudimentary knowledge of horses, no one is an infallible expert on them—as all who venture money on the Ascot Gold Cup lose—and the only man who appears to bet correctly (Bloom) is cast away as an outsider. Talk of betting on the races is presented as an indispensable part of Dublin's cultural fabric, every bit as common as discussions about the weather. In the barroom setting of "Lestrygonians," for example, the names of horses blend in seamlessly with those of alcoholic drinks (*U* 8.997–1025);[1] Nosey Flynn talks of the horse Zinfandel while Bantam Lyons orders a stone ginger and Paddy Leonard two small Jamesons—a linguistic slippage that carries through to the next episode when Shakespeare's classic lines are morphed into "My kingdom for a drink" (*U* 9.981). This also draws attention to the fact that racing in *Ulysses* is often more rhetorical than physical. Joyce was fond of quoting a statement Oscar Wilde made to W. B. Yeats: "We Irish have done nothing, but we are the greatest talkers since the Greeks." This view holds particularly true in the case of horse racing, where debate seems tantamount to participation.

Given Joyce's famed precision and comprehensiveness, it is also useful to consider the role of racing in his historical fidelity to 16 June 1904. Stanley Sultan argues that "the only reason for the date of Bloomsday that is in any way functional in the novel would seem to be the historical fact that a horse named Throwaway, a dark horse, in an upset that made the race a memorable one, won the coveted Gold Cup away from the famous Sceptre at Ascot on that day in that year" (456). As this is the sole nonfictional event of that day that directly influences the action of the book, extensive attention and precision are paid to its development, from the famed twenty-to-one odds on the winner to the 3:00 p.m. start time of the race. All four of the horses that ran in the race are mentioned in *Ulysses* (Throwaway, Sceptre, Zinfandel, and Maximum II), and each of these horses has particular thematic significance. It is at the end of "Lotus Eaters" that the first reference is made to this central sporting event of *Ulysses*:

—Ascot. Gold Cup. Wait, Bantam Lyons muttered. Half a mo. Maximum the second.
—I was just going to throw it away, Mr Bloom said.
Bantam Lyons raised his eyes suddenly and leered weakly.
—What's that? His sharp voice said.
—I say you can keep it, Mr Bloom answered. I was going to throw it away that moment.

Bantam Lyons doubled an instant, leering: then thrust the outspread
sheets back on Mr Bloom's arms.
—I'll risk it, he said. Here, thanks. (*U* 5.532–41)

The misunderstanding between Bloom and Bantam Lyons—with the latter assuming the former has offered him a betting tip on the horse Throwaway—sets in motion a butterfly effect that is reliant upon the enormous cultural significance of horse racing. In addition to its role in *Ulysses*, Joyce would
later weave horse racing into *Finnegans Wake*, where "the Thousand to one
Guinea-Gooseberry's Lipperful Slipver Cup" features a horse named "Rata-
tuohy" (*FW* 342.24)—most obviously a tribute to the RHA artist Patrick Tuohy,
who painted Joyce's portrait but also both a reference to the common French
dish comprised of leftovers and a near anagram to "Throwaway."

Beyond such linguistic gamesmanship, though, the extent of precise racing
references and terminology in both works is evidence that Joyce's interest in
horse racing is for more than its contribution to historical accuracy; it is instead tied to a deep cultural interest in the sport as an institution. James Atherton notes that "usually horse racing is referred to in the *Wake* as a generally
known activity, an inescapable but somewhat unimportant background feature
whose popularity is somewhat absurd" (53), and the same could certainly be
said of its role in *Ulysses*. The inescapability is made evident by the consistent
chatter from newsstands ("*Evening Telegraph, stop press edition! Result of the
Gold Cup races!*" [*U* 13.1174–75]), which gives the impression that all of Dublin was hanging on this race. The absurdity, meanwhile, is highlighted by the
newsboys' cries in "Circe," where the "Result of the rockinghorse races" is given
top billing over the "Safe arrival of Antichrist" (*U* 15.2140–41).

Horse racing additionally offers a decided insight into Irish national identity in the face of British colonial hegemony, although in a more subtle way
than the other sports of *Ulysses*. For example, boxing—another highly popular
competition heavily aligned with gambling—is highlighted in *Ulysses*' account
of the Keogh-Bennett boxing match, where it is equated with overzealous,
misguided nationalism (*U* 12.960–87). Although the Irish "pucker" defeats the
English "redcoat" in this fight, the bout is ultimately suggestive of Irish subjugation, as it offers a symbolic victory of no political or material significance.

Unlike boxing, or politically charged GAA sports such as hurling and Gaelic
football, or equally typecast English sports such as rugby, soccer, and cricket,
horse racing in *Ulysses* represents a comparatively neutral sport with respect to
nationalist bias. This is somewhat surprising, as in the early twentieth century

Irish horses were generally held to be one of the country's great sources of pride and among the best—if not *the* best—bred in all of Europe. Writing of the time, Stephen Gwynn states that, of all the animals of Ireland, "its glory is the horse. I have seen myself representatives of the German, French, Italian, and Spanish Governments on their way to pick up Irish blood for their cavalry studs" (313).[2] Despite the Ascot Gold Cup being an English race—contested mostly by English riders and English-owned horses—there are no charges of political betrayal leveled against Irishmen discussing the race. In *Ulysses*, while the Irish are interested in horses, they are not necessarily interested in Irish horses.

In spite of this, much as David Lloyd asserts that Yeats' work at the time offers "a symbolist aesthetic [that] is inseparable from the politics of cultural nationalism" (60), in *Ulysses* the horse offers a symbol with an indelible connection to colonial politics. All three of Throwaway's challengers in the 1904 Gold Cup carry such underlying political connotations. Maximum II was the defending champion of the race, having won the 1903 Gold Cup, and was owned by the Frenchman Jacques de Brémond, whose other famous racehorse was the ironically named winner of the 1901 Prix Royal-Oak[3]—Jacobite. Zinfandel, on the other hand, would rebound from a second-place finish in the 1904 Gold Cup to win the race the following year; he was owned by the 8th Baron Howard de Walden (whose family is still among the richest in England) and was sired by Persimmon, the most famous stud of King Edward VII's stable.

Sceptre, although never a winner of the Gold Cup, was perhaps the most famous racehorse of the time; she was also sired by Persimmon, and in 1902 she became the first—and to date only—horse to win four British Classic Races outright. Despite the phallic implications of her name, Sceptre was a female racehorse who was given a royal name in honor of Queen Victoria at the end of her reign.[4] Sceptre was originally owned by Hugh Grosvenor, the 1st Duke of Westminster, who was named Master of the Horse by William Gladstone in 1880 and who made a name of for himself in the 1880s in his public opposition of Gladstone's Home Rule Bill for Ireland. She was sold in 1903 to Sir William Bass, whose family fortune originated from his namesake's brewing company; Bass Pale Ale, when mixed with Guinness Stout, is to this day called a Black and Tan, much the same as the temporary royal constable Black and Tans whose mission was to suppress revolutionary activity in Ireland. In such a way, thoroughbred racing's traditional categorization as the "sport of kings" is repeatedly reinforced in the blue-blooded lineage and ownership of the rest of the Gold Cup's field. Accordingly, at the end of *Ulysses'* first episode, Stephen remembers to be wary of both the "hoof of a horse" and the "smile of a Saxon" (*U* 1.732).

However, this passage is just as surely warning against faith in the actual hooves of horses or—more specifically—against the certainty of the outcome of any horse race. In theory, horse racing is an event in which betting odds exist to level the racing field, pitting oddsmaker and bettor evenly against one another. In reality, of course, the odds in horse racing favor bookie far more than bettor, rendering horse racing equivalent to the Irish colonial struggle. While the oft-repeated odds on Gold Cup winner Throwaway were twenty-to-one (which no character in *Ulysses* actually takes advantage of), the betting odds on Zinfandel—the runner-up in the Gold Cup—were only five-to-four, offering maximum risk for minimal gain.[5] Mark Osteen emphasizes that "no character wins regularly on horses, and those associated with betting are among the least attractive characters in the novel" (266–67), such as Nosey Flynn, Bantam Lyons, and Lenehan.[6] On the other hand, those who abstain from gambling are often projected as the book's most admirable figures, including the responsible barkeep Davy Byrne, who "never put anything on a horse" (*U* 8.815–16), and Bloom himself, who "never backed a horse in anger in his life" (*U* 12.1552–53). Losses are all too common, and the occasional win is an excuse for recklessness. This is evident in Corny Kelleher's apology to the Watches on Stephen's behalf in "Circe": "Won a bit on the races. Gold Cup. *Throwaway*. (he laughs) Twenty to one. Do you follow me?" (*U* 15.4813–15).

Such behavior directly illustrates Jean Baudrillard's theory of the fulfillment of desire. Baudrillard speculates: "If you had fifty million dollars, what would you do with it? Chaos. Faced with the disposal of free time at will, the same immediate panic surfaces in us. How do we get rid of it?" (204). The temporary chaos created by winning a horse-racing bet aligns itself usefully with this trend, as "every fulfillment of desire in value returns to the contrary extremity" (Baudrillard 207). As such, gambling on horse racing is effectively described in "Lestrygonians" as a coin flip in which "Heads I win tails you lose" (*U* 8.827).

This system of tragic economics highlights the national significance of horse racing and helps explain its ironic standing as a preeminent Irish sport of the day. From a pure GAA sporting perspective, the popularity of horse racing is somewhat perplexing given that it provides no physical benefits, is driven by no political motives, and provides little (if any) pure entertainment, given that no one in the book attends or listens to the race. Instead, the universal interest in horse racing among the characters of *Ulysses* exists largely because of its potential to generate money. For obvious reasons, the opportunity to instantly acquire large financial sums for minimal risk proves alluring to many of Dublin's denizens. The economic logic that emerges from such a belief keeps the

Ascot Gold Cup at the forefront of *Ulysses'* plot, as horse racing is linked with gambling throughout the book, effectively categorizing racing as more of a lottery than a sport.

However, these long odds are a reality that does not escape the bettors in *Ulysses*, as losing in many cases presents a perversely attractive option.[7] Boylan wagers only two quid on Sceptre but makes a point of telling Molly he has lost twenty—the better to maintain his reputation for profligacy. Losing is also an opportunity to solidify one's place within social circles, as collective losses generate a sense of community. Indeed, there are unifying condolences all around Barney Kiernan's when the Gold Cup results are announced, from Joe Hynes' statement that Throwaway would "have won the money only for the other dog" (*U* 12.1233–34) to Lenehan's declaration that "We're all in a cart" (*U* 12.1222).

By (presumably) gambling on a long shot and winning big, Bloom establishes himself as an outsider among the patrons. In the cultural environment of "Cyclops," the only way Bloom "wins" is if he bets—and loses—on Zinfandel, Sceptre, or Maximum II. Although his transgressions are both unfounded and unintentional, by winning extravagantly and refusing to stand a round of drinks for the house Bloom has violated most every unwritten rule of horse racing's subculture. As Mark Osteen explains, "Issuing from a drive towards self-sacrifice, gambling both creates solidarity with other gamblers and enacts the larger culture's impulses toward self-destructive expenditure" (265). It is with a view toward this larger culture that the Gold Cup becomes economically significant beyond the obvious symbolism of its name and casts horse racing—both ironically and unfortunately—as the quintessential sport of Irish colonialism.

It bears mentioning that such self-destructive expenditure on horse racing is occasionally countered by Joyce with a corrupt eye toward the acquisition of wealth. There were actual instances where racing was used as a method of investment by brokers who relied on inside tips or racing fixes to generate revenue; both the 16 June 1904 editions of the *Evening Telegraph* and the *Freeman's Journal*, for example, contain an ad for Stephens and Henderson that offers to "Increase your income" with "no racing or stock dealing, but legitimate method." Most notable among *Ulysses'* characters on this matter is Bella Cohen, who has an arrangement with "the vet her tipster that gives her all the winners and pays for her son in Oxford" (*U* 15.1288–89).

It is this alternative attitude of opportunism that Bloom has apparently adopted toward horse racing. In "Ithaca," when Bloom contemplates a get-rich-quick scheme, it is no coincidence that horse racing is the first option he considers:

What rapid but insecure means to opulence might facilitate immediate purchase?

A private wireless telegraph which would transmit by dot and dash system the result of a national equine handicap (flat or steeplechase) of 1 or more miles and furlongs won by an outsider at odds of 50 to 1 at 3 hr 8 m p.m. at Ascot (Greenwich time), the message being received and available for betting purposes in Dublin at 2.59 p.m. (Dunsink time). (*U* 17.1672–78)

Bloom has no qualms about winning large sums of money off horse racing, but he is only willing to "gamble" on an absolute sure thing, where risk is driven to the minimum for a cash windfall. As he represents "the scientific" (*U* 17.560), Bloom is not willing to gamble on sports (an inexact science at best), but he is willing to gamble on numbers and technology (both of which carry a high degree of certitude for him).

This is not the only time horse racing offers particular insight into *Ulysses'* characters. Richard Ellmann records that Joyce once told his friend Daniel Hummel that "human beings sometimes appear to me to take the shape of animals" (*JJII* 428), and Joyce uses equine images repeatedly throughout *Ulysses* to describe the book's most prominent characters. Molly, for instance, is characterized by Lenehan as "a gamey mare" (*U* 10.566–67), despite her aversion to horse racing. In her sole specific racing reference, Molly erroneously refers to the Gold Cup as a "steeplechase" (*U* 18.956)—it is in reality a flat race—and displays an obvious distaste for the sport in general.[8] Recognizing the culture and behavior that racing engenders, she thinks, "when do you ever see women rolling around drunk like they do or gambling every penny they have and losing it on horses" (*U* 18.1435–38).

This is a key point, as horse racing in *Ulysses* is consistently correlated with the masculine mainstream. The episode considered the most masculine in *Ulysses*, "Cyclops," is also the one most heavily laden with racing references, and the most effectively masculine and blue-blooded antagonists of *Ulysses* are generally linked to horses. On *Ulysses'* opening page, Buck Mulligan's face is described as "equine in its length" (*U* 1.15), and the episode ends with the aforementioned warning about Haines ("hoof of a horse, smile of a Saxon") (*U* 1.732). In the following episode, Mr. Deasy's royalist sympathies are made evident by the décor of his office, in which "framed [. . .] images of vanished horses stood in homage" with their noble English owners on their backs (*U* 2.300).

In contrast to this, Bloom and Stephen are both marginalized and feminized by their general disinterest in horse racing and the equine references tied to their respective characters. While Joe Hynes' character notably terms Bloom "a bloody dark horse" (U 12.1558), Vincent Cheng suggests that when Stephen famously says, "History is a nightmare from which I am trying to awake," one can read the term "night *mare*" (i.e., dark horse) into his comment (106)—effectively aligning *Ulysses*' two major characters while also feminizing them. With this in mind, it is significant that the names on Molly's list of alleged lovers in "Ithaca" are also inclined to horses, as Boylan and Lenehan appear alongside "a farmer at the Royal Dublin Society's Horse Show" (U 17.2135). Boylan, Bloom's foremost challenger for Molly's affections, carries a repeated association with horses, given that he is the son of a horse dealer and that the pub where he and Bloom have previously encountered one another is the Bleeding Horse. He very vocally bets on Sceptre and effectively represents the mainstream masculine conscience of Dublin. Indeed, when Throwaway beats Sceptre in the Gold Cup, it can be read in a Freudian sense as Bloom getting the better of Boylan.

Although Sceptre is thoroughly ensconced by the characters in *Ulysses* as the race's favorite, the "Oxen of the Sun" episode details the race with her running "out freshly with O. Madden up. She was leading the field" until "in the straight on the run home when all were in close order the dark horse Throwaway drew level, reached, outstripped her" (U 14.1128–33). Much like Throwaway, Bloom is an underdog competing against a number of blue-blood favorites, as the Gold Cup race assumes an ironic significance in *Ulysses*' underlying narrative. In such a way, perhaps the most apt categorization of Bloom is the aforementioned description of him as a "dark horse" (U 12.1558). Much as the citizens of Dublin gamble wrong on the Gold Cup's outcome, Bloom also notably defies their expectations. Despite being an outsider in mainstream society who falls behind in the course of *Ulysses*, he ultimately heads his adversaries—however dubiously—by its finish, as the book ends with Molly's passionate recollection of Bloom's proposal and her acceptance. The mainstream challengers may claim victory on either side of this moment, but on 16 June 1904, both Bloom and Throwaway emerge victorious.

"It's Better to Be Born Lucky"

While not of the scope or fame of Joyce's *Ulysses*, Lawrence's "The Rocking-Horse Winner" nevertheless offers an equally compelling take on the culture of horse racing and its narrative and symbolic possibilities. While the work started out with an admittedly simple premise—in a May 1926 letter to Ada Clarke, Lawrence describes the text as "that little story about the boy who betted on the horse races" (Ellis 667)—"The Rocking-Horse Winner" is, according to James Cowan, "possibly the most frequently anthologized of Lawrence's stories" and "among the most widely discussed works in critical studies of the author" (122). It was the first of Lawrence's works to be adapted into a film (1949) and, despite its relative brevity, is driven by many of the same thematic issues as Lawrence's earlier novels. In fact, Lawrence viewed "The Rocking-Horse Winner" as a rewriting of his 1913 novel, *Sons and Lovers*, in which a son named Paul also falls ill and is obsessed with his mother's approval and well-being. While composing "The Rocking-Horse Winner," Lawrence told his wife, Frieda, that he felt his attempt to justify his mother's all-consuming love prevented him from effectively dealing with the issue in his earlier work, admitting, "I would write a different 'Sons and Lovers' now; my mother was wrong, and I thought she was absolutely right" (F. Lawrence 56).

In spite of such biographical origins, Lawrence does not share Joyce's fidelity to actual history when it comes to his story's horses. While "The Rocking-Horse Winner" does refer to many of the major races of the day—including the Epsom Derby, the Grand National, and the Ascot Gold Cup—their actual results take a back seat to fiction. Sansovino, for example, was an actual horse, albeit one that did not win the Gold Cup as the story suggests; he instead won the 1924 Derby, a race in which he was the favorite. Beyond that, there is no historical record of Singhalese, Malabar, or any other significant horse in the story.

Instead, it is the main characters in "The Rocking-Horse Winner" that have a real-life foundation, as—in addition to Lawrence's relationship with his own mother—Lady Cynthia Asquith and her family offered Lawrence an effective model for his story's narrative. Lawrence became familiar with the Asquith family as the result of business; "The Rocking-Horse Winner" was first intended for Lady Asquith's anthology, *The Ghost-Book*, which was published in September 1926.[9] However, this relationship would turn more personal as he became familiar with her firstborn son, who grew up with a pronounced social disorder (which was labeled—probably appropriately—as autism), and allowed Lawrence to witness firsthand the social dilemmas this presented for the family. In addition, Rosemary Davies emphasizes that "the Asquiths were poor relations compared to the social set to which they belonged by birth" (124), allowing Lawrence to find "in the Asquith household the ingredients for his story on destructive materialism" (121).

In "The Rocking-Horse Winner," Paul's mother tells him that they are also "the poor members of the family" (RHW 791), and their wealth is a veritable façade, as "there was always the grinding sense of the shortage of money, though the style was kept up" (RHW 790). Thus, although Paul's family lives in relative luxury in a fine house with servants, the house is filled with the haunting (and unspoken) phrase: *"There must be more money! There must be more money!"* (RHW 791). Everyone in the house—from the adults to the children to the puppy to the wooden rocking horse—hears this unspoken voice, and it comes to dominate the affairs of the house and the lives of those who inhabit it. It is in this impending void that horse racing assumes prominence with its ability to generate large sums of money instantaneously. Much the same as in *Ulysses*, "The Rocking-Horse Winner" reveals the cultural ubiquity of horse racing to be an overriding economic significance.

The use of the rocking horse in Lawrence's story also likely originates from the Asquith household. Prior to her association with Lawrence, Lady Asquith had worked as a secretary for J. M. Barrie, who notably owned a rocking horse (which he describes buying in *The Little White Bird* [1902]), which presumably influenced Lady Asquith to buy one for her son. Davies explains that "a behavior trait among children afflicted with autism is forward-backward rocking motion of their bodies," and, as a result, "it is likely John would have been given a rocking horse, and that he would have used it long after he outgrew it, given his condition" (126).[10]

This raises the significance of the rocking horse itself, which W. D. Snodgrass considers "the story's chief structural feature" (191) and an object that has a rich history with respect to both class and nationalism. Before becoming industrially produced in the late nineteenth century, rocking horses had been luxury items that had been the toys of future nobility (most notably by England's Charles I). England was home to the world's most famous maker of rocking horses, J. Collinson and Sons of Liverpool, which was visited personally by Queen Victoria in 1851; it was then that she stated her preference for the dapple gray variety of rocking horse, which is considered the quintessential English rocking horse to this day. The rocking horse was thus a source of British pride and identity, with a royal heritage to support its widespread popularity.

In "The Rocking-Horse Winner," Paul rides his horse in an eerie, possessed manner—which Lawrence describes as a "mad little journey" (RHW 793)—until he knows which horse will win. Paul's rocking horse as described in the story is the model that originated in the 1880s, which featured a wooden horse suspended by straps and springs from a stationary frame.[11] As such, Daniel

Watkins argues that "the rocking horse is a brilliant symbol of non-productive labor, for even while it moves it remains stationary" (298). Paul's riding is nevertheless so frenzied that "it made [his sisters] peer at him uneasily," so that while he was riding they "dared not speak to him" (RHW 793). "In this context," Watkins argues, "work is not a means of meeting basic human needs, but rather only a way of producing greater sums of money, and thus it is clearly socially unproductive" (297).

As a moneymaking venture, though, racing is depicted in "The Rocking-Horse Winner" as an incredibly lucrative venture. As opposed to the characters in *Ulysses*, who universally lose money on the sport, Paul has both the ability to predict racing winners and an uncanny knack for knowing how much to wager. Paul and Bassett emphasize that they only try to bet when they are certain of the outcome, admitting that "it's when we're not quite sure that we go down" (RHW 796). In truth, Paul is prone to the same folly as most gamblers when he loses a bet, as he begins to reach on races that he is not sure of, but he bets conservatively enough that it has little effect on his accumulated wealth. Much as Leopold Bloom is only willing to wager on a sure thing in his get-rich-quick scheme in *Ulysses*, Paul makes a point of risking significant money only when he is certain of the outcome.

Paul picks Daffodil for the Lincoln Handicap, in spite of the fact that he "was an obscure horse comparatively" (RHW 794). In truth, Daffodil is not a true long-shot horse, as the eventual win only pays four-to-one odds, but throughout the story Paul bets on horses with progressively longer odds. Paul gambles heavily and successfully on Lively Spark, who is described as "quite an inconsiderable horse" at ten-to-one odds (RHW 797). His ultimate selection for the Derby, Malabar, pays out at fourteen-to-one odds, making Paul more than seventy thousand pounds (and giving him more than eighty thousand pounds collectively)—an incredible financial windfall that stems from an initial ten-shilling risk.

In such a way, Paul's run of success can only be accounted for through extraordinary luck, which becomes a highly associative factor in "The Rocking-Horse Winner." Paul's mother is unlucky, she says, because she married an unlucky husband; conversely, Paul considers his Uncle Oscar lucky because Oscar loaned him the ten shillings that he wagered on his first winner. "It's better to be born lucky than rich," Paul's mother tells him, because "if you're lucky, you will always get more money" (RHW 792). In the wake of his mother's comment, Paul steadfastly declares, "I'm a lucky person. [. . .] God told me" (RHW 792) and makes it his obsession to prove this statement correct.

That God supposedly told Paul of his gift endows it with a sort of religious reverence, and Paul and Bassett accordingly speak in hushed tones about his newfound ability. Paul is hesitant to state the true extent of his winnings, emphasizing to his uncle that this knowledge must stay between them. Paul's Uncle Oscar warns him that "a bird in the hand is worth two in the bush" (RHW 800), and Paul understands enough about the precarious nature of luck to be secretive and superstitious about it, but he is nevertheless confident in his future ability to pick winners; "I'm sure to know for the Grand National," he declares, "or the Lincolnshire; or else the Derby. I'm sure to know for one of them" (RHW 800).

While Paul's uncle plays a supervisory role in the story, and Bassett offers a lower-class peer for Paul, Paul's father plays a noticeably minor role. Thus, in spite of the highly masculine nature of horse racing, a woman and a child are the main characters of "The Rocking-Horse Winner." As a result of his father's bad luck, it is left to Paul and his mother to provide for the family financially; this realization drives Paul to his obsession with picking horse-racing winners and is all the more complicated by his desire to provide for the family anonymously. When Paul's mother tells him, "If you were me and I were you [. . .] I wonder what we should do!" (RHW 801), the irony is palpable, given that Paul is the family's primary breadwinner, while his mother is generally a petulant spendthrift. Paul's uncle is understandably delighted that his nephew has developed an interest in racing—a thoroughly masculine and adult institution—in view of the fact that he occupies a feminized and infantile home. However, while predicting races offers Paul his only avenue into adult socialization, it is still an isolationist and juvenile pursuit, one that requires him to ride a toy horse alone for hours at a time. For Paul, Snodgrass observes, "such control of the world as he can gain is useless because he has lost the knowledge of what he wants, what he is" (195).

Such anonymous subservience in "The Rocking-Horse Winner" casts racing in the same colonial light as in *Ulysses*, and, while the horses in Lawrence's story are mostly fictional, their names are a testament to a similarly tragic system of economics and life. Snodgrass, in his definitive analysis of Lawrence's story, observes that Singhalese (the first horse on which Paul wins) and Malabar (the last) are both names that refer to British colonial regions in India, and that one could go so far as to consider a third horse, Mirza, to suggest the British colonial region of Mirzapur. Furthermore, Paul's "secret of secrets was his wooden horse, that which had no name" (RHW 801); instead, the rocking horse's name changes in accordance with the intended winner of the next major race. A new name emerges in this void for most impending races, only to be replaced by another void that must ultimately be filled with the name of another winner.

"The Rocking-Horse Winner" consequently stands as an allegory on accumulative capitalism, with Paul's mother offering a prime example of what Baudrillard calls the "radical necessity of lack" (207). As stated earlier, Baudrillard insists that "every fulfillment of desire in value returns to the contrary extremity" (207). In spite of Paul's winning, the house nevertheless begins "whispering" more than it ever has, to the point that these voices eventually escalate to the level of "a chorus of frogs on a spring evening" (RHW 800). Paul can make himself a winner, but he cannot do the same for his mother, who is unable to make suitable money of her own accord. Even when she earns several hundred pounds sketching furs and dress materials, she is dissatisfied that her drawings command only a fraction of what is earned by the other lady in the studio. Wealth, in such a way, is a competitive pursuit for Paul's mother, offering a material goal that can never be fully satisfied. Paul's winnings may buy new furnishings, a private tutor, and a spot at Eton, but they do not secure any long-term financial prosperity or domestic happiness. When he anonymously donates five thousand pounds to be given to his mother in yearly installments of one thousand pounds, she desultorily asks if she can receive it immediately in a lump sum.

Seven years after the publication of "The Rocking-Horse Winner," Yeats would conclude that "Lawrence is an emphasis directed against modern abstraction. [. . .] Of course happiness is not where he seems to place it. We are happy when for everything inside us there is an equivalent something outside us" (810). In "The Rocking-Horse Winner," Paul's focus is wholly manifested in money begetting the need for more money, as he feels that the only way for his mother to acknowledge his value is by his acquisition of wealth and the consequent proof that he is lucky. As soon as Paul discovers that Malabar is the horse for the Derby, he passes out unconscious with a brain fever. When he is revived, he makes a point of sharing his secret with Hester for the purpose of validation:

> "I never told you, mother, that if I can ride my horse, and *get there*, then I'm absolutely sure—oh absolutely! Mother, did I ever tell you? I am lucky."
> "No, you never did," said his mother.
> But the boy died in the night. (RHW 804)

This again aligns significantly with Baudrillard's theory of the fulfillment of desire. "When the demand for always more utility and satisfaction is confronted with the possibility of its immediate realization, it evaporates," Baudrillard explains. "The whole package of motivations, needs and rationality that is so conveniently supposed to constitute human nature simply flies apart" (205). So long as the family is in dire financial straits, and so long as his luck remains unproven to his mother, Paul has a goal that provides his impetus for living. However, his only real emotional connection with his mother is through his role in her economic providence; once that has been secured, he promptly perishes.

Paul's surreal compulsion eventually culminates in his demise, as he establishes himself as lucky in racing but unlucky in life; in such a way, "The Rocking-Horse Winner" is grounded in addiction every bit as much as mysticism. Lawrence, much like Joyce, is not anticapitalist so much as he is simply averse to material obsession. For all his affluence, Paul's Uncle Oscar is not an obsessive capitalist but merely a pragmatic opportunist; he does not need the winnings from racing to live on, and so it remains a sport to him. For Paul, on the other hand, horse racing is such a compulsion that it becomes inextricably tied to his life force. Before his final collapse, Paul's mother poignantly warns him: "I think you care too much about these races. It's a bad sign. My family has been a gambling family, and you won't know till you grow up how much damage it has done" (RHW 801).

The irony, of course, is that although Paul will never get to grow up, he will nevertheless experience firsthand the destructive results of an obsession with gambling. Despite the initial promise of the situation, Paul quite literally gambles his life away, rendering his ability to pick racing winners a Faustian bargain. As Oscar says to his sister at story's end: "You're eighty-odd thousand to the good and a poor devil of a son to the bad. But, poor devil, poor devil, he's best gone out of a life where he rides his rocking horse to find a winner" (RHW 804).

"Truth Stranger Than Fiction"

Both *Ulysses* and "The Rocking-Horse Winner" utilize horse racing as a central narrative and symbolic vehicle, as the sport makes an ironic winner out of Leopold Bloom and an ironic loser out of Paul. Despite the initial outcomes of these texts, their end results defy the oddsmakers and come to define these two dark-horse individuals. This dramatic significance draws attention back to the original "dark horse" of *Ulysses*—Throwaway—who competed in the Ascot Gold Cup on Bloomsday against Sceptre, Zinfandel, and Maximum II. The aforementioned account of the race in *Ulysses*' "Oxen of the Sun" episode gives the impression that Throwaway came from behind in the race and was fortunate to head his favored opponents down the stretch. The *Evening Telegraph* of that day offers a markedly different account of what actually happened[12] and demonstrates that the long shot's win was as decisive as it was unexpected:

> It was not surprising to see Zinfandel a better favourite than Sceptre; last year's winner being quoted at tens, and Throwaway on offer at twenties. However, the despised one created a great surprise, as with the exception of being once headed by Sceptre, he made all the running, and won in the style of a thorough stayer. ("Ascot Meeting" 3)

Horse racing is likewise a subject that has exhibited a high degree of staying power in these respective works of Joyce and Lawrence. While much of the political and social structure of the early twentieth century has been irrevocably altered over the last hundred years, the racing institutions of *Ulysses* and "The Rocking-Horse Winner" have remained largely intact, with no single event better exemplifying this than the lone race mentioned in both works—the Ascot Gold Cup. The Gold Cup is still the premier race of the day, run at the same time (3:00 p.m.) and day (Thursday) that it was a century earlier. The race continues to generate extensive media coverage and large-scale wagering across Britain and Ireland, and it often plays out in accordance with Bloom's "truth stranger than fiction" assessment of the 1904 race (*U* 17.323). The 2006–2009 races were swept by the only four-time winner in the Gold Cup's history, in a nod to literature, irony, and the cultural crossover between Britain and Ireland that would no doubt have delighted Joyce and Lawrence alike.

[The horse's name: Yeats.]

Notes

1. This connection between alcohol and horse racing is further evident in the reference to the "Vintners' sweepstake" earlier in the episode (*U* 8.826). Much the same as Bloom considers drinking to be "the curse of Ireland" (*U* 12.684), horse racing is seen as an equally destructive addiction, as Davy Byrne laments, "It ruined many a man, the same horses" (*U* 8.824–25).

2. A statement that supports the citizen's praise of "our [Ireland's] farfamed horses even today" (*U* 12.1252–53), which he holds to be the finest in the world. This is as close as any character comes to politically implicating the Gold Cup, but it abruptly ends

there. The citizen's primary interest in the Gold Cup appears to be coercing a round of drinks out of Bloom, and he does not include the event in the rest of his diatribe on Irish nationalism.

3. The Prix Royal-Oak could be considered a French equivalent of the Ascot Gold Cup, as it is a Group 1 flat race founded in 1861 that is open to thoroughbreds three years and older and run annually at the end of October.

4. This is in complex relation to Lévi-Strauss' argument in *The Savage Mind* that "the names assigned to racehorses are words from discourse which rarely, if ever, describe them" (206). While Sceptre is, ironically, a filly, she is also from a veritable royal lineage and grows up to dominate the major races of the time, rendering her name decidedly appropriate in the context of her entire career. Meanwhile, there has rarely been a more aptly named racehorse than Throwaway, a nondescript challenger competing against a star-studded field who is shunned by every gambler in *Ulysses*.

5. In contrast to the action in *Ulysses*, Slack contends that "habitual, frequent, and even some occasional gamblers are not often happy with 'sure things' and oddsmakers' favorites; such wagers either do not have a great enough return on the odds or they are simply unappealing to many bettors' whimsical natures" (5)—which makes it all the more surprising that no character in *Ulysses* actually bets on Throwaway.

6. Going back to the "Two Gallants" story in *Dubliners*, Lenehan is described as "a leech" whose name "was vaguely associated with racing tissues" (50). Accordingly, in the "Aeolus" episode of *Ulysses*, he is seen emerging from the newspaper office "with Sport's tissues" and declares Sceptre "a dead cert for the Gold cup" (*U* 7.387–88).

7. For an in-depth treatment of this trend, see Osteen's chapter, "'Cyclops' and the Economy of Excess," in *The Economy of* Ulysses.

8. In "Circe," Bloom does provide a relatively fond recollection of an outing years ago when Molly "won seven shillings on a three year old named Nevertell" (*U* 15.546–47). It is also instructive that in this case Bloom originally misremembers the site of Leopardstown as the "Fairyhouse races" (*U* 15.541), only to be corrected by Josie Breen, who gives the proper name.

9. Interestingly, Lawrence writes that while it had sold for fifty pounds in America, the story only merited fifteen pounds in England for Lady Asquith's book (Ellis 667).

10. This is a subject of consistent concern for Paul's mother in "The Rocking-Horse Winner," as from the beginning of the story she asks him, "Aren't you growing too big for a rocking-horse? You're not a little boy any longer, you know" (RHW 793).

11. This newer model is in contrast to the traditional rocking horse, in which a wooden horse is mounted on a pair of bow rockers. This older model had declined in popularity by the time of "The Rocking-Horse Winner," largely as a result of safety concerns. There is little to merit the distinction between the two models in Lawrence's story, beyond the sounds that "came whispering from the springs of the still-swaying rocking-horse" (RHW 791), which probably accounts for why images associated with the story sometimes feature the older bow-rocker model.

12. This would have been the account of the race that Bloom read that evening in the cabman's shelter at Butt Bridge, which he recounts in "Ithaca" (*U* 17.325–26).

Works Cited

"Ascot Meeting," *Evening Telegraph* 16 June 1904. www.harenet.co.uk/splitpea/LastPink. pdf. Accessed May 27, 2014.

Atherton, James S. "Sport and Games in *Finnegans Wake.*" *Twelve and a Tilly: Essays on the Occasion of the 25th Anniversary of* Finnegans Wake. Ed. Jack P. Dalton and Clive Hart. Evanston: Northwestern UP, 1965. 52–64.

Baudrillard, Jean. *For a Critique of the Political Economy of the Sign.* Trans. Charles Levin. St. Louis: Telos, 1981.

Cheng, Vincent. "White Horse, Dark Horse: Joyce's Allhorse of Another Color." *Joyce Studies Annual* (1991): 101–28.

Cowan, James C. *D. H. Lawrence: Self and Sexuality.* Columbus: Ohio State UP, 2002.

Davies, Rosemary Reeves. "Lawrence, Lady Cynthia Asquith, and 'The Rocking-Horse Winner.'" *Studies in Short Fiction* 20.2–3 (Spring/Summer 1983): 121–26.

Ellis, David. *D. H. Lawrence: Dying Game 1922–1930.* Cambridge: Cambridge UP, 1998.

García León, Rafael I. "Reading *Ulysses* at a Gallop." *Papers on Joyce* 3 (1997): 3–8.

Gwynn, Stephen. *Ireland: Its Places of Beauty, Entertainment, Sport, and Historic Association.* Garden City, NY: Doubleday, Doran, 1928.

Holt, Richard. *Sport and the British: A Modern History.* Oxford: Clarendon, 1989.

Lawrence, D. H. "The Rocking-Horse Winner." *The Complete Short Stories of D. H. Lawrence.* Vol. 3. New York: Viking, 1961. 790–804.

Lawrence, Frieda. *Not I, but the Wind.* Carbondale: Southern Illinois UP, 1974.

Lévi-Strauss, Claude. *The Savage Mind.* Chicago: U of Chicago P, 1966.

Lloyd, David. *Anomalous States: Irish Writing and the Post-Colonial Movement.* Durham, NC: Duke UP, 1993.

Osteen, Mark. *The Economy of* Ulysses: *Making Both Ends Meet.* Syracuse, NY: Syracuse UP, 1995.

Slack, John. "Regular Hotbed: *Ulysses*, Gambling, and the Ascot Gold Cup Race." *Aethlon* 11.2 (Spring 1994): 1–11.

Snodgrass, W. D. "A Rocking-Horse: The Symbol, the Pattern, the Way to Live." *Hudson Review* 11.2 (Summer 1958): 191–200.

Sultan, Stanley. *The Argument of Ulysses.* Columbus: Ohio State UP, 1964.

Watkins, Daniel P. "Labor and Religion in D. H. Lawrence's 'The Rocking-Horse Winner.'" *Studies in Short Fiction* 24.3 (Summer 1987): 295–301.

Yeats, W. B. *The Letters of W. B. Yeats.* Ed. Allan Wade. London: Rupert Hart-Davis, 1954.

Contributors

Hidenaga Arai is professor at Kumamoto University. His publications include "The Mediator Split: The System of Oppositions in *The Marriage of Heaven and Hell*," in *Enlightened Groves: Essays in Honour of Professor Zenzo Suzuki*; "The 'Core of Asia' and the Core of Evil in D. H. Lawrence's *St. Mawr*," in *D. H. Lawrence: Literature, History, Culture*; and *Literature along the Lines of Flight: D. H. Lawrence's Later Novels and Critical Theory*.

Zack Bowen (1934–2010) was an internationally respected James Joyce scholar and chairperson of the Department of English at the University of Delaware for ten years. His scholarly books include *Musical Allusions in the Works of James Joyce: Early Poetry through* Ulysses; Ulysses *as a Comic Novel*; and *A Reader's Guide to John Barth*; he coauthored, with David L. Wilson, *Science and Literature: Bridging the Two Cultures*.

Martin Brick is associate professor of English at Ohio Dominican University. His research primarily focuses on religion and authors of the twentieth century, and he has published in *James Joyce Quarterly, Genetic Joyce Studies, Virginia Woolf Miscellany*, and *Christianity and Literature*.

Johannes Hendrikus Burgers is assistant professor at Queensborough Community College, part of the City University of New York. His research focuses on the intersections between transnational modernism, racial theories, sexology, and aesthetics, topic on which he has published recently in the *Journal of the History of Ideas* and various edited collections including *Art and the Artist in Society* and *Decadence, Degeneration, and the End: Studies in the European Fin-de-Siècle*. He is currently researching the relationship between anti-Semitism and modernism.

Gerald Doherty (1930–2014) was a senior lecturer in English at the University of Turku from 1972 to 1995. He published widely on modernist writers in *PMLA, Modern Fiction Studies, James Joyce Quarterly, Irish Renaissance Annual, European Joyce Studies, D. H. Lawrence Review,* and many other journals and collections. He is the author of *Theorizing Lawrence; Oriental Lawrence;* and *Pathologies of Desire.*

Enda Duffy is professor of English at the University of California, Santa Barbara. His interests include postcolonial literatures and cultures; modernism and postmodernism; Irish literature; cultural studies; and James Joyce. He is the author of *The Subaltern Ulysses* and *The Speed Handbook: Velocity, Pleasure, Modernism.* He is also the coeditor, with Maurizia Boscagli, of *Joyce, Benjamin and Magical Urbanism,* which appeared as volume 21 of European Joyce Studies. *The Speed Handbook* was joint winner of the Modernist Studies Association Book Prize for 2010.

Earl G. Ingersoll is Distinguished Professor Emeritus at the State University of New York, College at Brockport. He is the author or editor of more than a dozen books, including collections of interviews with Margaret Atwood, Lawrence Durrell, Doris Lessing, and Rita Dove. His works on Joyce and Lawrence include *Engendered Trope in Joyce's* Dubliners; *D. H. Lawrence, Desire, and Narrative;* and *Windows to the Sun: D. H. Lawrence's "Thought-Adventures."*

Louise Kane is associate lecturer at De Montfort University, England. Her primary research area is modernist periodical studies; her monograph project focuses on the exploration of new methodologies through which to approach British little modernist magazines. Her publications include chapters on Holbrook Jackson's *To-day* and middlebrow culture and the early periodical publications of Wyndham Lewis.

Matthew J. Kochis is assistant professor of writing at Holy Family University. Previously, he was a Mellon Post-Doctoral Fellow of Digital Humanities at Dickinson College, where he advised faculty and students on creating digital projects. He has published an article in the *D. H. Lawrence Review* and has frequently presented at national and international James Joyce conferences. He is currently an executive officer of the D. H. Lawrence Society of North America. As digital editor for the Modernist Versions Project, he has uploaded high-quality scans of the first edition of James Joyce's work as it was published in 1922 by Sylvia Beach's Shakespeare & Company bookstore (see http://web.uvic.ca/~mvp1922/you/).

Eleni Loukopoulou completed her doctorate in 2011 at the University of Kent, Canterbury, on the topic of James Joyce and London. Work drawing on her research has appeared in the edited collection of essays *Irish Writing London.* She has published essays in the *James Joyce Quarterly*, the *Journal of Modern Periodical Studies*, and the *Literary London Journal* and has contributed to the modernist section of the *Routledge Annotated Bibliography of English Studies.* She is currently researching Victor Gollancz's Left Book Club series of books (1936–48) and the communities of reading it created.

Heather L. Lusty is assistant professor in residence at the University of Nevada, Las Vegas. She works on twentieth-century war literature, science in world literature, postcolonialism(s), and classical revival studies. She is currently revising two projects examining currency and state-sponsored architectural projects as national identity. She was an organizer for the Modernist Studies Association annual convention in Las Vegas, Nevada, in 2012, and is an executive member of the D. H. Lawrence Society of North America.

Carl F. Miller is assistant professor of English at Palm Beach Atlantic University, where his primary research interests are in twentieth-century comparative literature, critical theory, cultural studies, and children's literature. He has other recent publications on the influence of the Cold War on the 1980s graphic novel, the role of sport as identity in Harper Lee's *To Kill a Mockingbird*, the crisis of the bildungsroman in Sherwood Anderson's *Winesburg, Ohio*, and the significance of philosophical ethics in Dr. Seuss' *Horton Hears a Who!*

Jennifer Mitchell is visiting assistant professor of English at Weber State University. Her work on modernism, young adult literature, and queer theory has appeared in various edited collections and journals including *Bookbird, Journal of the Fantastic in the Arts,* and the *Journal of Bisexuality.* In her first book, *Everyday Masochisms: Nineteenth-Century Fiction, Modernism, and the Vicissitudes of Desire*, she contends that there is a strong literary reaction to early influential sexologists whose diagnoses of masochism as deviant became increasingly pervasive.

Margot Norris is Chancellor's Professor Emerita at University of California, Irvine, where she taught literature, culture, and the art of the twentieth century. She has published extensively on James Joyce, the animal in modern literature, and twentieth-century war literature. Her books on Joyce include *The Decentered Universe of "Finnegans Wake"*; *Joyce's Web*; *Suspicious Readings of Joyce's "Dubliners"*; and *Virgin and Veteran Readings of "Ulysses."* She has also edited the Norton Critical Edition of Joyce's *Dubliners*, published in 2006.

Index

Page numbers in italics refer to illustrations.

The Florida James Joyce Series

EDITED BY SEBASTIAN D. G. KNOWLES

The Autobiographical Novel of Co-Consciousness: Goncharov, Woolf, and Joyce, by Galya Diment (1994)

Bloom's Old Sweet Song: Essays on Joyce and Music, by Zack Bowen (1995)

Joyce's Iritis and the Irritated Text: The Dis-lexic Ulysses, by Roy Gottfried (1995)

Joyce, Milton, and the Theory of Influence, by Patrick Colm Hogan (1995)

Reauthorizing Joyce, by Vicki Mahaffey (paperback edition, 1995)

Shaw and Joyce: "The Last Word in Stolentelling," by Martha Fodaski Black (1995)

Bely, Joyce, and Döblin: Peripatetics in the City Novel, by Peter I. Barta (1996)

Jocoserious Joyce: The Fate of Folly in Ulysses, by Robert H. Bell (paperback edition, 1996)

Joyce and Popular Culture, edited by R. B. Kershner (1996)

Joyce and the Jews: Culture and Texts, by Ira B. Nadel (paperback edition, 1996)

Narrative Design in Finnegans Wake: *The Wake Lock Picked*, by Harry Burrell (1996)

Gender in Joyce, edited by Jolanta W. Wawrzycka and Marlena G. Corcoran (1997)

Latin and Roman Culture in Joyce, by R. J. Schork (1997)

Reading Joyce Politically, by Trevor L. Williams (1997)

Advertising and Commodity Culture in Joyce, by Garry Leonard (1998)

Greek and Hellenic Culture in Joyce, by R. J. Schork (1998)

Joyce, Joyceans, and the Rhetoric of Citation, by Eloise Knowlton (1998)

Joyce's Music and Noise: Theme and Variation in His Writings, by Jack W. Weaver (1998)

Reading Derrida Reading Joyce, by Alan Roughley (1999)

Joyce through the Ages: A Nonlinear View, edited by Michael Patrick Gillespie (1999)

Chaos Theory and James Joyce's Everyman, by Peter Francis Mackey (1999)

Joyce's Comic Portrait, by Roy Gottfried (2000)

Joyce and Hagiography: Saints Above!, by R. J. Schork (2000)

Voices and Values in Joyce's Ulysses, by Weldon Thornton (2000)

The Dublin Helix: The Life of Language in Joyce's Ulysses, by Sebastian D. G. Knowles (2001)

Joyce Beyond Marx: History and Desire in Ulysses *and* Finnegans Wake, by Patrick McGee (2001)

Joyce's Metamorphosis, by Stanley Sultan (2001)

Joycean Temporalities: Debts, Promises, and Countersignatures, by Tony Thwaites (2001)

Joyce and the Victorians, by Tracey Teets Schwarze (2002)

Joyce's Ulysses *as National Epic: Epic Mimesis and the Political History of the Nation State*, by Andras Ungar (2002)

James Joyce's "Fraudstuff," by Kimberly J. Devlin (2002)

Rite of Passage in the Narratives of Dante and Joyce, by Jennifer Margaret Fraser (2002)

Joyce and the Scene of Modernity, by David Spurr (2002)

Joyce and the Early Freudians: A Synchronic Dialogue of Texts, by Jean Kimball (2003)

Twenty-first Joyce, edited by Ellen Carol Jones and Morris Beja (2004)

Joyce on the Threshold, edited by Anne Fogarty and Timothy Martin (2005)

Wake Rites: The Ancient Irish Rituals of Finnegans Wake, by George Cinclair Gibson (2005)

Ulysses *in Critical Perspective*, edited by Michael Patrick Gillespie and A. Nicholas Fargnoli (2006)

Joyce and the Narrative Structure of Incest, by Jen Shelton (2006)

Joyce, Ireland, Britain, edited by Andrew Gibson and Len Platt (2006)

Joyce in Trieste: An Album of Risky Readings, edited by Sebastian D. G. Knowles, Geert Lernout, and John McCourt (2007)

Joyce's Rare View: The Nature of Things in Finnegans Wake, by Richard Beckman (2007)

Joyce's Misbelief, by Roy Gottfried (2007)

James Joyce's Painful Case, by Cóilín Owens (2008)

Cannibal Joyce, by Thomas Jackson Rice (2008)

Manuscript Genetics, Joyce's Know-How, Beckett's Nohow, by Dirk Van Hulle (2008)

Catholic Nostalgia in Joyce and Company, by Mary Lowe-Evans (2008)

A Guide through Finnegans Wake, by Edmund Lloyd Epstein (2009)

Bloomsday 100: Essays on Ulysses, edited by Morris Beja and Anne Fogarty (2009)

Joyce, Medicine, and Modernity, by Vike Martina Plock (2010; first paperback edition, 2012)

Who's Afraid of James Joyce?, by Karen R. Lawrence (2010; first paperback edition, 2012)

Ulysses *in Focus: Genetic, Textual, and Personal Views*, by Michael Groden (2010; first paperback edition, 2012)

Foundational Essays in James Joyce Studies, edited by Michael Patrick Gillespie (2011)

Empire and Pilgrimage in Conrad and Joyce, by Agata Szczeszak-Brewer (2011)

The Poetry of James Joyce Reconsidered, edited by Marc C. Conner (2012)

The German Joyce, by Robert K. Weninger (2012)

Joyce and Militarism, by Greg Winston (2012)

Renascent Joyce, edited by Daniel Ferrer, Sam Slote, and André Topia (2013; first paperback edition, 2014)

Before Daybreak: "After the Race" and the Origins of Joyce's Art, by Cóilín Owens (2013; first paperback edition, 2014)

Modernists at Odds: Reconsidering Joyce and Lawrence, edited by Matthew J. Kochis and Heather L. Lusty (2015)